T0163861

FEW CALL IT **WAR**

"Robert Hicks has written a masterpiece in the study of religiously motivated terrorism. He has been fair in his critique of all religious violence, including movements within Judaism and even Christianity, yet avoids the type of moral equivalence that political correctness calls for—where a lone wolf like Timothy McVeigh is regarded as no less dangerous than the leaders of al Qaeda or ISIS."

—Robert L. Brennemann, PhD, Professor, Intercultural Studies, North Central University, Author, *As Strong as the Mountains: Kurdish Cultural Journey*

"In a time when political leaders are reluctant to talk about faith, Dr. Hicks opens our eyes to the truth about 'religious terrorism'. He brings great academic acumen as a history professor and practical experience as a military chaplain to answer the question "For what would I be willing to kill someone?" A must read for those of all faiths, no faith, and evangelicals who love their country"

—Chaplain, Major General Charles C. Baldwin, USAF (Retired)

"The mixture of political ideology, religious values, and the willingness to engage in premeditated violence against innocent people for political gain is the combustible cocktail of religiously motivated terrorism. Dr. Hicks presents a highly readable and well-documented account of the use and abuse of religion for violent political ends. He reminds us that no religion is immune from violence and that values have consequences. This is a book well worth reading. You will not be disappointed"

—Timothy J. Demy, ThD., PhD, Co-author, *In the Name of God: Understanding the Mindset of Terrorism*

"Chaplain Hicks factors in what so many 'experts' leave out... the critical role religion plays in the modern terrorist mind. His concluding 'out of the box' counter measures are worth the price of the book"

—Major General, John M. White, Air National Guard (Retired), Former ANG Assistant to Air Combat Command, Commander

"Chaplain Hicks has written a book that must be read by military personnel, law enforcement officers, and anyone who seeks to understand the terrorism we are seeing around the world every day. This is an objective and thoroughly researched book that dives deep into the details of the world's main religions and describes how both in the past and today these religions impact the nature of extremist terrorism that far too many seem to be afraid to tie to its religious roots and motivations. It is refreshingly frank and informative and I highly commend it to everyone who wants to learn more about extremism and religiously motivated terrorism."

—Tom Hastings, former US State
Department Counterterrorism Official, ,
FBI Crisis Management Specialist, (Retired)

FEW CALL IT

WAR

Religious Terrorism:
Then and Now

Robert Michael Hicks

New York

FEW CALL IT **WAR**

Religious Terrorism: Then and Now

Published in New York, New York, by Morgan James Publishing. Morgan James and The Entrepreneurial Publisher are trademarks of Morgan James, LLC.
www.MorganJamesPublishing.com

The Morgan James Speakers Group can bring authors to your live event. For more information or to book an event visit The Morgan James Speakers Group at
www.TheMorganJamesSpeakersGroup.com.

This work published in association with Steven Webb Literary, Marble Falls, Texas.

Shelfie

A free eBook edition is available
with the purchase of this print book.

CLEARLY PRINT YOUR NAME ABOVE IN UPPER CASE

Instructions to claim your free eBook edition:
1. Download the Shelfie app for Android or iOS
2. Write your name in **UPPER CASE** above
3. Use the Shelfie app to submit a photo
4. Download your eBook to any device

ISBN 978-1-63047-785-1 paperback
ISBN 978-1-63047-786-8 eBook
ISBN 978-1-63047-787-5 hardcover
Library of Congress Control Number:
2015914862

Cover Design by:
John Weber

Interior Design by:
Bonnie Bushman

In an effort to support local communities and raise awareness and funds, Morgan James Publishing donates a percentage of all book sales for the life of each book to Habitat for Humanity Peninsula and Greater Williamsburg.

Get involved today, visit
www.MorganJamesBuilds.com

Habitat
for Humanity®
Peninsula and
Greater Williamsburg
Building Partner

Dedication

Charis Cathryn Hicks Pierson
March 19, 1971-February 10, 2004

Table of Contents

Acknowledgements

In 2003 my F-16 Fighter unit was deploying to Operation Iraqi Freedom. I did not go with them because my Commander thought it best I stay back to support those not deploying. In addition, my daughter Charis was receiving a bone marrow transplant at MD Anderson Hospital in Houston, Texas. So I stayed, to support our unit in Montgomery, Alabama, and to spend many weekends in Houston to be with my daughter in her fight against cancer. My wife was her primary caregiver in her room most of the time. On one of my weekend visits, the Iraqi air war had just begun and I was intently interested in watching updates on my daughter's TV in her room. I commented to my wife, "I need to watch this to see how it is going." I thought Charis was asleep, but she opened her eyes and said, "Dad, I'm in the middle of a war *here*." How true. We all have different wars. So this book, about a war that few call by its name, is dedicated to my courageous daughter who fought her own unique war. She is my hero, and a warrior in her own right.

The book you have in your hand was begun more than ten years ago, prior to 9/11. So my memory may fail me on some of the persons who had a part in stimulating my thinking on the subject of terrorism. My trips to the Middle East were certainly part of my education on the subject, as were the professors and fellow students at the USAF War College, not to mention the outstanding personnel at the Air University Library at Maxwell Air Force Base, Montgomery, Alabama. Their helpful service on any topic always went beyond my expectations. I think if asked they would have written my papers for me during my study there.

I need to thank my mother-in-law for the use of her North Carolina Mountain home where the early development of the book took place. The cool mountain air stimulated my thinking and enriched the conditions needed for intense concentration and writing. Likewise, I was blessed to be able to do a complete rewrite and update of the material while sequestered in the Lake Lure mountains of North Carolina. A wonderful lake house was graciously provided for my wife, my daughter Ashley, and me. A hearty "thank you" goes to Patty Sturgeon for allowing us the rich time to use her Red Bird retreat as a respite for Ashley and Cynthia and for me, to complete the book.

It's been a long haul working on this book, but Steve Webb, my literary agent, is the one who finally connected me with Morgan James. Thank you Steve, for your patience with me, and never giving up thinking this book needed to be published. To present a book to a publisher it also needs to be proofread many times, correcting the typos, finding grammatical and spelling errors, and reading through often unintelligent sentences. Carol Crawford did an amazing job in taking chapters written over many years on several different computer systems and putting them together in a fashion that makes the book more readable and shorter. Great job, Carol! For the people with whom we have dealt at Morgan James, including Megan Malone, accept our gratitude for a job well done. A special thanks goes to Terry Whalin, Senior Acquisitions Editor, without whom this book would not have occurred!

Finally, there are those who had to stand by for years watching me on the computer, asking, "When you will get this book published?" My family, close relatives, and professional friends were what kept me working on the book believing it was worth the delays and time spent. I was always encouraged by my son Graham and my daughter Ashley, who always thought their dad was on the right track with this book. And of course, there is the most important person in my life who keeps me going in all areas, my wife, Cynthia. She is a soldier in her own right putting up with me for, as of this writing, 46 years. Her children rise up and call her 'blessed," and her husband praises her saying "many daughters have done nobly but you excel them all."

Robert Michael Hicks
August 15, 2015

"As the century comes to a close, terrorism is becoming the substitute for the great wars of the 1800s and early 1900s."
—**Walter Laqueur**, Political terror expert prior to 9/11

"When the enemy, in this modern era, cleverly uses the cloak of religion, we are reluctant to name the threat . . . We dare not speak the name of the enemy coiling around our necks."
—**S. Eugene Poteat**[1], *Journal of Intelligence Studies*

1   S. Eugene Poteat, "Refusing to Identify or Name our Enemies," *Intelligencer, Journal of U.S. Intelligence Studies*, Fall/Winter 2010, Vol. 18, Number 1, p. 3.

CHAPTER ONE
The Blinders Were On Prior to 9/11

Awakened by a boom . . . boom . . . boom, I quickly looked at my watch. It was 5:30 in the morning. Rushing to the door of my thatched enclosure, I saw nothing. I had no idea what had happened until I dressed and walked to our kibbutz breakfast at eight o'clock. Over a Mediterranean breakfast of boiled eggs, cheese, and juice, I learned the news. A cadre of Islamic terrorists had come ashore across from Camp Achiev,[2] where I was spending the night with other students. They had been spotted by Israeli naval forces.

The booms I had heard were the sounds of Israeli gunboats zeroing in on the hostile intruders. The only populated area in the region was the very camp in which I was spending the night. The targeted victims were self-evident. Within an hour or so, news cameras were on scene reporting the incident. The speed with which they arrived amazed the whole community at Camp Achiev. It was my first close call with Middle East terrorism.

---

2   Achieve is one of several ways the Hebrew can be translated. On a current map of Israel it is located at tel Akhziv.

It's one thing to read about such events or to watch the repeated images on television. But when I realized the terrorists were coming for me and my companions, everything changed. After the explosion a deflated dinghy was pulled ashore, loaded with all kinds of explosives, AK-47s and grenades. It was a direct confrontation with reality and with my own mortality.

An appalling irony immediately struck me. I was in Israel in 1980 to study its geography with primary interest in Biblical history. Suddenly I was confronted not with identification of Biblical sites but with contemporary geopolitical issues. In that moment over breakfast, I felt like a naïve victim of something much larger than myself. Being a student of ancient history did not make me immune to current history.

Years later I led a small group of adults on a tour of Israel. I had planned a day of walking around the old city of Jerusalem, complete with lectures at the famous Biblical gates. While driving from our hotel to the old city, we turned toward the New Gate passing the Notre Dame Hospice. Suddenly an angry crowd of black-hatted Hasidic Jews confronted us with stones in hand. As I waited for the light to change I noticed the car in front of our VW bus had Palestinian license plates. Immediately, the Hasidic Jews hurled stones at that car. I looked over at my guide, a former student, friend, and reservist in the Israeli army. I blurted out, "What do I do now?" Without acknowledging my request or even looking at me, he lowered his head and started praying! As I looked to him desperately for direction, he merely prayed for God's protection. I had to confess later that I was looking for some military tactic to get us out of there, not prayer! But his prayer must have worked. As the Hasidic crowd pounded the car in front of us with stones, not one rock hit our bus. As we drove around the corner, we breathed a sigh of relief, realizing we had been spared, while also wondering about the fate of the Palestinians in the car. At that moment I again realized the ever-present realities of being in the Middle East. Terrorism not only comes from the PLO (Palestinian Liberation Organization) Muslims, but also from Israeli Jews . . . religious, orthodox, yarmulke-wearing Jews.

But a particular group of Christians needs to be included in the list of terrorists as well.

While I was serving as National Guard Chaplain my commander asked me to evaluate the conscience of one of our unit members. Racist literature had been found at various locations on our base, and it had been attributed to this individual. As

Chaplain, I was tasked to evaluate the sincerity of this individual and his religious beliefs. When I spoke with him, his beliefs were very apparent. He felt America had been taken over by political correctness that had excluded and devalued the rights of white Anglo-Saxon males. He believed the US Constitution duly authorized state National Guard units (militia) for the protection of a state's citizens. As such they were the only hope for the restoration of distinctively white Anglo-Saxon values. The discovered literature expressed themes of white supremacy, the dominance of Christian Identity and the necessity of arming for a coming conflict with federal government authorities. In short, the beliefs he advocated were just as violent as the Muslim and Jewish acts I had encountered in the Middle East. The only difference lay in the "Christian" justifications he claimed from the Bible. In short, I became fascinated by the commonalities in attitudes and actions I observed in these diverse religious groups.

While my fellow guardsman was relieved of his commitment to the National Guard based upon his racist views, I realized there was not much difference between his Christian Identity beliefs and the views of the PLO in Lebanon or some of the orthodox Jewish settlers in Israel. Striking commonalities existed between the views of right-wing religious Jews in Israel and the Islamic and Christian groups who justify violence in the name of God.

Years later, I was equally shocked to learn that a Japanese religious cult conducted the first use of a weapon of mass destruction. As I watched the news coverage and read the literature detailing the release of lethal sarin gas in a Tokyo subway, I had to drastically change my view about Eastern religions. The information that surfaced was that the group, Aum Shinrikyo, was anything but a passive group that only practiced meditation. In fact, they were apocalyptic, genocidal, and messianic. Aum surprised even the most sophisticated intelligence networks by their clandestine underground operations. The impact of their significance was made pale only by the horror of the Oklahoma City Federal Building bombing which happened a few weeks later.

This raises a fundamental question. What do a decorated Gulf War veteran, a Jewish rabbi, a Saudi billionaire's son, and a blind Japanese acupuncturist have in common? To the average observer they are as diverse as oil and water. Upon deeper investigation they have a surprising common attribute. They are all terrorists! Not only are they terrorists, they are terrorists of a particular, very unique kind . . . true believing *religious* terrorists, individuals whose faith in God apparently directs them to justify violence in God's name. The violence to which they are committed flows from the passion of their religious convictions and respective faith histories. As such they are unique and far more difficult to understand than the traditional political terrorist. In the opinion of this writer, they are potentially far more lethal.

Prior to 9/11 most Americans viewed the sporadic expressions of terrorist violence as inhuman and shocking. The events might have captured our attention for a few days, but then after bingeing on the coverage, we returned to our routines without giving much thought to the deeper significance of the violence. The press did not help either. They were quick to place labels on terrorists in the void of meaningless, irrational events. "Religious Fundamentalists," "Extremists," "Right-Wing Radicals," and "Militants," became convenient sound bites to explain the complexity and severity of these terrorist actors. Pop psychology "experts" portrayed terrorists as wide-eyed, drug-induced fanatics or undereducated disenfranchised poor . . . both being used by clandestine political players to carry out political ambitions. This is where most academics stuck to the purely political approach in trying to understand this new breed of terrorism. The approach resulted in a political oversimplification that failed miserably to explain the religious complexity of the nature of this violence. It doesn't grant the crucial, fundamental premise that sincere, religiously motivated individuals can carry out violent acts in the name of God . . . a terror in the name of Heaven that few call war. It is to this premise that this book is written.

My interest in the subject of religious terrorism began very early in my educational experience. While studying history, I was surprised by the extreme violence that took place at the hands of supposedly godly men. (Few women are found, though there have been women terrorists.) The Christian Crusades, the Catholic Inquisitions, the Thirty Years' War, medieval pogroms against Jews, the religious wars between the popes and Protestants, and of course, the expansion of Islam by the sword of Mohammed, all seem to go against the nature of religion. Yet the history is there. During the sixties and seventies, I followed from a distance the terrorist acts of the fringe left. They were somewhat predictable, in-your-face terrorists who wanted everyone to know about their cause. Marxist and various Liberationists daringly hijacked airliners and kidnapped famous people for the notoriety it gave their cause. Groups like Black September, the Italian Red Guard, the Weathermen, and the Irish Republican Army were easy to understand because of their very clearly pronounced political agendas.

But during the past decade and a half, somewhat imperceptibly, a new kind of terrorist was born. This was a terrorist not motivated by mere political objectives. The hearts and motives of these perpetrators were elsewhere. Some didn't even care if their organizations or groups got credit for their violent acts. Knowing their objective to strike deep into the psyche of their enemy was pleasing to their God was in itself enough acknowledgement. No other credit or recognition would be required.

It was in the context of this cultural shift that I attended the United States Air Force War College. One of the first electives I took was entitled simply "Terrorism." Throughout my study in the course, I kept noticing what I considered religious underpinnings for many of the issues in discussion. Religious factors were significant players in the liberation movements in Central and South America and apartheid in South Africa. Likewise, religion dominated Middle East conflicts and played a significant role in understanding the conflicts in the Balkans. The renewal of the Russian Orthodox Church and its collusion with the new, more "democratic" Russian government, along with the "ethnic" war against Muslim Chechnya, illustrated the role religion was still playing in Russia.[3] If religious tensions between Pakistan and India and the religious conflicts in the Sudan, Indonesia and North Africa are also factored in, it seems almost every hot spot in the world today has a religious dimension to it.

More recently, most of the Middle East has seen revolutions against long-serving leaders in the so-called Arab Spring. From Tunisia to Egypt, Bahrain to Baghdad, including now Libya and Syria, it would be naïve to think religion is not playing a role in events. Iraq is being split by the Islamic State of Iraq and Levant (ISIS or ISIL). Its leader, Al Baghdadi, has called for an Islamic Caliphate. Iran continues to support its Shia consensus in Baghdad proper but is being surrounded by ISIS. The Kurds in the north have fought well and reversed some ISIS advances,

---

3   The symbol of the hammer and sickle is gone. What is now found throughout Russia is the double-headed eagle, the old symbol of Czarist Russia that depicts the twin heads of State: The Czar and the Russian Orthodox Church. On a visit to the Kremlin after the fall of the Soviet Union I noticed the Patriarch of the Russian Orthodox Church had an office just down the hall from the President's office in the Kremlin.

but only time will tell what the long term results will be: true democracies or religious states modeled after medieval caliphates?

My War College professor finally grew tired of my questioning and offered, "Look, I know a lot about terrorism, but very little about religion. Why don't you do your research project for this course on the subject of religious terrorism?" This volume was born in that exchange.

As it turned out, I wrote my War College thesis on "Right-Wing Religious Terrorism." Upon completion of the year I was offered an opportunity to stay and teach on the subject the following year. Most of the material and insights found in this book have their origin in the research done at the Air University Library (Maxwell AFB, AL) during those two years. Subsequent conversations with professors and fellow military officers filled in the gaps in research. These conversations included senior officers of all the armed services, international officers, DOD, CIA, FBI, and Department of State officials. Though classified sources were consulted in the research, all material found within this book is unclassified and available in the public domain. Conclusions or connections made by the author are his alone, and not to be taken as official statements by any of the branches of the US military or Department of State or other government agencies. I have tried to source my conclusions and connections with a reasonable amount of evidence for both the benefit of the reader and the conscience of the author.

The importance of this book arises from the emerging milieu of the twenty-first century. The Reverend Richard John Neuhaus somewhat prophetically observed in 1997, "The twenty-first century will be religious or it will not be at all . . . At the threshold of the third millennium, it seems that the alternatives to religion have exhausted themselves . . . The perversity of the human mind will no doubt produce other ideological madnesses, but at the moment it seems the historical stage has been swept clean, with only the religious proposition left standing."[4]

With the ideological stage empty, religion has not only filled the vacuum, it has filled it with a vengeance. This conflict that few call war did not begin on 9/11, and it did not end with the killing of Osama bin Laden. Harlan Ullman, a DC policy adviser, cautions about the current American propensity for not *doing war*:

---

4   Richard John Neuhaus, "The Public Square: The Approaching Century of Religion," *First Things*, October 1997, Number 76, p. 1.

"The Achilles' heel is our geostrategic thinking and fixation on winning battles not wars." He goes on to point out, "limited uses of force through no-fly zones . . . and pre-emptive strikes, illustrates our failure to think seriously about wars, only battles."[5] The vengeance continues and constitutes a holy terror, justified with heavenly credentials.

My year at the USAF Air War College was one of the finest educational experiences I have enjoyed. However a critique of the program lies in its omission of religion as a key player in the study of international relations, foreign policy and national security issues. Whatever subjects were discussed, the academic lenses given to us to evaluate issues were routinely the political, economic and military lenses. If religion was addressed at all, it was under a subcategory of cultural issues. It was not given the independent value it deserves.

At a 2011 symposium on the Role of Religion in Foreign and Public Policy, two former State Department speakers hit the nail on the head. They both confessed the official policy of the US State Department was this: *Religion is a problem in doing foreign policy, therefore it is off limits to discuss.* The perspective of these Georgetown University professors was: *If religion is the problem, then it is also the solution and absolutely must be addressed.*

What is even worse: religious discussion is also taboo in our own Supreme Court. Dahlia Lithwick, writing about Justice Antonin Scalia, says, "In a country averse to political debates about competitive faiths, nowhere is frank discussion of religion more taboo than at the US Supreme Court . . . it is not something that's talked about in polite company."[6] Not only does our State Department have blinders on when it comes to religion, but even our Supreme Court out of politeness sees it as a taboo subject.

The problem goes to the heart of our educational and political systems. Political scientists and government bureaucrats rarely study religion, and theologians are rarely interested in national security issues or foreign policy.[7] I hope this work will bridge the gap.

---

5   Harlan Ullman, advisor to the Atlantic Council, "Win Wars, Not Battles," *Defense News*, June 3, 2013, p. 21.
6   Dahlia Lithwick, "Scalia v. Scalia," *The Atlantic*, June 2014, p. 48.
7   Author in attendance at this symposium: "The World and Religious Affairs: Afghanistan, Pakistan and Beyond," Berkley Center for Religion, Peace and World Affairs, Georgetown University; held at Fort Jackson, SC, April 12 – 15, 2011.

"More than at any point in human history, the interest of nations and peoples are shared. The religious connections we hold in our hearts can forge new bonds among people or tear us apart."
—**President Barak Obama**, UN General Assembly[8], September 22, 2009

---

8   Quoted in The National Security Strategy, The White House, May 2010.

CHAPTER TWO
This Kind of Terror is Not New

Early Religious Terrorism

What is surprising about the subject of religious terrorism is most of the earliest examples of terrorism are religious in nature. Some have argued that the Bible records one of the earliest terrorist acts in Jail's covert act of driving a tent peg through the skull of Sisera, the commander of the Canaanite army, while he was asleep (Judges 4:21). From the writings of Jewish historian Flavius Josephus, we learn of the *sicarii*, a Jewish political-religious faction that attacked fellow Jews who were not in favor of revolting against the Roman occupation. The Sicarii would attack during religious holidays and celebrations by hiding daggers (the *sica*) under their coats and murdering selected political enemies.

In the eleventh century a Shia Muslim sect called the Ismailis established an entire Order of Assassins active throughout Persia, Syria, and Palestine. They viewed

Sunni Muslims as traitors and killed both Sunnis and Christians through clandestine actions. A Christian leader, the Marqui Conrad of Montferrat, who ruled Jerusalem at the time, was killed by a small group of dagger-carrying "emissaries" disguised as Christian monks. In offering advice to the King of France, a Christian priest advised, "I name the Assassins, who are to be cursed and fled. They sell themselves, are thirsty for blood, kill the innocent for a price, and care nothing for either life or salvation."[9]

Likewise, Walter Laqueur notes, "In India, the motivation of the *thuggee*, from which we get our word *thug*, who strangled victims, was apparently to make an act of sacrifice to the goddess Kali."[10] His point: Up until the present secular age, terrorism was fundamentally religious in nature. Only during the past century have politics and religion been separated and made into the doctrine of complete church and state separation in the United States. This is a misunderstood and misapplied Jeffersonian concept that does not appear in the Constitution. However, the history of the world is otherwise. Ancient history is upon us again, making current political conflicts into what few call war . . . religious war.

Current Religious Terrorism

To begin this chapter I want to take us back to a lesson we should have learned from the Balkan wars that took place prior to 9/11. The United States and its NATO allies have been involved in the Balkan conflict for over a decade now. After the peacekeeping efforts of the United Nations failed miserably in the former Yugoslavia, NATO under American leadership sent its troops in to stop the killing and stayed to keep the peace. Many are still there. Once the peace was secure in Bosnia, the warfare and ethnic cleansings simply moved to Kosovo, claimed by Serbia as their province. Those who study the region were not surprised by the "ethnic cleansing" as it was usually cited. One CIA analyst predicted in a 1993 intelligence assessment that the Bosnian war would result in a permanent redrawing of the Balkan borders. He noted, "I believe we are moving toward a greater Serbia, a greater Croatia, and a greater Albania as a result of this war." What these "greaters" meant at the time is that parts of Bosnia and Albania and all of

---

9   Bernard Lewis, *The Assassins: A Radical Sect in Islam*, Basic Books, 1968, p. 1.
10   Walter Laqueur, *The New Terrorism*, pages 10-12. Also see, Bernard Lewis, *The Assassins: A Radical Sect in Islam*, pp. 20-37, Oxford University Press, 1967.

Kosovo were on the table to be swallowed up by someone else.[11] Callahan's astute understanding of the region, however, reduced the Balkan conflict to mere "ethnic conflict." He writes, "the multiethnic state of Yugoslavia . . . with ethnic grievances simmering for decades just under the surface of official solidarity and national unity, was nothing but a façade."[12]

What observers failed to understand or comment upon was the distinctive religious character of this conflict. It is indeed an ethnic conflict, but ethnicity is deeply rooted in religious histories. Serbians for the most part are members of the Serbian Orthodox (Christian) Church. Kosovo was considered by the Serbs a Muslim or Albanian section of Serbia but having a (Christian) Eastern Orthodox minority which needed to be protected. Albania and parts of Catholic Croatia are also Muslim. Mixed into this conflict were a few Catholic and Orthodox Christians in Bosnia. "Ethnic" violence eventually spread to Macedonia. This should have surprised no one. Macedonia is claimed as northern Greece by the Greeks, southern Serbia by the Serbs, western Bulgaria by the Bulgarians, and eastern Albania by the Albanians.[13] So is this simply ethnic conflict or something more?

Each claim is rooted in the religious conflicts of earlier days. Each group viewed their section of real estate as holy ground and found a divine mission in preserving holy sites and settling old scores. Author Robert Kaplan explains, "To the (old) Catholic powers of Europe, and also to many Croats, it mattered not that Serbs and Croats were fellow Slavs. The Serbs were Eastern Orthodox and therefore, as much a part of the hated East as the Muslim Turks."[14] What is still amazing is the almost outright refusal on the part of government and media to give religion its due regard in the conflict. Reducing conflict to mere ethnicity does nothing to help the situation. In fact, it only furthers the confusion and lack of understanding. Why is it easier for Westerners to accept the phrase *ethnic cleansings* rather than an outright religious terrorism in the name of God? Most admit to inhuman executions on both sides of the conflict, but does this in some way help our consciences to call it *ethnic violence* rather than a religious war? Or perhaps, as completely secularized Westerners, we no longer see religion as being a relevant player in the public square?

---

11   David Kanin, CIA Chief Analyst for Yugoslavia, quoted in *Unwinnable Wars: American Power and Ethnic Conflict*, by David Callahan, p. 70.

12   David Callahan, *Unwinnable Wars*, p. 12.

13   See Robert D. Kaplan, *Balkan Ghosts*, Vintage Books, 1994, Chapters Two and Three. Pp. 49-70.

14   Ibid., p. 25.

What this book will try to establish is how religious groups in all of the major faith traditions (Christian, Jewish, Islam, and Eastern religions) have a significant tradition of violence in their respective histories. In addition, currently these religions have groups within them who are not only prone to using violence in the name of God but have already done so. Few see this as war. Though religions are normally viewed as being life affirming, benevolent and peace loving, what will be shown in this book is that violence in the name of God is not new. It is firmly rooted in the history and sacred writings of each religion. Many religious groups today find their justification in using violence in the teaching of their founders, their sacred scripture, and interpretations by its clergy or leaders. This was true even before we watched the Word Trade Center collapse.

Called *sectarian violence* in Tual, Indonesia, an Orlando Sentinel 1999 article recorded, "violence erupted for a second day where witnesses said Muslims hurled homemade bombs at Christians. The number of dead and injured was unclear."[15] The article did not appear on the front page but was hidden many pages later in a small two inch box.

On a back page, obtaining a little more space, is the conflict in the ancient African country of Sudan. The country has always been split between the Muslim north and the Christian and animist[16] south. A 1998 Wall Street Journal article recorded attempts by the Sudanese leadership to impose Islamic law on the entire country and make Sudan an Islamic state. Nina Shea writes, "Even the best accounts often fail to note that religion, that is, religious persecution of the most deadly sort, is at the heart of the current crisis."[17] Shea puts the death figure at 1.5 million with the displacement of millions more. Included in the report are witnesses of body hackings, with the capturing and enslaving of children and young women. This made the violence in the Balkans pale in comparison. The leadership in Khartoum openly called the violence a *Jihad* or holy war against the non-Muslim south. Ms. Shea concluded by saying, "Nowhere in today's world is religious persecution more appalling." But then Sudan rarely appeared on anyone's journalistic screens! Ms. Shea made her comments in 1998, yet the

---

15 *Orlando Sentinel,* April 25, 1999.
16 Animists honor and worship the spirit world as existing in all natural forces: stones, wind, fire, animals, etc.
17 Nina Shea, "A War on Religion," *Wall Street Journal,* July 31, 1998.

Sudan continues to suffer in 2014.[18] In 2013, south Sudan became the newest nation in the world. Yet, Christians and animists in South Sudan still suffer persecution from the Muslim north, while intertribal rivalry has created a civil war in the southern new country. Much of the population has fled to next door Kenya as a refuge from the violence.

More recently, the navy yard gunman Aaron Alexis opened fire on fellow workers killing twelve and wounding many more. Immediately, Alexis' interest in Buddhism seemed at odds with his actions. A *Washington Post* article reported, "Some saw the tragedy as an opportunity to publicly air some difficult topics that Buddhists most often discuss only among themselves . . . that image of being a peaceful religion." An ethicist quoted in the article said this image "is a myth."[19]

When the first attack on the World Trade Center took place in 1993 it should have been a wake-up call to most Americans. Ramzi Yusef, an Egyptian engineer, masterminded the attack, but it was a blind Muslim Brotherhood cleric who provided the "spiritual direction and benediction." An obscure Saudi millionaire helped finance the operation. The name Osama bin Laden was not well known at the time, but it would be shown to be behind the early attacks on American embassies and of course 9/11. But this attack was not the beginning, but only the fruit of a much larger religious revival. Later in the book I will show how the Islamic revolution, which began in Iran under Ayatollah Khomeini in the late 70s, was only the beginning of a global religious revival designed to bring the West to its knees. A new golden age of Islamization had been ignited as most of us sat and watched our game shows and complained about the price of gas.

When I tell people I am working on a book on *religious terrorism*, they naturally assume I am talking about Islamic terrorism. A mistake indeed! Unfortunately, religious terrorism is not limited to just one faith group. Violence with some kind of divine benediction takes place right under our noses even by those claiming to be Christians. Right here in good ol' USA.

In a lengthy 1997 article, *U.S. News & World Report* observed, "Characters like James Dalton Bell are giving federal agents fits these days. Bell, they believe, is one of the new generations of tinkerers and technicians, of college-educated extremists

---

18 More recently, South Sudan became its own independent nation, but much of the violence still continues.

19 "Buddhist community ponders apparent link between their community and Navy Yard shooter," Post Local, *Washington Post*, September 18, 2013.

threatening to use biological, chemical or radiological weapons to achieve their goals." In the same article, threats are noted as being made by "militia" members in Minnesota to use biological toxins to assassinate federal agents.[20]

Likewise, federal agents arrested Larry Wayne Harris after he obtained vials of bubonic plague. Who is Harris? An Ohio microbiologist and member of the Aryan Nation.[21] Aryan Nation and other militia groups are usually painted as white supremacist groups, putting them in the category of hate groups or extremist right-wing political groups.

On March 29, 2010, in a raid by a joint task force operation by FBI and ATF, a previously unknown group called the "Hutarees" was arrested in Washtenaw County, Michigan. This militia consisted of nine indicted individuals who called themselves "Christian soldiers" preparing for the coming Antichrist and being ready to defend themselves using swords (arms). They quoted Jesus in Luke 22:35-37, saying that he (Jesus) wanted his disciples to take swords. (www.hutaree.com). The action that brought them to the attention of law enforcement was planning to kill a police officer and then, as a trap, following up the murder by exploding a device at the funeral targeting fellow law enforcement officers attending.[22]

The reality is that these "Christian" groups have their own unique "Christian ideology" and are often led by ordained clergy, who believe they are doing God's work. It is commonly accepted that Timothy McVeigh, the architect and co-actor in the Oklahoma City Federal building bombing, was significantly influenced by this militia theology.[23] The extent to which these "Christian Identity" doctrines have infiltrated mainstream Christianity in America will be shown in this book.

Concern over the use of chemical weapons as an instrument of terror has always been on the intelligence radar screen of Western governments. However, the intelligence on such issues usually focused on rogue nations or the former Soviet Union. What was envisioned was the use of such weapons in wartime scenarios and not upon civilian populations.[24] But the first contemporary use of a chemical

---

20 "Terrorism's Next Wave," David Kaplan, *U.S. News & World Report*, November 17, 1997, p. 28.
21 Kaplan, p. 30.
22 "The Hutarees: Exposure and Vulnerability," Fred Burton and Ben West, Stratfor Global Intelligence Online, April 1, 2010.
23 "Parallels Between the *Turner Diary* Bombing and the Oklahoma City Bombing," *Klanwatch Intelligence Report*, The Southern Poverty Law Center, June 1995, p. 4.
24 Mustard gas was used on the battlefields during World War I by both the Allied and Axis forces, but not used on civil populations.

weapon capable of mass destruction was not used on a military battlefield but in a Tokyo subway. It took a religious group to unloose the genie of chemical weapons on innocent civilians. The group Aum Shinrikyo, or Supreme Truth, led by a blind acupuncturist turned religious guru, was found to have a high-tech laboratory capable of producing various nerve agents, like sarin, anthrax and botulin toxins. Ph.D. scientists who gave up prestigious university jobs to join the cult gave direction to the chemical labs. Kaplan's article on terrorism called them "New Age fanatics," an interesting label for such an educated group![25]

The Middle East has always been a hotbed of violence. As soon as the Jewish State was declared in 1948, violence between Israel and its Arab neighbors erupted leading to all-out war. The conflict was understood as a war between the Palestinian "soldiers" trying to regain their lost territory and that of the State of Israel trying to defend the security of its boundaries. All that changed in February of 1994. A religious Jewish Orthodox settler named Baruch Goldstein took his automatic weapon to the Tomb of the Patriarchs in Hebron, a site sacred to both Judaism and Islam, and proceeded to massacre twenty-nine Muslim worshippers. Goldstein was a devotee of Rabbi Meir Kahane who believed that killing Palestinians was justifiable in the eyes of God in order to take control of the Jewish people's God-given land.

Equally it was not surprising the assassin of Israel's Prime Minister, Yitzhak Rabin, was also a member of a Kahane group. Yigal Amir, a Bar-Ilan University student, admired and was profoundly influenced by the action of Goldstein.[26] First, the killing of Muslim worshippers by an Orthodox Jewish physician, then the killing of the Jewish Prime Minister by an Orthodox, Talmud-studying University student . . . what has happened here? Political motivations may be intertwined, but the ultimate source of this Jewish violence seemed rooted more in their faith in God than any particular politics. To the truly faithful of any faith group, religion *is* their politics! What will be pursued further in this book is the extent to which the "settlement" or "Kahane" movement has captured both the religious political Right in Israel and some American conservative evangelicals.

The year 2013 saw Islamists attack a Christian school in Nigeria killing thirty (twenty-nine students and their teacher) by the Boko Haram group.[27] In addition,

---

25 Kaplan, *U.S. News & World Report*, p. 30.
26 See Michel Karpin & Ina Friedman, Murder in the Name of God, p. 16-17.
27 "Nigeria: 30 Killed in School Attack," Stratfor Global Intelligence, July 6, 2013.

the kidnapping of 300 Nigerian school girls received world attention. (At this time of writing they are still missing, and many believe they were sold into slavery or became the "wives" of Haram soldiers.) In India nine simultaneous explosions hit the Hindu Mahabodhi temple complex, injuring the monks serving there. Intelligence sources say the town of Bodh Gaya had been targeted by Islamic terrorists based in Pakistan.[28] On August 25th of the year a mob of 1,000 Buddhists burned down dozens of Muslim homes in Northwest Myanmar. Sources say roughly thirty-five houses and twelve shops were destroyed. Security concerns have existed in the country for some time due to conflicts between Muslims and Buddhists.[29] Finally, in the midst of the ongoing violence in Egypt between Islamists and Christians, a Coptic priest was killed in El Arish by an unknown assailant.[30] This year (2015) the Islamic State executed 21 Egyptian Christians working in Libya on the shores of the Mediterranean. One of the killers warned, "*crusaders* would never be safe."[31]

Except for the Libya beheading above, most of these events are not usually covered or even mentioned in the daily news cycle. But almost every day, attacks like these take place, or go unreported and have serious religious connections. Stratfor reported "in Belgium the murder of three Jews with one wounded in a shooting at the Jewish Museum in Brussels, May 24, 2014."[32] Likewise, on Sunday June 8, 2014, two police officers were shot and killed while having lunch at a Las Vegas pizza buffet. A third was also killed at the nearby Walmart. Their killers? Jerad and Amanda Miller, a sort of lone wolf "Patriot-Militia" couple with views espousing antigovernment and citizen rebellion.[33] Mark Pitcavage of the Anti-Defamation League reported in the article, "We are five years into the largest resurgence in right-wing antigovernment groups since . . . the Oklahoma City bombing." White Supremacist literature was also recently found on the Ft. Carson, Colorado Army Base. Recruiting "propaganda flyers" were found "urging troops to join the drive to create a *white nation* in the Pacific Northwest." Current and former members of

28 "India: 9 Explosions Hit Temple Complex," Stratfor Global Intelligence, July 7, 2013.
29 "Myanmar; Buddhists Set Fire to Muslim Homes, Shops," Stratfor Global Intelligence, August 25, 2013.
30 Egypt: Coptic Priest Killed in Sinai, Sources Say," Stratfor Global Intelligence, July 6, 2013.
31 "Libya: Islamic State Executes 21 Egyptian Christians," Stratfor Global Intelligence, February 15, 2015.
32 Stratfor Global Intelligence, "Belgium: 3 Killed, 1 Wounded In Shooting At Jewish Museum," May 24, 2014.
33 Kelly Riddell, *The Washington Times*, June 9, 2014.

the military have long been recruited by Neo-Nazi and white supremacists for their "tactical skills and ideological beliefs."[34]

In short, terrorism is global with incidents named in ninety-four countries in 2013.[35] Most of these were religiously inspired. In 2015, two Pakistani churches were bombed in Lahore killing fourteen and wounding another seventy-eight, one of which was a suicide attack.[36] In Nigeria, a female suicide bomber killed another ten, wounding thirty others in a bus station attack in Damaturu. Boko Haram claimed responsibility.[37] The Somali terrorist group al Shabaab called for militants in America to attack shopping malls in the US, Canada and United Kingdom. Homeland Security Secretary Jeh Johnson responded saying, "his department takes the threats seriously."[38] Just recently, (2015) the FBI arrested six men in Minnesota and California for planning a terrorist attack. The threats were traced to a Somali Jihadist recruitment cell in Minneapolis.[39] Even though some may not want to call these attacks and actions "war," it is more than apparent these groups are seriously engaged in armed conflict against Americans, the West, and in particular Christians, Jews, and Muslims who don't embrace the radical ideology

Purpose of This Book

The design of this book is to take a look at two very complex fields: the field of religion and the subject of religious violence. It will give an overview of the history of religious violence, illuminating this modern kind of terrorism as an act of war. What terrorism is to one individual may not be terrorism to another, so the definitional problem must be carefully considered.

I will present representative case studies of current religious terrorist groups and take a look at one example from each of three major faith groups.

Most would think religious terrorists from different faith groups would have little in common. But the truth is just the opposite. Though the content of their beliefs varies greatly, each terrorist group demonstrates "uncommon commonalties,"

---

34 *Army Times*, "White Separatist Propaganda Turns Up at Ft. Carson," June 10, 2014.
35 "Infographic: Where Terrorists Attacked in 2013," *War on the Rocks Newsletter*, June 11, 2014, (warontherocks.com).
36 Stratfor Global Intelligence, March 15, 2015.
37 Stratfor Global Intelligence, February 15, 2015.
38 Stratfor Global Intelligence, February 22, 2015.
39 Stratfor Global Intelligence, April 20, 2015.

commonalties many people of faith can see in themselves. Bottom line: what would I really be willing to kill for?"

I will also address the growing concern about moral equivalency. If there are common elements among all terrorists, are they then all the same? Finally, some countermeasures will be addressed. A final look will be given to the role churches, synagogues, mosques and other places of worship play in being both a breeding ground for terrorist attitudes and as well, playing a significant role in reducing terrorist tendencies among their adherents. In fact, as noted in the first chapter, if religion is the problem then that is where most of the solution must lie!

Religious terrorism is not going away. Every year more atrocities take place at the hands of religious people.[40] It is difficult for a secular society to see religion as playing a significant role in anything. Equally, with political correctness in vogue, one cannot say publicly or officially anything negative about another's religion. (Although it seems Christianity and especially evangelicals are the lone exception.) The accepted academic version of pluralism and multiculturalism restrains most evaluators from saying one religious tradition is more inherently prone to violence than another. Even to raise the question can bring charges of prejudice, bigotry or legal action.

The enlightened age of the Western world somehow has imparted the view that all religions are equal if not the same. Therefore, to suggest religion can play a very powerful role in motivating a person toward violence denies the common logic of benevolent humanism and the Enlightenment. In the absence of clear political motivators, religion has filled the ideological vacuum. One religion editor observes, "With the Cold War over and global capitalism triumphant, religion has become the engine that drives the world's political and military struggles . . . That's because faith, the essence of religious commitment, makes a formidable motivator." Quoting another source he continues, "In the absence of other forms of opposition, religion is now a great repository for anybody who feels disenfranchised by modern institutions, cut off . . . or turned off, alienated from the so-called blessing of modern civilization and materialism."[41]

---

40   Groups motivated in part or in whole by a salient religious or theological motivation committed 10 of the 13 terrorist spectaculars in 1996. Bruce Hoffman, "Terrorism Trends and Prospects," *Countering the New Terrorism*, RAND, 1999, p.17.

41   "On a String and a Prayer," Mark I. Pinsky, *The Orlando Sentinel*, December 14, 1997.

The U.S. State Department lists forty-seven terrorist organizations. Of those listed, thirty-four are distinctively religious terrorist groups.[42] The rest are mostly the old Marxist style revolutionary groups like the Shining Path in Peru and the FARC in Columbia. These are just the ones intelligence sources know about. As noted earlier, no one saw the violent activities of Aum Shinrikyo coming. So how many other groups are out there like Aum?

When we Americans think of terrorism, we wrongly assume the only threat is a threat imported from another country. What we are not informed about tends to be of little or no concern to us. Fellow townspeople who attend the local patriot group, the members of the mosque in the suburb next door, or the Zionist or Christian groups raising money to rebuild the temple in Jerusalem don't get much notice from us. Yet all these groups could potentially promote attitudes leading to supporting or doing violence . . . either in their own communities or outside it. The details presented in this book will demonstrate America can be a breeding ground for terrorists as much as any other place on the globe. Remember it was Major Hasan Nidal, an American Army psychiatrist, who killed thirteen of his own fellow soldiers at Fort Hood while wounding another thirty-two. It was two Boston area college student brothers who performed the Boston Marathon bombing. Richard Abanes cautions even American Christians, "Undiscerning Christians have helped create a movement that is a bizarre mish-mash of evangelicalism, Christian terminology, apocalypticism, white supremacy, anti-Semitic legends, hate-filled rhetoric and violence!"[43] If Abanes is correct, it calls religious communities to exercise more care in their words, thinking, sermons, definitions, and behaviors.

So what is religion? What is terrorism, and what is religious terrorism? The next chapter will take a look at these emotionally charged, complex terms.

---

42   "The State Department Terrorist List," November, 2010.
43   Richard Abanes, *American Militias: Rebellion, Racism and Religion*, InterVarsity Press, 1998, p. 221.

CHAPTER THREE
A Brief History of Religious Terrorism
Fanatics or Freedom Fighters:
Faithful Zealot or Religious Terrorist?

"The religious imperative for terrorism is the most important defining characteristic of terrorist activity today."[44]
—Bruce Hoffman, *Inside Terrorism*

We often hear the expression, "one person's terrorist is another person's patriot or freedom fighter." This clash of perspectives raises multi-faceted difficulties in trying to define what constitutes a terrorist act. Likewise it begs the question as to what constitutes a truly religiously motivated terrorism.

---

44 Bruce Hoffman, *Inside Terrorism*, Columbia Univ. Press, 2006, p. 82.

Difficulties in Defining Religious Terrorism

In the process of defining this unique kind of terrorism we encounter several problems. First is the problem of preciseness. When the Israeli Air Force targets Hezbollah in southern Lebanon or the Hamas leadership in Gaza, should this action be called a *conflict between two nations* (Israel and Lebanon or Palestinian Gaza) or a type of *religious war* because it pits Jews against Muslims; or is it just a *military operation*, or *pre-emptive strike* against a sub national or transnational entity? (Southern Lebanon has been under Syrian administrative control providing cover for Iranian sponsored Shiite religious "freedom fighters;" likewise Gaza is ruled by Hamas which makes claims to represent all Palestinians.) The war with ISIS and others may bring about changes in the Lebanon/Syria/Iranian connection. For those living in the Lebanon and Gazan villages attacked, it is considered *Zionist terrorism*. In such cases calling the action all-out *war* or *conflict* might be too imprecise, while calling it a *pre-emptive strike* might be too precise on political terms. So the nature of the action gets lost in a foray of linguistic battles between the various parties; each having its own lexicon and vocabulary to justify the point of their actions. When a national entity, Israel (though a Jewish state) drops bombs on an "Islamic group" living in a third country, Lebanon and Gaza; what should it be called? Is it religious, political, a combination of both, or something other?

A second difficulty has to do with inclusivity. Who should be included in a label and who should be excluded? Mainstream journalists have a unique proclivity in not being able to distinguish groups within groups and consequently often include people in terrorist categories who are not. Words like *Islamic terrorists* transmit the connotation that all Muslims are terrorists. Even a subcategory like *Shiite* (a branch of Islam) *terrorist* or *Shiite extremist* gives the mistaken impression that all Shiite Muslims are extremists. Likewise, saying a *Christian militia group* was responsible for a terrorist act or *Jewish Orthodox settlers* were linked to terror activities imparts the same mistaken inclusive language. Not every Orthodox Jewish settler in Israel is a terrorist or militant; neither is every American Christian militia group prone to violence. Many are just middle-aged men playing around in the woods in camouflaged uniforms with paint guns!

Therefore, when defining *terrorism*, special care must be given to the problem of inclusivity. It takes more time and harder journalistic work to carefully distinguish the differences in religious groups. What is at stake is not only the personal integrity of the journalist but also the unique integrity of the religious group. It is a great temptation to lump sincere, religious people of the same kind into a splinter group with violent associations.

Approaches to religion lie in two extremes on a spectrum. One extreme is the position claiming total objectivity. University World Religion texts fall in this category. In academia the worst thing a scholar can do is to insert a personal opinion, therefore most texts at least give the appearance of information that is historically accurate, truthful, and free of personal bias.[45] Most informed people know this is impossible. One cannot speak or write one sentence without tapping into some personal belief or value. Another extreme also creates special problems in the study of religion. This is the problem of total subjectivity.

While teaching a course on Terrorism at the War College I required students to write a research paper on any subject related to religious terrorism. I required the paper to include at least ten different source materials. All the students performed to my expectations except one, an international officer. His paper was all personal opinion about a particular religious group (his own). The only source material quoted was verses from his religion's sacred scripture. When asked about his lack of research he responded that his religion did not permit the reading of non-religious books! This is total subjectivity. What he knew about his religion was totally from his own experience. Within his faith group (so he said) he could not be faithful and do otherwise. My assignment was trying to *Westernize* him and make him unfaithful to his God. As a *Westerner* I viewed his position as subjective and unlearned. We probably failed each other.

The objective versus subjective problem is also related to the tension between adherents and non-adherents. The objective/subjective issue naturally flows from the difference in being a religious adherent or having no experience with religion at the practice level.

Those within religious groups wonder whether a non-adherent can truly sympathize and appreciate the mysteries of their religion. I admit this concern from my own evangelical Christian tradition. It seems no matter how much coverage the press gives to evangelicals they never quite get it right. We are all

---

45 Though most scholars admit there is no such thing as total objectivity in any field, they write books having the appearance of lacking personal feeling about the data they provide.

right-wing fundamentalists with borderline personalities and suspicious politics. I often wonder whether any objective journalist could do justice to this multi-faceted community who call themselves *evangelicals*.[46] No one can prove to what degree being an adherent to a particular religion affects one's objectivity. Likewise, I don't believe trying to be objective about religion necessarily means being unsympathetic or understanding about someone's faith. In every religion there is enough mystery that total objectivity will fail. Likewise, I can't conceive of an absolute subjectivity. All beliefs come from multiple sources through the process of history. A pure faith is only a hypothetical assumption. This should lead us to caution in the process of defining.

A final problem confronts us when trying to define religious terrorism. Related to the adherent issue above but differing in the way religions are experienced, is the cognitive versus intuitive aspect of religions. Some faith groups form their beliefs around a set of cognitive facts or tenets. Their religion is then experienced through a those facts whether they are the Bible, the Koran, or the life and teachings of Buddha. Other religions experience their reality through the medium of human intuition or going within the human psyche. Animism, religions of nature and some Hinduism would be in this category.[47] Some pop-psyche and New Age thinking could also fall into this quasi-intuitive-religious category. These two categories (objective and subjective) are not pure in themselves. In practice, a full range of experiences exist that combine aspects of the cognitive and intuitive. The lines are not clear in practice. Religion always operates on the basis of some facts, beliefs, or ideology while generating some expression to the tenets in outward behavior or experience.

If religious experience is difficult to define, likewise, so is terrorism. As stated earlier, one person's terrorist can be another's faithful zealot.

Defining Terrorism

Early definitions of terrorism exclusively focused on the political nature of violent acts. Wardlaw's 1982 work defined terrorism simply as "the use of terror for political

---

46 If politics is rarely covered by the media without some bias, it really gets laughable when it comes to religion. Reporters either don't know what to say about it so they say nothing, or what they do say is "off the wall." As media critic Michael Medved noted, "When it comes to religion, reporters aren't biased, they are just ignorant!"

47 Early Hinduism was essentially a naturalistic animism, while later Hinduism became more philosophical and analytical.

ends."[48] Even though he grants that all terrorist acts are moral and symbolic in nature, he basically affirms the political nature of the violence. In like fashion, the United States up to 9/11 viewed terrorism mostly through a political or criminal lens. It still seems to lean more heavily on the political end of the spectrum rather than the religious.

The United States Department of State defined terrorism officially as: "the pre-meditated *politically* motivated violence perpetrated against noncombatant targets by subnational groups or clandestine agents intended to influence a *political* audience."[49] Notice I have highlighted the word *politically* because this tips the hand as to where the State Department was coming from at the time of definition (1996). In their view, terrorism was politically motivated and intended to send a political message to a political audience. From the outset this seems to oversimplify the problem. The FBI definition prior to 9/11 makes the same omission. A 1994 definition states, "Terrorism is the unlawful use of force or violence against persons or property to intimidate or coerce a government, the civilian population, or any segment thereof, in furtherance of political or social objectives."[50]

The Department of Defense definition now at least goes further and sees terrorists as possibly fulfilling "religious objectives." The DOD statement reads "terrorism is the unlawful use of, or threatened use of force or violence against individuals or property to coerce and intimidate governments or societies, often to achieve political, *religious* (emphasis mine) or ideological objectives."[51] A former member of the National Security Council defined terrorism as, "an act or threat of violence against noncombatants with the objective of exacting revenge, intimidating, or otherwise influencing an audience." [52]In these definitions we see a massive failure to grant genuine religious motivations or intents making religion a significant factor. This is one of the key difficulties in countering this unique brand of terrorism.

---

48   Grant Wardlaw, *Political Terrorism: Theory, Tactics and Counter-measures*, Cambridge Univ. Press, 1989 p. 3.
49   *Patterns of Global Terrorism*, United States Department of State, April 1996.
50   Quoted in *Understanding Terrorism*, by SAA Andrew Bringuel, FBI Academy, Behavioral Science Unit, Courses Materials, 2011.
51   Quoted in *The New Terrorism*, by Walter Laqueur, p. 5.
52   Jessica Stern, *The Ultimate Terrorists*, Harvard Univ. Press, 2000, p. 11.

Elements of Terrorist Acts

Academics studying the nature of terrorism divide terrorist events into multiple components or critical attributes. In every event there is an *act* of terror, *the actors* involved, *a target*, and an *audience*, along with *the message or meaning* of the act. To understand how these events are studied let's take, for illustrative purposes, the Oklahoma City Federal Building bombing. This terrible event killed 168 people and injured another 500 in the April 19 explosion in 1995. It continues to be the second worst act of terrorism on American soil.

The act itself is easy to identify. A homemade fertilizer bomb composed of ammonia nitrate and kerosene was loaded into a rented Ryder truck and placed in front of the Murrah Federal Building in downtown Oklahoma City. A delayed detonation device exploded the contents of the truck as the driver and perhaps his passenger walked away in separate directions. The detonation was so close to the building it brought down the entire frontal façade of the building and caused damage to surrounding buildings. That's the act or the element of what happened.

So who were the actors involved? Immediately, the attack was rumored to have been Middle East Islamic terrorists. But we now know that Timothy McVeigh, a US Army Gulf War veteran, was the primary actor in the act even though Middle East connections have not disappeared altogether.[53] He had a co-conspirator in Terry Nichols, an ex-army buddy.

The target here is equally easy to identify. The Federal Building in Oklahoma City represents the United States Government. But why this building at this time? As the facts came to light later, it housed the regional offices of the FBI, where some of the very agents who had worked the Waco standoff-turned-fiasco were currently serving. With this knowledge it then seems reasonable to conclude the attack was not just on a building but on what the building represented and who was working in the building at the time. Even the date of the attack had an ominous connection to Waco and the infamous FBI shoot-out at Ruby Ridge.[54]

---

53   See "Secret War Alleged" by Cliff Kincaid in the Washington Watch section of *The American Legion Magazine* March 1999, p. 48. The author quotes McVeigh's former attorney who now believes Iraqi agents were behind the explosion with links through McVeigh's co-conspirator, Terry Nichols!

54   Both these events were on the same date, which has now become known among patriot groups as *militia day*.

Understanding the audience is not quite as clear. An audience is the group to whom the message of the attack is being sent. In this case, it could be the United States Government, the FBI, a handful of FBI agents, Attorney General Janet Reno, various patriot groups, or the entire American populace! Any, all, or none of these may in fact be the likely audience.

Likewise, understanding the message or meaning of the act is just as problematic. What was the meaning or message the Oklahoma City bombing sent to whoever its audience was? Was it payback for the FBI and ATF debacle at Waco? Was it the message that the federal government is too powerful, or that the government had become so corrupt that it is worthy of being destroyed building by building? Who knows except the one unrepentant perpetrator![55]

The above approach to understanding terrorist acts is very helpful in clarifying most of them. However, when encountering any religious terrorist we need further clarification on the subject of audience. Who is the terrorist trying to influence? One intelligence analyst has called the beheading of American and British journalists *Terrorism as Theatre*, saying, "beheadings by a British-speaking ISIS terrorist sends the message of: "We don't play by your rules." Orange suited prisoners reminds us of mistreatment of Muslim prisoners at Guantanamo Bay. The British accent illustrates "We are as sophisticated as you." Using YouTube illustrates this is a message to the entire West. And the actual beheading is a statement, "We will triumph without any constraints."[56] Whatever message the religious terrorist is sending, the aspect of divine audience and religious motivation must also be factored into the discussion. A message may be sent to governments, groups, or individuals. But for the true religious terrorist, his or her audience is ultimately and in some way connected to a belief in God or some divine entity.

What the true believing religious terrorist does, he does in order to obtain a kind of divine benediction or divine favor based on his understanding of God's will. If the Divine is the audience, the terrorist doesn't care about whether the public at large gets the message or even if the right organization gets the credit. Of course, there is rarely a one hundred percent perfect religious motivation. Other

55 McVeigh received a death sentence and was executed in June of 2001. Terry Nichols received life imprisonment and is still serving 161 consecutive life terms. Fellow Army buddy Michael Fortier testified against both McVeigh and Nichols and pleaded guilty to knowing about the attack beforehand but telling no one. Fortier plea bargained and was sentenced to twelve years in prison. He was released in 2006 and is currently in the witness protection program.

56 Robert Kaplan, "Terrorism as Theatre," Stratfor Global Intelligence, August 27, 2014.

factors commonly exist. However, to those truly motivated by their religion, the perceived pursuit of divine benediction and the satisfaction gained by the actor in accomplishing the violence is reward enough. This is probably the most dangerous aspect of the religious terrorist, and the one that usually gets overlooked by government agencies trying to counter terrorist acts.

What Is Religion?

If it is difficult trying to define what a terrorist act is, it is equally difficult to define what religion is. Religion is one of those words that everyone thinks they know the meaning of until they have to define it. At first blush, it would seem that religion has to do with faith in God. But of course, this definition just begs another question, what does the term *God* mean, and what does *faith* mean? Hindus believe in millions of gods, and Buddhists don't believe in a personal God as Judeo-Christianity does. We even use the word *religious* to describe any range of behaviors from obsessive-compulsive workaholics to those who *religiously* care for their pets. New Age devotees may never step into a house of worship but still consider themselves very *religious*. Likewise, I know evangelical Christians who pride themselves in saying they hate religion and the last thing they want to be known for is being religious![57]

Perhaps a safer definition of religion would be one focusing on the ultimate concern of the person, whatever that may be. One individual's ultimate concern could be provision for his family, while for another it is making sure his or her life counts for something. If something is the ultimate concern of an individual (regardless of the content of the belief) we might say he is religious in that regard. Someone may be religious about caring for family or making some impact upon the world. In this sense, religion can be anything and everything, without being clearly definable.

One scholar, Dr. Robert Oden, has defined religion as, "A communicational system constituted by a supernatural being which relates to specific patterns of behavior."[58] I like Dr. Oden's definition because it is precise enough while still being a little indefinite. I like his emphasis on religion being a communication system.

---

57   They say, "I just believe in Jesus and read my Bible, but this is a personal relationship with God and doesn't have anything to do with *religion*."

58   Robert Oden, *God and Mankind: Comparative Religions*, Vol. II., Video Series, The Teaching Series Company, 1990, Arlington, VA.

A communicational system gets into specific beliefs, ideas, and propositions.[59] Religious people are carriers of all three. Even the things we deny end up being propositions about the nature of God or our belief system. The statement, "I do not believe in a God of love," is as much a statement of one's belief system as the affirmation of the statement. In this sense Madelyn Murray O'Hare's atheism was just as religious as the most ardent believer's faith.

The second element of Oden's definition is that he postures the belief in a supernatural being that is the ultimate source of religious ideas, beliefs, and propositions. In other words true religion is revelatory. However one conceives the divine, this divine Person communicates or reveals thoughts and ideas to human receivers. When received, these worshippers believe the ideas to be divinely given and more importantly believe they require some action on their part. Religion as a divine-human communicational system ultimately must affect *specific patterns of behavior.*"

True religion then requires the genuine believer to act on his beliefs. It is these specifically religious patterns of behavior that ultimately define and distance the believer from the nonbeliever. Religious people are judged not only by what they believe but also by what they do or don't do! Most people *believe* they should be benevolent toward their fellow man, but how many act on this belief? Likewise, a man may act on his own passions while not acting on any particular system of beliefs. This individual in the technical sense of religion would be considered acting merely on impulse or animalistic instincts. In truly religious people, beliefs and acts are unified while reinforcing each other.

The Good Samaritan story told by Jesus imparts a belief about helping people who are in critical need. In turn, the story requires the obedient Christian to act in kind. Therefore, when I see someone in need, I try to give aid. Likewise, when I help someone in need, it makes me feel good that I both helped another human being, and perhaps may have pleased Jesus by doing it. The revelatory message of God as found in the New Testament forms a back and forth communicational system between my God and me, which in the final analysis, if I really believe

---

59   I am using the word *proposition* in its standard philosophical usage, a use that proposes the grammatical statement of a subject, verb, and object complement. The statement or proposition can then can be believed, doubted or denied. In this sense, God *is* something. The something that is affirmed about God can be believed, doubted, or denied. Example: God is love!

it, affects my behavior. That's what religion is and does. But not all religions are the same.

Classification of Religions

If religion is hard to define, it is again equally difficult to classify. However, for the purposes of this overview of religious experience I will use five historically recognized and respected classifications. The first is *Tribal Animism*. Found throughout the world, the experience of animism involves: lack of written history, spontaneity of expression, motivation by fear and self-preservation, lack of written moral codes (only *taboos*), the presence of magic and manipulation of cosmic forces through ritual, and an all-embracing effect on the totality of life. Examples of animism can be found among the Quechan Indians (Bolivia), Haitian voodoo, Hawaiian *kahunas,* and Australian aborigines. In these expressions, animal sacrifice is common and at various times in their histories, these systems included human sacrifice and cannibalism. Here various forces of nature or innate spirits were viewed as being appeased by human or animal blood. Violence then was not uncommon.

The second category is *Naturalistic Religions.* Here the forces of nature (wind, rain, fire, sun, moon, stones, animals, and stars) are worshipped as gods or spirits who provide some control over human destiny. Traditional religions listed as naturalistic include, Taoism, Confucianism and Shintoism, and Native American worship. As such they do not make clear statements about the gods they embrace but see them as naturalistic influences on their lives. Though nature is violent (hurricanes, earthquakes, animal carnivores) generally, these religions have been less violent than tribalism.

Monistic Religions are very similar to the naturalistic but are more philosophically developed. Monistic religions include Hinduism, Buddhism and Jainism. In these systems, all reality is viewed as one, thus a fundamental *One-ism*, or monism, exists. Differences exist only as a thimble full of water taken from a river differs from the river itself. All reality is the same; differences are only subparts of a greater reality.

Monotheistic religions are better known, at least in the West. These include Judaism, Islam, some Zoroastrians, and some Christian groups like Unitarians. Here, a strict belief in one God is foundational; this one God is distinct from the creation and wholly other or apart from his creatures. Surprisingly, on the subject of violence, each of these groups has their own unique history of both extending and defending their faith through bloodshed.

Finally, there are the *Trinitarian* Christian religions consisting of creedal Christianity as expressed in the various orthodox, Catholic and Protestant confessions. These groups, though claiming to be monotheistic, believe the one God exists in three persons (Father, Son and Holy Spirit) or a tri-unity of being. On the subject of violence, the history of Trinitarians is no more passive than other groups. They have used the sword to defend, extend, and establish their "Christian" purposes.

One of the most common elements found in all religions is the experience of and belief in good and evil. In this sense, religion both affirms and explains the ultimate cosmic human conflict. Bruce Hoffman has acknowledged "religious terrorism tends to be more lethal than secular terrorism because of the radically different value system"[60] A major part of this value system is the powerful role good and evil plays in constructing one's world view. Religions may differ in details as to how they construct the good/evil paradigm (spiritual forces in conflict, religious phenomena, psychological, psychosomatic, psychic, occultic, or demonic, or some combination of all or part of the above) but the good/evil continuum exists all the same, and provides rich raw material for both believing and carrying out violent acts.

Religious Terrorism Defined

So how *does* one define religious terrorism and in what ways is the religious terrorist unique? Taking the Department of State definition and amending it to include the religious component, religious terrorism is then: "*the premeditated* **religiously** *or politically motivated violence perpetrated against noncombatant targets by subnational, transnational or antinational groups or clandestine agents, usually intended to influence or exact revenge*[61] *upon a political audience or* **to gain the honor, respect or benediction from a deity, and/or fellow religious observants.*" Knox Thames, a former State Department staffer on Policy and Religion, observes in the latest State Department Country Reports on Terrorism, "the Strategic Overview never describes terrorists with a religious modifier, such

---

60   Bruce Hoffman, *Countering the New Terrorism*, p. 19.

61   I include *revenge* based upon the research of Jessica Stern where she sees revenge against specific targets as a major factor in motivation. See *The Ultimate Terrorists*, p. 11.

as violent *religious* extremism or *Islamist extremism.*" The new *worrisome trend* of terrorist violence is said to be fueled by *sectarian motivations!*[62] This reflects the still ever-present hesitancy by Washington officialdom to say this brand of violence is connected to religious motivations.

My definition above makes the religious terrorist unique in the sense that he or she is motivated by distinctly religious concern, sees God as either the primary or secondary audience, and as a religious believer, has a faith that can cross any national boundary while respecting only those of the same faith. As a result the religious terrorist is far more potentially lethal while making counterterrorism activities more difficult. But this lethality is not new. The definition also demonstrates both a theological or vertical aspect (a belief system or ideology) plus the social aspect of functioning within some kind of ideological community (the horizontal aspect). These twin components reinforce each other to create attitudes toward violence that can result in terrorist acts.[63]

The religions of East Asia are also worthy of attention in this context, as evidenced by the reference in Chapter One to Aum Shinrikyo, but are beyond the scope of this book. So we will examine three major faith groups: Judaism, Christianity, and Islam. What will be found in the histories and teachings of the faiths we do consider is not a consistent doctrine of nonviolence as many assume. Even President Obama recently said, "First of all, ISIL is not Islamic. No religion condones the killing of innocents."[64] This seems either very naïve or our Commander in Chief needs a new speech writer! If any person wants to justify violence in the name of Heaven, he or she does not have to go very far in the histories of any of these major faith groups to find material for an argument.

---

62 Knox Thames, "Opportunities to Combat Violent Religious Extremism," *Small Wars Journal*, http://smallwarsjournal.com, December 12, 2014.

63 Later, the "lone wolf" terrorist theory will be considered. Basically, the theory denies the social component because the terrorist acts alone, belongs to no group, and is usually only influenced by the online ideologies. Unfortunately, many miss the humorous reality as to why we call the "social media" social!

64 Quoted in *The American Thinker*, Stu Tarlowe, "Obama's speech strategy: open with your biggest lie," www.americanthinker.com/blog, September 12, 2014.

CHAPTER FOUR
The History of Violence in Religion

"The idea of finding an acceptable code of behavior for contemporary terrorists is a contradiction in terms."

—**Walter Laqueur**[65]

T he former reigning opinion seemed to say religion and violence were very strange, if not incompatible, bedfellows. The thought that religious people can and do perpetrate violent acts was often met with perplexed looks. Prior to 9/11, I was speaking at a church one Sunday and happened to mention my work on religious terrorism. Afterwards, a woman came up and said, "I'm so glad you are dealing with this terrorism problem. I have experienced so much abuse by religious people!" It dawned on me she had absolutely no idea what I was talking about. When I explained that I was talking about actually killing people in the name of God, a confused look appeared on her face. Finally, I said,

---

65   Walter Laqueur, *The New Terrorists*, 1999 p. 281.

"like when the Muslims and Christians took swords and killed each other in the Crusades, or when European state churches drowned Anabaptists for believing in *another baptism*, or when American Christian Patriots want to kill racially mixed couples." Eventually, she turned and walked away, probably thinking what an odd Christian I was. I thought how illiterate we are about our own history and the realities of our current world. We don't connect the thought of religion with the experience of violence. In fact, the two not only coexist today, but have always coexisted.

9/11 was the not the beginning of a new era. Even former FBI agent Mike German admits, "Modern day terrorists follow strategies pioneered centuries ago."[66] But what made the 9/11 events shocking was where they took place. For years, violent attacks on innocents in the name of religion have routinely been noted around the world. It is eye opening to realize the types of terrorist events that have taken place in the past. These are not major events but ones that get tucked away on back pages of newspapers and magazines. Most never make it to the mainstream media. Former Army General Hugh Shelton, chairman of the Joint Chiefs of Staff once noted it is the "little conflicts" that the U.S. faces that are the "nastier dangers . . . posed by arsenals of asymmetric threats and a messier world . . . (these little conflicts) are dominated by failed states where internal strife would be the hallmark of contemporary security affairs."[67] Here are a few of the "nastier dangers" to think about.

On the West Bank of Israel, Orthodox Jews moved into a house in the Ras al-Amud section of East Jerusalem, apparently ousting a Muslim Arab family living in the house. The move "drew protests from both Israelis and Arabs and put Israelis security forces on alert. Dr. Irving I. Moskowitz, an American Jew, financed the entire operation.[68]

In Denver, a 39 year-old man was arrested as he intended to "incinerate" Colorado's largest mosque. He was arrested after fleeing the site in a car loaded with bomb-making materials, four guns and 1,000 rounds of ammunition. Suspect Jack M. Modig said to the arresting Sheriff, "I am an enemy against the Islamic nation and I was going to take care of business." In the past, the article reports, "Modig

---

66 Mike German, *Thinking Like a Terrorist*, Potomac Books, 2007, p. viii.
67 "Defense Trends: Russian, China, India Keys to Unity," *Air Force Times*, October 12, 1998.
68 "Jews Oust Arab Tenants from House in Jerusalem," *The New York Times*, September 16, 1997.

has expressed support for the far-right antigovernment philosophy espoused by the Freeman group in Montana."[69]

On May 27, 1999, a half page ad was taken out in *The New York Times* by the organization, *The National Association of Asian Indian Christians in the USA, Inc.* The ad is an appeal for freedom of religion in India. It claims overt violent "religious persecution of small Christian communities in India by right-wing Hindu fundamentalists." Although India is a democracy granting freedom of religion, nothing is being done about the atrocities being committed.[70]

Another article records persecution and violence against a Palestinian Christian for no other crime than being a witnessing Christian. *The Jerusalem Report* records, "A Palestinian Christian Arab named Muhammed Bak'r sits in a West Bank jail. His crime? Converting to Christianity from Islam and then distributing Bibles to Muslims. A friend who visited him says the suspect has been severely tortured."[71]

In a frightening brief, *The Air Force Times* records, "Government auditors trying to balance the books have discovered that inaccurate or unreliable inventory data has left the Department of Defense unable to account for some equipment. For example, 220 tanks, 10 helicopters, 25 aircraft, eight cruise missiles, and 21 ships are reported missing."[72] Makes one wonder where they went, who has them, and how in the world they got stolen or misplaced! Recent attempts to investigate if there was any follow up to this story revealed no further information. This was equally surprising.

In Sacramento, California, two antigovernment militiamen faced a hearing on weapons charges in an alleged plot to create a propane explosion so disastrous that it would lead to a government overthrow. More than 50 firearms, 50,000 rounds of ammunition and 30 pounds of fertilizer that could be used in explosives were seized when the men were arrested.[73]

Rabbi Abraham Cooper, of the Simon Wiesenthal Center, believes "the subculture of hate on the Internet is growing at alarming rates." Many of

---

69 James Brooke, "Colorado Man Is Suspected of Planning Mosque Attack," *The New York Times*, May 13, 1999.

70 "An Appeal for Freedom of Religion," *The New York Times*, May 27, 1999.

71 "Palestinian Christians say 'Land Dealer' really held for Missionizing," *The Jerusalem Report*, September 4, 1997.

72 "Anyone Here Lose a Tank?" *The Air Force Times*, June 29, 1998.

73 Wire report: "Hearing set for militiamen in giant-explosion scheme," *USA Today*, December 9, 1999.

these are Christian Identity groups like the World Church of the Creator, of whom three members have pleaded guilty to charges of beating and robbing a Jewish businessman. The Southern Poverty Law Center in Montgomery, AL, now counts over 1000 such "hate sites" on the Internet,[74] with over 1000 designated hate groups listed in 2012 . . . a 67 percent increase since the year 2000.[75]

In response to a growing concern chemical or biological agents could be used by terrorists on American soil, the National Guard has trained rapid reaction teams to respond to such events. "There is a real threat out there today," said Washington Air Guard Captain Terry Gram. "I believe we need to be prepared. Not every fire department and emergency medical system is totally capable of responding to a weapons of mass destruction incident."[76]

In sum, prior to the eventual day of September 11, as Sam Meddis cautions in an *USA Today* article, "Religion, not politics, has become the driving force behind much of the world's post-Cold War terrorism." Citing a former CIA counter-terrorism expert, he says, "There's no question an era has passed, the new breed are people who claim a direct pipeline to God . . . and that's much more dangerous. In the USA, where the antiwar violence of the Weather Underground has become a dim memory, "there are anti-abortion shootings and bombings by people who identify themselves with the Christian right. If you have the mandate of God, you are not prohibited by normal morality."[77]

Justification

It is now time to step back and ask what common elements in religion can lead a person to kill another human being with what they believe is divine authority. For the religions that do believe violence can be justified, how do they justify it? Can similarities be seen among their arguments? From our study thus far, I can identify five arguments or factors that become justifications for violence.

---

74 "U.S. hate groups top 1000," *SPLC Report*, Southern Poverty Law Center, Spring 2011, Vol. 41, Number 1.
75 "The Year in Hate and Extremism," *Intelligence Report*, Spring 2013, Issue number: 140.
76 "First Raid: New Guard Rapid Reaction Medics Train to Thwart Terrorists," *National Guard*, May 1999.
77 "Holy War is the way of Terrorism," *USA Today*, March 24-26, 1995.

Exaltation of the Warrior

Some religions develop a warrior class or a warrior ethic which becomes very powerful. The idea of the warrior and his lethal justification lies in the defensive nature of his role.

In other words, a warrior's violence in battle is justified by hostile threats or attacks by an enemy. The warrior is the front line defender of a nation's people, values and way of life. If these are threatened, the killing he does is a necessary function of his duty. For these defensive duties, the warrior is exempted from the normal consequences of killing. Our counterpart today is when a combatant kills in warfare it is not considered legal murder. The warrior is exempted from normal criminal civil law.

A direct application to terrorism is obvious. Most terrorist groups see themselves as warriors, fighting a defensive war against ungodly forces of evil. In this sense, they see themselves exempted from the norms and laws of society. As religious warriors they are doing their divine "duty." Here, the warrior tradition in their religion plays a powerful role in providing both a motivation and ultimate justification for their violent acts.

Belief in a Warrior God (Emulation Factor)

When I research some new religious cult one of the first things I look at is how they conceive their deity. Any religion that has supernatural or supra-natural deities has to describe them in some way. The possibilities are endless, but most resort to images or metaphors. Even in the Christian tradition, we describe God as a Father, a Judge or a Savior. One of the characteristics of cults is they usually focus in on one primary attribute to the exclusion or reduction of other attributes. Therefore, they might see God as a God of justice more than a God of love, for example.

Belief in a warrior god provides for the devotee or terrorist an emulation factor for violence. The logic goes, "if god is a warrior, and I want to be god-like or please this god, then I need to be a warrior." If God acts as a warrior, it is not much of a leap for the follower to act as a warrior and justify violence in the name of God. This is precisely the dynamic we will see later.

Sacred Writing Justification

One of the interesting things about human nature is our need or tendency to seek authority from outside sources for justification of our ways. Our acts are rarely independent in the purist sense. Some religious traditions have more sacred writings than others, but where writings exist, adherents will find justification for their actions in these writings. This is why knowledge of the sacred writings about such things as war, peace, life, death, murder, and revenge are so important. These sources are key determiners in how a specific faith group will view violence. Sacred writings may provide guidance to warriors, justification for violence, and the promise of a certain kind of afterlife.

Theology of Human Existence

To do violence to another human being ultimately strikes at the heart of how one conceives human life and existence. An interesting phenomenon is how a military must dehumanize or even demonize its enemy in order to justify killing him. Names like, "communists, Nazis, gooks, japs and towelheads" all provide not-so-subtle attempts to lower the level of existence of another human being to the point where he is *killable.*

World Order Vision

The groups that worry me the most are those who have a universal vision for the world. In other words, they do not keep their religion to themselves, but are under a perceived divine obligation to extend their faith until some new world order is established. One of the interesting things about the demise of the Cold War is that the order of the world has changed significantly. The clearly defined bi-polar world of communism versus the free world no longer exists.

Today, there is no clear political vision for the world. In the gap, world alliances such as NATO, the United Nations (UN), European Union (EU) and the World Trade Organization (WTO) have tried to fill the vacuum with new economic and military agreements. NATO has expanded to include the Baltic, Eastern Europe and several Balkan states. (Turkey is on hold.) Some nations within the UN would like to see the eclipse of American domination and the emergence of the UN as the leader of governance for the world. Europe tried to emerge as the new bipolar balance to America but is now faltering due to serious economic problems starting with Greece and Portugal. The Russian takeover of key areas of the Ukraine has also complicated relations among Eastern and Western Europe nations. China has emerged as more of a world player but has not yet really surpassed the US in domination, even as the World Bank and World Trade Organization try to replace the US as financiers for emerging growth. However, none of these attempts have provided a comprehensive, sensible ideological vision for the world.

Obviously, the group or religion where most or all of these factors exist has the greatest potential for developing a radical ideology for violence. As stated earlier, as educated, enlightened Americans, we do not like to think about the fact that one religion may be more prone to violence than another. It's just not politically correct to assume such. But this is precisely the case I am making in these chapters. Some religions have more history of violence than others, and have more raw materials in their sacred writings to provide religious justifications for violence. Just because it is there, does not mean the individuals within that religion are more prone to violence. All it does mean is that the historical and sacred literature justification is there waiting for some guru in the right circumstance to claim "inspiration" from the material (or from their divine source) and use it to justify a more militant vision of the future

In reaction to the secular century of both capitalistic and dialectical materialism, the world is hungry for a spiritual vision. In response, this century may turn out to be about whom or what can provide the most satisfying ideology for spirituality. That makes religion a key factor for the future. As one writer said, "God is back,"[78] but unfortunately the DC beltway leadership is slow in realizing this. Commenting on the Washington culture, writers John Mickelwait and Wooldridge report, "Washington diplomats and think tanks remain locked in their Westphalian box (separation of church and state). Looking back, former Secretary of State Madeleine Albright cannot remember during her adult years any leading diplomat speaking in depth about the role of religion in shaping the world." In her own words, Ambassador Albright admits she did not "view the great issues of the day through the prism of religion, either my own or that of others . . . I did

---

78 Quoted in *God is Back*, by John Mickelwait & Adrian Wooldridge, Penguin books, 2009, p. 358.

not consider spiritual faith a subject to talk about in public."[79] It's no wonder we have problems. Our leaders are out of touch! The current Obama administration seems to ignore or downplay the religious realities of the Middle East by repeatedly issuing the mantra of Islam as a religion of peace. Unfortunately, this strategy (if that is what it is) has not changed the reality on the ground no matter how many times the Administration has repeated it.

The purpose of the following chapters is to demonstrate the long-standing tension that has existed between the traditions of peace and the traditions of violence in the major religions.

I will look at Judaism, Christianity and Islam. In doing this survey, I do not claim to be an expert on each of these religions . . . how could anyone? I am very dependent upon the referenced source material. I do hold a master's degree in theology and have done doctoral and postdoctoral work in theology and religious studies. However, just as I would not claim to be a "master" of my own religious traditions or Biblical sources, so I would not claim expert opinion on such a wide range of religious traditions.

This review is critical in order to understand the world and mindset in which the current terrorist lives.

So, let's turn for a deeper look at Judaism, Christianity, and Islam.

---

79 Madeleine Albright, *The Mighty and the Almighty*, Harper Collins, 2006, p. 7. She also says after the publication of Samuel Huntington's *Clash of Civilizations*, she and other foreign policy professionals had to adjust their lens of how to view the world!

CHAPTER FIVE
Zionists, Crusaders and Jihadists
History of Violence in Religions of Middle-Eastern Origin

"Let me him who has no sword, sell his robe and buy one."
—**Jesus**, Gospel of Luke 22:36

The *Western religions* of Judaism and Christianity plus Islam are *all* of Middle Eastern origin and have much in common with Middle Eastern customs and value systems. Historian and Middle East expert Bernard Lewis argues, "Christianity and Islam are both religions of very much the same kind with a common history, with common background and a large measure of common beliefs . . . when a Christian said to a Muslim or a Muslim to a Christian "you are an infidel and will burn in hell," each understood exactly what the other meant . . . this kind of dialogue would have been meaningless between a Christian or Muslim on the one side and a Buddhist or Confucian on the other!"[80]

One of the ironies of being in the Middle East is how both Israelis and Arabs have the same greeting. Jews in Israel say, "Shalom Aleichem," while their Arab neighbors say, "As salaam alaikum." Both mean the same thing, "peace be unto you." In other words, both acknowledge the value of peaceful relations among men. Their histories speak otherwise.

Peace and Violence in Judaism

There is an aspect to the history of Judaism that rarely receives attention. Realities of both peace and violence have coexisted throughout much of Jewish history. Let's take a look at three major periods of Judaism: the Biblical, Revolt and Rabbinical periods.

Biblical Period

The Jewish Bible (Christian Old Testament) is based on the sacred Hebrew literature of the Law, Prophets and Writings (or Wisdom literature). These texts offer a vast experience of violence, bloodshed, murder, and war while also affirming the value of human life. The history begins where God is the first to shed blood by slaying an animal in order to clothe the first couple with animal skins (Genesis 3:21). The first murder is, likewise, essentially an act of "religious violence." Cain is so jealous of his brother Abel's divine favor, he kills him (Genesis 4:8). Later, Abram, Patriarch of the Hebrew nation, leads 318 armed men into warfare against a coalition of kings in order to rescue his nephew Lot.

After the Egyptians were miraculously defeated in the Jewish exodus, the Hebrews celebrated the victory in the name of Yahweh, their Warrior. They sang, "The Lord is a Warrior; Yahweh is His name, Thy right hand O Lord, is majestic in strength; thy right hand, O Lord, shattered the enemy."[81] (Exodus 15:3-6).

During the nation's sojourn in the wilderness, some of the men of Israel took Midianite wives, and when one of the women was brought to Moses, Phinehas

---

80 Bernard Lewis, *Faith and Power: Religion and Politics in the Middle East*, Oxford University Press, 2010, p. 155.

81 George Ernest Wright, Old Testament Professor at Harvard, regards the image of God as Warrior as basic to the Biblical conception of God. Willard M. Swartley, *Slavery, Sabbath, War and Women*, Herald Press, 1983, p. 103.

took a spear and ran it through the women's Israelite husband (Numbers 25:7-18). In response, God tells Moses to be hostile to the Midianites (Numbers 25:17). Later, Phinehas leads an army of 12,000 armed men and completely destroys the Midianites, burns their cities, and captures their spoil.

When the tribal nation entered the Promised Land, General Joshua led a 40,000 man army of conquest (Joshua 1:1-5, 4:13) destroying whole towns including women and children (Joshua 6:21, 8:25). These wars were called *herems* or holy wars with specific bans on looting. Where looting took place there was to be swift justice (Joshua 7:16-26). Joshua personally killed kings, hung their bodies on trees (Joshua 10:23-24), and took no captives (Joshua 10:28, 48). The assumption throughout this literature is what the Israelites did in warfare, God did. Or putting it another way, what God was doing, he was doing through the agency of his warrior Israelites (Joshua 10:42, 23:3). The complete destruction of cities is equated to obedience to God as commanded through His spokesman, Moses (Joshua 11: 10-15). In Joshua's final charge to his people he tells them to continue fighting to possess the remainder of the land. In so doing, God is the one who goes before them to do the warfare, as Longman and Reid note, "The central principal is that God is present in the battle with his people as a warrior" (Joshua 23:4-5).[82]

During the time of Israel's tribal Judges, Othniel wages a war against King Aram. Judge Ehud pulls off a clandestine dagger attack on the King of Moab. Next, Deborah, the first feminine military leader, leads an army of 10,000 warriors against Sisera, commander of the Canaanite armies. The text records an intriguing musical blessing on Jael, the wife of Heber, for killing a sleeping Sisera in her own home by driving a tent peg into his skull. He asked for water, but she gave him milk and a tent peg! She is honored as, "Most blessed among women" for her act of violence (Judges 5:l, 24). Compare this with Luke's recorded benediction upon Mary, the mother of Jesus! "Blessed among women are you" (Luke 1:42).[83]

The history of Israel's kings is no better. Both King Saul and King David were warrior kings. In fact, David had so much blood on his hands, God denied him his deepest longing, to build a house for God (I Samuel 17:45).

---

82 War, during this time was equated with worship. "War was worship for Israel," say Tremper Longman and Daniel Reid, *God Is a Warrior*, Zondervan press, 2010, p. 20.

83 Luke 1:42, where Elizabeth offers this blessing upon Mary and upon receiving Mary's greeting Elizabeth's child leaping in her womb.

The law sections of the Torah record ethical codes for warfare. There should be an offering of peace made to an enemy before waging war; a way of escape must be provided; and destruction was to be limited. Fruit-bearing trees were not to be touched. Options were offered for noncombatant status (Deuteronomy 20). The Wisdom literature recognizes the reality of bloodshed and conflict, and is probably best summarized in, "there is a time to kill, and a time to heal . . . a time for war and a time for peace," (Ecclesiastes 3:8).

The Poetic sections record an emphasis on peace and praying for peace (Psalm 122:6), while also praying to God as Warrior to smash the ungodly nations (Psalm 17:13). In addition, the Psalms and Prophets envision a growing suspicion about military strength, "Some boast in chariots and some in horses, but we will boast in the name of the Lord," (Psalm 20:7). An increasing yearning for a time of permanent peace (when swords will be beat into plows, Isaiah 2:4) is also expressed in the Prophets and sees its fulfillment in a future Messiah, or Anointed One, who will establish peace and justice (Isaiah 9:6).

Thus, as noted in other religions, the sacred writings of Judaism seem to be divided on the subject of violence. It depends on where one goes in the literature as to what is taught and recorded. From the Biblical period of Judaism, we now turn to the period of Jewish Revolts.

History of Jewish Revolt

I remember my first trip to Israel and my rigorous hike up to the Masada fortress. Our guide had a "thing" about soft American tourists taking the cable car up, so our small group hiked up the historic incline. Our guide was trying to instill in us the powerful symbol Masada represents to the Israelis. Israeli soldiers are sworn in on top of Masada after climbing it as we did. Masada is the poignant symbol of Jewish armed revolt.

The period of Jewish revolt can be dated to the Greco-Roman transition period between the closing of the Jewish canon of sacred literature (second century BC) and the birth of Christ. During this time Antiochus Epiphanes of Greece tried to establish a sovereign Greek culture in Palestine (Israel). A Jewish militant named Judas Maccabee saw the imposition of Greek culture as defiling the Jewish way of life and defiling the sacred Jewish temple in Jerusalem. When Antiochus Epiphanies sacrificed a pig in the temple, it was the last straw for Judas Maccabee. He organized an army of followers to revolt against both Greeks and any fellow Jews who resisted them. In 165 BC, he achieved victory, had the temple cleansed and rededicated to God. The Jewish festival of Hanukkah commemorates this victory.[84]

Later, under Roman rule, a Jewish scholar, Johanon ben Zakkai, led a passive resistance movement against the Romans. He gained such a following that to get rid of him the Romans allowed him to move further north from Palestine to establish a Jewish center of learning at Jabneh-Jamnia. But passive resistance did not get rid of the Roman occupation or the invasion of Roman culture into Israel. Increasingly, Roman occupation was seen as destroying Jewish life, beliefs, and their worship of the true God. Roman Emperors were increasingly deified, and required to be worshiped as such. The Jewish population could no longer go along with it.[85] Between 63 CE and 135 CE, a series of Jewish armed revolts took place. First, to quell the revolt, Rome marched a full army on Jerusalem and in a bloody consummation destroyed the city in 70 AD. The Jewish historian Josephus, a personal witness, recorded 110,000 deaths by famine and sword, with another 97,000 Jews being enslaved and dispersed throughout the Roman Empire.[86]

The revolts, however, did not end. Surviving Jews fled to the wilderness and organized into guerrilla warfare groups. In a brazen act of courage, they stormed the heights of Masada, a Roman outpost and playground for its Emperors and Governors. From there, they made attacks against the Roman occupying forces between 132 and 135 AD. Now, Rome had had enough. They marched their legions to Masada and laid siege against it. The Jewish fighters would not surrender. As the Roman legions climbed the precarious heights, the Jewish men killed their families, then each other, with the last remaining alive committing suicide. Masada functions for the Israelis today as Pearl Harbor, the Alamo, and 9/11 do for Americans. "Remember Masada" is a very deep emotionally laden phrase in Israel.

These incidents of Jewish revolt have played a very important part in more recent history. After the British Mandate fell apart and British troops pulled out of Palestine at the end of World War II, Jewish leaders surfaced and used the *new Jew* identity as a powerful motivator to establish a Jewish state. Groups that had been

---

84   See *A History of Jews*, Cecil Roth, Schocken Books, New York, Revised, 1989, Chapter 7, The Struggle Against Hellenism, pp. 70-80.

85   *A History of the Jews*, Roth, p. 110.

86   Figures quoted in *Heritage: Civilization and the Jews,* Summit Books, 1984, by Abba Eban, p. 87.

organized to fight against the Germans now turned their sights on their British occupiers. Armed violence and guerilla warfare was the norm. Groups like the Stern gang, Haganah, and the Argun, of whom the later Prime Minister Menachem Begin was a member, all saw the new Jewish identity as a fighter and warrior. The *new Jew* was not the compliant, passive, non-resistant Jew of the previous rabbinical period, but a Jew with a gun! This new Zionism was not a vision where God fought for Israel, or where God would establish peace through a Messiah, but a vision where a homeland for Jews could be obtained through military might. The slogan "No more Masadas" helped create the Jewish state.[87]

Rabbinical Period

Today, Judaism is divided into four major groups: Orthodox, Conservative, Reform and Reconstruction. However, the last three groups are products of the last century. Before the nineteenth century, Judaism was Orthodoxy, or Rabbinical Judaism. Rabbinical Judaism sees itself as preserving the divinely inspired traditions of the earliest fathers of the faith. Predominately, it has centered on the synagogue and learning centers which blossomed after the Diaspora (the scattering of Jews to the world after the fall of Jerusalem in 70 AD). It was during this time traditions were kept alive, sacred texts were studied, and rabbinical opinions became the next generation's law. As Roth observes, "The national idea was henceforth not the priest, warrior, or the landowner, but the student."[88] The Rabbinical teaching or Talmud formed the basis of authority for Orthodox Judaism. So what did the rabbis teach about peace and violence?

Fundamentally, the concept of Shalom or peace prevailed, making Orthodoxy essentially nonviolent. Biblical admonitions like, "Seek peace and pursue it," (Ps 34:14) predominated. One opinion states, "Peace even takes precedence over all other commandments." The tradition of "Thou shall not kill (murder)" was so determinative, some rabbis felt constrained to put peaceable interpretations

---

87   This obviously is an oversimplification of a very complicated period. The UN along with American and Russian support were all involved. Political Zionism had been in development since the late 1890s. But the Holocaust probably demonstrated to the world that the only solution to the "Jewish Problem" was a land for Jews alone. Theodore Herzl, the founder of political Zionism did not even care if the Jews obtained land in Palestine or not. Places in South America and Africa were also seriously considered. So this vision was far more driven by politics than sincere religious commitments.

88   Roth, *A History of the Jews*, p. 125.

to passages about violence. In short, destructive action was to be avoided and forgiveness was viewed as better than revenge. Where destructive action could not be avoided it was viewed as a "tragic necessity." One opinion observed; "Whoever sheds blood diminishes God's presence in the world." War and the killing of enemy soldiers were regarded as unfortunate necessities and the failure of peace.

The Rabbinic sage Maimonides does, however, distinguish between two types of war. "Milchemet Reshut" is *optional war* that must be approved by the Sanhedrin, or seventy elders. "Melchemet Mitvah" is *obligatory war* or commanded war that is defensive. In this regard, the wars of conquest under Joshua were seen as obligatory wars because of their specific command of God. The wars of David were viewed as optional without clear divine authority. Hence, the bloodshed was on David's hands alone.[89] Rabbinical opinion is divided on the subject of *pre-emptive war*, or wars of prevention.[90]

In short, rabbinic consensus includes offering a way of escape for an enemy with an offer of peace before waging war. Military service should be compulsory and universal with compassionate exceptions, and in honor of Sabbath-keeping, only *defensive war* is allowed on Sabbath. In some rabbinical circles, the tradition of the Suffering Servant (Isaiah 53) was interpreted as a nonviolence doctrine. "He who gladly accepts the suffering of this world, brings salvation to the world."

One can easily see from this condensed overview of rabbinical teaching that the tradition of nonviolence ruled. The command not to take life was viewed as the supreme social command in regulating relations among men and between nations. Whereas in the Biblical Period the virtues of peace were yearned for, violence and warfare were the norm, including the concept of holy war (herem). This violence was subject to moral critique by both the Biblical prophets and later rabbis. Prior to the destruction of Jerusalem and the fall of Masada, armed resistance was common. As was seen, political Zionism in this century authorized both open and clandestine warfare for the establishment of the Jewish State. Today, conflict exists between the

---

89 Mishneh Torah: Hilchot Melachim 5, 1., *The Torah*, Herbert Danby, Oxford Univ. Press, 1st Edition, 1933.

90 Pre-emptive attacks are usually argued as defensive thus qualifying as legitimate defensive measures. However, this argument is a slippery slope to negotiate. Striking first then no longer means a "first strike," since the intention or planning to attack by the other side is viewed as an attack in fact. This raises serious questions about the role of intentionality and planning in warfare. The United States military has hundreds of "off the shelf" plans for various contingencies around the world. Do these plans imply intentionally and legitimate "first strike" threat in fact?

secular and religious Jews in Israel. Within both of these groups exists a division on the subject of militant violence. Secular Jews are divided between the once called *Peace Now* activists who encourage nonviolent demonstrations, and the older *Zionists* who believe that peace only comes by ruling with a gun. The religious are divided between the traditional nonviolent approach of the medieval rabbis and the newer *settlement* movements (Land of Israel) lead by Orthodox rabbis, who believe political Israel has sold its soul in giving away *the land of Biblical Israel* for the sake of peace.

For those who wish to justify violence in the name of God it is easy to turn to the Torah (Old Testament) and see God as the Supreme Warrior, who fights for Israel through his human agents. The history of both successful and unsuccessful Jewish revolts can be used to stir the passions and visions of dedicated Jews. This history mixed with the current religious view that Israel's secular leaders have sacrificed their right to rule by giving away sacred land makes for a very volatile situation in Israel.

Peace and Violence in Christianity

I became a Christian while studying at a state university, not the most benevolent environment for encouraging the faith of a new convert! It was the late sixties, and the anti-war movement was growing in strength. Vietnam, though a far distance from Kansas where I was studying, was every day coming closer via modern news footage and commentary. As a new Christian, the question most asked by my football and fraternity buddies was "how could I justify being a Christian in light of the *Christian* Crusades and Spanish *Christian* Inquisitions? At the time, all I really knew was that I loved Jesus for his dying for my sins. It wasn't until much later I realized the depth to which this issue was a problem to those who are not on the inside of the fold of Christianity. Our history has also been violent!

The Early Teachings of Jesus and the Disciples

Christianity was born in the cradle of Judaism, and the simple essence of Christianity lies in its founder, Jesus the Messiah or Christ. Jesus, of course, was Jewish if the original documents are allowed to stand as is.[91] Therefore, Jesus appears in the

---

91 This is ironic because in modern Israel, most Hasidic or Ultra-Orthodox Jews are exempted from military service in order to study Torah. The State also gives them a stipend to do nothing but study. Such a deal!

milieu of first century Jewish messianic expectations. A strong element within that tradition was that the messiah would be a military leader (Psalm 2). Literature from the period saw the messiah as "a lion who would destroy the Roman Empire." Even the disciples of Jesus struggled from time to time with this expectation. Jesus finally had to clarify, if ". . . my kingdom was of this world, my servants (disciples) would be fighting" (John 18:36). An obvious affirmation toward nonviolence! One disciple, Judas Iscariot, who would ultimately deny Jesus, might have been a former laughable revolutionary. Iscariot means "dagger,"raising the possibility Judas previously had been an assassin or *dagger man* before becoming a disciple.[92]

However, Jesus did not behave like a military messiah with a literal axe to grind against Rome. He rejected Satan's offer of an earthly kingdom (Roman), called Matthew, a tax-collector employee for Rome to be a disciple, healed a Roman Centurion's son, and actually encouraged the paying of taxes to Rome. For his own *messianic* entrance into Jerusalem, he chose to ride an unassuming young donkey rather than the white stallion of a conquering leader. When arrested, He forbade his disciples from resisting with force saying, "All those who take the sword will perish by the sword" (Matthew 26:52). This was in response to the action of one of his disciples in cutting off the ear of the high priest's servant! In addition, he taught, "Blessed are the peacemakers," and "those who are persecuted" (Matthew 5:9-10). He went beyond the Jewish teaching of *love of neighbor* and taught *love of one's enemy*. He neither looked nor acted like a military messiah. In the minds of most, the messiah should be willing to use violence to redeem Israel from the bane of Rome.

The Apostle Paul taught, "Repay no one evil for evil," and "if your enemy is hungry, feed him, and if thirsty, give him drink" (Romans 12:17-21). In the earliest New Testament writings there is no mention of armed warfare or use of violence by the early church. The last New Testament book depicts a suffering church in a hostile world waiting until Jesus returns from Heaven to make war with the armies of the world. These earthly armies are not slain by Christians fighting for God, but by the simple blast of Jesus' voice (Revelation of John 19:11-21).

So how is it that some Christians justify violence in the name of Jesus? The answer lies in how one reads the teaching of Jesus and the admonitions by later New Testament writers. If the premise is correct (and I believe it is) that Jesus

---

92 The dagger was the primary weapon of choice for assassination during this time.

fundamentally was a nonviolent person and never encouraged violence, the reality is his teachings and actions were profoundly threatening to the religious/political establishment of the day. He challenged all branches of religious authority as to their hypocrisy (Matthew 21:45-46), so they sought to seize and kill him. In addition, some today claim Jesus was making a very overt politically activist statement in taking a whip to the Temple compound and overthrowing the tables of the moneychangers (John 2:13-17). A whip can certainly be viewed as a weapon, and disruption of the financial system a serious threat to the economy and State. It can also be noted that Jesus did not prevent his disciples from carrying swords, and on one occasion in fact, encouraged it (Luke 22:35-38). Some might see this as mere self-defense, but it could also affirm an argument toward civil defense as well. Likewise, he never told the Roman centurion to resign his command and become a pacifist. St. Paul saw a legitimate, divine authorized role for the State to bear arms but makes no comment about whether Christians should be involved in the sword-bearing task (Romans 13:1-7).

So can the use of violence be authorized on the basis of the teaching of Jesus and his early disciples? For this writer, it seems clearer to hold to the view that fundamentally Jesus taught and lived out the principle of nonviolence.[93] On the whole, Jesus' disciples, particularly Paul, saw Christian warfare as spiritual rather than taking place purely on the physical level (Ephesians 6:10-20, 2 Corinthians 10:3-6).

The Teachings of the Early Church Fathers after Jesus

As seen in the other religions, later generations often depart from the teachings of their founders, or at least re-interpret the teachings in light of new situations. For almost two centuries after the time of Jesus, no Christian would serve in the military of Rome. They did not want to be involved with the direct worship of the Emperor, and as well, believed that a soldier of Christ does not fight. However, early theologians like Tertullian and Origin wrestled with whether Christians should serve in the military. Both believed God had ordained the State, and agreed on the subject of Christian involvement in bearing arms. Tertullian thought carrying the sword was a direct violation of the teaching of Jesus, whereas Origin taught

---

93 When Jesus first gave his requirements for service to his disciples, carrying a sword is not mentioned (Matthew 10:9-10). Apparently, he wanted his disciples to be totally dependent upon God while preaching and healing.

Christians should fight the enemies of the State by prayer.[94] Later, Cicero's Greek *Just War* arguments emerged into Christian ideology, particularly with Augustine and Aquinas. Wars could be justified, but Christians should still not be a part of them. This all changed when Constantine became Emperor of Rome. Upon his supposed conversion to Christianity, he had his entire army baptized and placed the Greek letters *Chi-Rho* (Christ as Lord and Savior) on all Roman shields. From this period on, the fortunes of the church were tied to that of the State. As a result, it was then a Christian's duty to serve in the military, although clergy were exempted. Defense of the Empire could be thought of as Just War sometimes called Holy War.

St. Augustine argued war was an instrument of divine judgment on wickedness by the State, but believed personal pacifism was still the rule for Christians. He felt puzzled by the Sermon on the Mount and the teaching of Jesus about *turning the cheek* (Matthew 5:39). Clovis, a Frankish military hero during the medieval period, exalted the virtue of Peter drawing his sword in defense of Jesus. Likewise, Charlemagne fought against *pagan infidels* with papal blessing, and used the sword for forced conversions upon the Saxons. Clergy did not hesitate to take up the sword in these wars against the encroachment of pagans into Christian lands. However, there were sensitivities about bloodshed in light of Jesus' teaching, so a forty-day period of penance was required after taking lives. Warfare was also prohibited during Advent, Lent, Easter and Pentecost. Historically then, this leads us to the infamous Crusades.

The Late Middle Ages and The Crusades to Retake the Holy Land

The Crusades are still hotly debated. Though the series of eight crusades is usually spun as a series of religious holy wars, there were many other considerations. Commerce, trade routes, the power of popes, and the jealousy of kings, mixed with the promise of wealth for soldiers, all contributed to the warfare. A scholar of Muslim history reports concerning the last unsuccessful crusade, "the finest flower of European chivalry gathered together for a crusade (in 1396), as much secular as religious in impulse, whose objective was to check Bayezid's lightning advance and eject the Turks once for all from the Balkans."[95] But fundamentally,

---

94   See *War and Christian Ethics*, Arthur F. Holmes, Editor, for further discussion. pp. 48-54, Baker Book House, 1974.

95   Lord Kindross, *The Ottoman Centuries*, Morrow Quill Paperbacks, 1977, p. 66.

the "Christian" concern was over Muslim occupation of the Holy Land in addition to stopping the advance of Islam into Europe. After all, the Muslim advance from 632 on was centered on conquering the lands that were Christian and mostly part of the Christian Byzantine Empire. Cambridge University scholar Christopher Catherwood observes, "From the death of Muhammad, right up until the second attempt by the Ottoman Turks to capture the city of Vienna in 1683, the boot was firmly on the Islamic foot, with the Muslim powers on the offensive and those of Christianity on the defensive."[96] Therefore, the first Crusade, authorized by Pope Urban II, was called, a "righteous war against the infidel, promising those who participated blessings in Heaven and temporal rewards of booty."[97] It turned a monk and mystic like Bernard of Clair Vaux from a monastic pacifist into a leader of a military order.

Such groups as the Knights Templar, Hospitallers, Knights of St. John, and the Teutonic Knights, all date their origins to this twelfth century period. Clair Vaux, one of the greatest moral forces of his day, saw no contradiction between his faith and taking the sword to infidel Muslims. Members of the Templar Order saw their duty in prayer and warfare. Their meals consisted of prayer and readings from the books of Joshua and Maccabees. St. Bernard is recorded as instructing, "*killing for Christ* was malecide not homicide (killing evil rather than killing people), the extermination of the ungodly is therefore desirable; indeed *to kill a pagan is to win glory since it gives glory to Christ.*" One writer notes these warriors were, "part monk and part warrior. These Soldiers of Christ saw themselves as consecrated defenders of the True Faith, dedicated to humble piety in cloister and absolute ferocity in battle . . . the blending of Christianity with the influence of the Nordic/Teutonic militarism created the ideological basis for European knighthood."[98]

The Crusades and the development of such Orders multiplied over time and culminated in the infamous and tragic Children's Crusade where thousands of small children died in route or were slaughtered by the Muslims. By the end of the Crusader period, contemporary opinion argues Muslims universally viewed Christians as militaristic imperialists. The Muslim historical record is largely silent in this regard. However, many within Islam today maintain this view toward the

---

96   Christopher Catherwood, *Making War in the Name of God*, Citadel Press, 2007, p. 12.
97   I often wonder why it took so long for the Christian nations to respond to the massive loss of Christian lands!
98   Reynold P. Franca, "Pious Warriors," *Military History*, August 2000, pp. 62-63.

"Christian West."[99] Amin Maalouf, editor of a Beirut daily, admits, "the Arab East still sees the West as a natural enemy. Against that enemy, any hostile action, be it political, military or based on oil, is considered no more than legitimate vengeance . . . and to be viewed "as an act of rape."[100] What is forgotten is from the seventh century to the final siege on Vienna in 1683, it was Muslim imperialism and expansionism that dominated most of the Middle East and Eastern Europe.[101] As Bernard Lewis expresses, tongue-in-cheek, "When the peoples of Asia and Africa (Muslims) invaded Europe, it was not imperialism. When Europe attacked Asia and Africa, it was!"[102] Catherwood notes concerning the first siege, "Had Vienna fallen to the Turkish siege in 1529 . . . then the heartland of Europe would have been open to Islamic invasion for the first time since Charles Martel defeated the Muslim armies back in 711."[103]

The Reformation and the Further Development of Just War Theory

After the Crusades, justification for violence among Christians moved from what some thought of as holy war during the Crusades, to the development of *Just War* theories during the Reformation. Debates developed about use of *indiscriminate weapons* like crossbows and siege machines, but in time both Catholic and Reformation churches formalized *Just War* criteria. In short, violence could be authorized with Christian justification if there was just cause (usually defensive not offensive), right intention to advance some good, declaration of war by legitimate ruling power, fought with proper means, with a reasonable chance of success and as a last resort. Some Christian groups like Mennonites, Brethren, Quakers and some Anabaptists saw in warfare, "nothing but homicide and robbery by consent." Most continue their passive peace traditions to this day.

In England, Oliver Cromwell brought his Puritan Christianity into politics and established the Reformed faith through force of arms by overpowering what he called "ungodly princes." Examples such as Cromwell surely had some impact

---

99 Bernard Lewis, *Faith and Power,* p. 7.

100 Amin Maalouf, *The Crusades Through Arab Eyes*, Schocken Books, New York, 1984, p. 266.

101 This of course, begs the question. In the next section, it will be seen that Islam was just as militant and imperialistic!

102 Lewis, *Faith and Power*: Religion and Politics in the Middle East, Oxford Univ. Press, 2010, pp.175-176.

103 Catherwood, p. 131.

on the American Revolution, justifying the American colony's revolt against a tyrannical King George. However, Christians during the American Revolution were not unified. Some were loyal to the king on the basis of Romans 13, while many were outspoken patriots, and saw it their divine duty to fight against the king. Others were sincere pacifists and out of conscience fled to Canada until the conflict was over.[104]

So what can be concluded about the use of violence in Christianity? Jesus was fundamentally nonviolent in approach while being very aggressive in caring, healing and restoring the downtrodden. His one act of "disruption" was an attempt to restore His father's house to a place of prayer and cleanse the temple compound of crass merchandising. He was courageous in confronting what he saw as the evils and hypocrisy of his day. It was because of these actions, along with his claim to be the Divine Son of God, that he was put to death. Later New Testament writers affirm the legitimate authority of the State to use violence in order to protect and establish justice.

Early Christianity is in stark contrast to the early period of Islam. Catherwood again observes, "While the first century of Christianity saw martyrdoms of converts being thrown to the lions in the Circus, or used as human torches by the emperor Nero, the first generation of Muhammad's followers were engaged in creating one of the biggest land empires that the world has ever seen."[105] Christian church history has been divided on the use of violence in war. Christian views still range from nonviolent pacifism, noncombatant activism (serving as medics or chaplains), including preventative war theories. When Christians have decided to use violence, they have usually fought on some kind of just principles (even in the Crusades). In the most extreme cases, wars of aggression (fought to take over lands that were never theirs) were not viewed as Christian. Finally, most Christians agree on the basis of Jesus' teaching about wars, that their increasing numbers signal the coming apocalypse and His eventual return (Mathew 24).

In the final analysis, those looking to justify a Christian theology of violence can do so. There is plenty of evidence in the history of the Church, especially during some of her darker moments. Though perhaps little justification can be

---

104 See *The Minutemen: The First Fight*, John Galvin, Brassey's, 1996, for an excellent treatment of the varying responses by American clergy.

105 Catherwood, p. 14.

found in the life and teaching of their founder Jesus, this has not stopped the Church through the centuries from utilizing the same kind of arguments for violence found in other religions.

Peace and Violence in Islam

Muslims I have known argue of all religions Islam is the simplest. In one sense, they are correct. To become a Muslim all one has to do is to confess, "There is no god but Allah, and Mohammed is his Prophet." After that, it is just a matter of keeping the other four pillars of faith (the first being the declaration). The pillars are: prayer five times a day; fasting during Ramadan; at least one pilgrimage to Mecca; and almsgiving, or acts of charity.

Today Islam is divided into two major groups, the Shi'ites, who claim they are the direct descendants of Muhammad through his cousin Ali. The other group, Sunnites (aka "Sunnis"), defends the traditional practices of Muhammad, while believing his teachings are expressed in the community of teaching clerics without having any direct successor. (There are also many differing sects in both groups; too many to comment on here.) They also differ on the issue of a coming Mahdi, or guided one, who will lead the world to justice. Though the Koran has nothing to say about a Mahdi, the Hadiths (traditions ascribed to the Prophet) describe the Mahdi as a Redeemer who will rule seven, nine, or nineteen years before the Day of Judgment. His reign will coincide with the second coming of Jesus. Shiite *Twelvers* believe the Mahdi is the twelfth Imam who was born and then hidden until his *Occultation* is revealed in the End Times. Some Shia, like the Ismailis, don't buy into the Occultulation doctrine. Sunnis believe the Mahdi is a successor of the Prophet Muhammad who is yet to come.

However, both traditions reference the concept of Jihad, literally translated as *effort or striving*. It is here differing opinions about the legitimacy of violence are seen in Islam. First, Jihad is to be thought of as an extension of a Muslim's overall response or submission to God. (Islam means submission). Therefore, Jihad is always viewed as striving in the way of Allah. The history of Jihad is rooted in the inter-tribal raiding practices of Arabs during the early life of Muhammad. Raiding, *ghazi,* was the sport of Arabian tribal culture. The *raid* was what tribes did to each other for recreation, sport, and entertainment. A raid obligated the raided party to return the favor.[106]

Muhammad then faced the option of letting the practice continue, abolishing it, or controlling it. He chose the avenue of control. What he banned was inter-tribal raiding within the community of Islam. If a tribe did not want to be raided, they had to adopt the new religion of Muhammad, or continue to be raided. Any tribe accepting Islam was protected from being raided by other tribes. An attack against one Islamic tribe was then viewed as an attack against all.[107] In other words, the original concept of Jihad was defensive in nature and designed to end the random raiding practices in Arabia. Defensive violence was then justified.

This view is enshrined in the Koran. The Koran opposes the use of violence as a direct means of conversion while protecting the faithful from being attacked. For killing a believer the Koran says, "he that kills a believer by design shall burn in Hell forever" (4:93). During certain periods, Jews and Christians found protected status (dhimmi) within Islam from their enemies. However, they were taxed when Muslims were not, and there were restrictions on their worship centers, dress, bearing of arms, riding horses and occupations.[108] Spanish Jews were often protected by Muslims during the Inquisitions, and Buddhists in Punjab were welcomed by Muhammad ibn Qasin as relief to Hindu persecution.

Muslim literature defines two general kinds of Jihad, one of preaching and persuasion and the other of war. Islamic jurists distinguish four types of Jihad: one of *the heart*, or one's personal fight against evil; *the tongue*, in support of what is right or wrong; *the hands*, in support of right and wrong only to a greater degree; and *the sword*, to be used against unbelievers and enemies of the faith. Here, it is incumbent upon the believer to offer their lives and wealth in support of Jihad (61:11). In reference to this kind of violent Jihad, the Koran states, "Allah loves those who fight for His cause in ranks as firm as a mighty edifice," (61:4), and "As

---

106 See Robert Lacey's, *The Kingdom: Arabia & the House of Sa'ud*, Avon Books, 1981, *pp. 145-146* for an enlightening account of this tribal institutional practice.
107 Lacy, p. 27.
108 Bernard Lewis, *The Crisis of Islam*, The Modern Library, Random House, 2003, p. 46. Those of dhimmi status had to pay the jizya (tax), wear distinguishing garments or badges, no new houses of worship could be built, and no existing ones could be repaired. The tradition of Jews wearing a distinctive Star of David goes back to this period of dhimmi status under Islam.

for those slain in the cause of Allah, He will not allow their works to perish, he will admit them to the Paradise," (47:8).

The idea of lands not brought under Islamic control comes from the division of the world into two spheres: Dar-al-Islam, the territory under Islamic rule, and Dar-al-Harb, a territory of war. In other words, to the Islamic mind, there are only two categories or ways to view the world: those under the dominion of Islam and those that are not. Those not under its dominion are viewed as living in the domain of war. Dar-al-Islam is where Muslims have full citizenship, while those of other faiths may have partial rights and toleration. Dar-al-Harb is the realm of the infidel or nonbelievers in Islam. By definition, this kind of Jihad is directed against polytheists, apostates, and any enemy of Islam. A positive Jihad is one that seeks to establish an Islamic theocratic state.

It should be noted that Jihad is usually not a pillar of faith in Islam to be kept by every believer. Jihad, when called for, is a collective obligation that falls on the entire community of Islam and not any particular individual. In theory, this means no one individual can declare a Jihad for the entire community of faith. Technically, only a Caliph (leader of Sunni Muslims) or Imam (leader of Shi'ite Muslims) can declare a Jihad. With this declaration, an invitation to accept Islam must also be given. Supposedly, Osama bin Laden was criticized by some clerics after his first fatwa because he did not ask the Western infidels to repent and become Muslims. The invitation to become a Muslim is good for only three days, however!

Muslim jurists subdivide military Jihad into four further categories: 1) against polytheists, where they are ordered to fight against them until they say, "there is no god but Allah." 2) Against believers: apostate believers are to be viewed as Dar-al-Harb; dissenting believers are to be threatened with Dar-al-Harb unless they restore themselves to each other; believing bandits should be executed, their hands and feet cut off or banished from the land. 3) People of the book (Jews and some Christians) might embrace Islam and become full citizens or maintain their beliefs and accept Muslim rule. 4) Strengthening and protecting the believers (rabat), where "one night spent on rabat is worth a thousand spent in prayer."

To engage in military Jihad the requirements are: to be a believer (though exceptions are made); an adult male, sound in mind and body, free, economically independent; having parental support, good intention, with retreat as only a last resort. This of course, is what is required in the ideal. However, the requirements are often ignored. For an all-out military Jihad, the Koran and subsequent jurist opinion limits the Jihad. Noncombatants are to be spared unless they are cooperating with the enemy. Animals are protected, but inanimate objects like crops and trees can be destroyed. Poisoning of wells is permitted.[109] One fifth of the spoil goes to the state, with the remainder being kept by the participant. Out of necessity, Jihad can be waged on holy days and months; "to war at that time is bad, but to turn aside from the cause of Allah, and in the sacred Temple and to drive out its people, is worse in the sight of Allah (12:214).

Though the concept of Jihad always played a vital role in Islam prior to 9/11, Islam was not necessarily thought of among Western nations as a warlike religion. In the late seventies I found the Arab population positive and open to Westerners, however today that has changed. The commonly accepted view is that the Christian Crusades forever changed the relations between Christians and Muslims, and has imparted a superficial militant view toward each other's religion. Esposito rightly observes, this is a failure "to distinguish between illegitimate use of religion by individuals, and the faith and practice of the majority of the world's Muslims."[110] Many of us know Muslims who are peace-loving, and in some countries long traditions of peaceful relations have existed. Muslim law encourages arbitration as the best and fairest way of settling disagreements especially to prevent fighting against each other (4, 62). Some Islamic sects have dropped altogether the necessity of observing Jihad (Maziyariyya), and have focused on the spiritualizing aspects of Jihad and the weaning of the soul away from desires and evil (or violent) impulses. There exists also a growing development in the concept of Jihad as that of active concern for the weak and oppressed, but these are of more recent development. Catherwood points out, "the current day split between the peaceful and aggressive forms is entirely modern. Jihad, as traditionally understood and practiced by hundreds of years of Islam has always been primarily an expression of warfare; and not the internal-struggle aspect."[111]

Therefore, Judaism, Christianity, and Islam all have a history along with their sacred writings, illustrating the dual co-existence of violence and peace. For one wanting to justify violence in the name of God, there is plenty of evidence in

---

109 This provides a powerful argument within Islam for the use biological or chemical weapons.
110 John Esposito, *The Islamic Threat: Myth or Reality*, Oxford Univ. Press, 1995, p. 250.
111 Catherwood, p. 9.

the history of each religion to justify it. Likewise, a tradition of peace can also be argued from these same writings with examples from the behaviors or statements from their founders. So on one occasion Jesus says "go without a sword," then later "take a sword" (Luke 22: 35-36). Likewise, it is said of Muhammad in one place "turn away from those who join false gods with Allah (15:94) and in another place "slay the infidel wherever you find them" (2:91).[112] In the Jewish Torah, a tribute is made of Joshua who "left no survivor but utterly destroyed all who breathed just as the Lord, the God of Israel commanded" (Joshua 10:40); mixed with the Psalmist encouraging "Depart from evil and do good; seek peace (shalom) and pursue it" (Psalm 34:14).

Sacred Writing Justification

The Biblical Torah tradition of Judaism (Christian Old Testament) is profoundly bloody, especially the wars of conquest and the continuing battles waged by Israel's judges and kings. Offensive war is justified as "holy war" during the conquest even though offers of peace are made to some groups. Limitations were imposed in terms of booty and care for the ecological environment.[113] By the end of the Biblical period, the prophets began to look for One to come (the Son of Man, the Servant of Yahweh), who would establish peace and justice.

The documents of Christianity (New Testament) do not justify or record as much violence as do the Jewish scriptures. The most violent acts in the gospels are the unjust executions of infant males in Bethlehem, the cruel beheading of John the Baptist and the Roman crucifixion of Jesus himself. Jesus did not lead an armed revolt against Rome, nor did he authorize his followers to do so. At the most, he may have justified self-protection in the bearing of a personal sword. If this is the case, then personal self-defense is justified for the Christian but Jesus makes no statement beyond. Some Christians believe "turning the other check" (Matthew 5:39) as taught by Jesus is a prohibition of self-defense while others believe it is only a prohibition of the required co-equal retaliation of Jewish law. Later New Testament writers are silent about the use of arms but encourage obedience to government authorities who have the right to rule with the sword. In St. John's

---

112 The Islamic legal concept of "abrogation" comes to play here where later revelation abrogates or makes invalid earlier statements.

113 Just because the legal sections of the scripture prescribed these ethical considerations does not mean they were followed.

Revelation, John sees a vision of Jesus as the slain Lamb of God, returning to destroy the armies of the world and setting up His rule.

In Islam, the Koran justifies armed conflict for the sake of protecting Islam, disciplining errant believers, or extending the realm of Dar-al-Islam. As the Koran says, "Prophet, make war on the unbelievers and the hypocrites and deal sternly with them. Hell shall be their home, evil their fate" (66:9). For those fighting and dying in authorized warfare, paradise is the promised Muslim reward.

View of God as Warrior

The Biblical and Revolt periods of Judaism demonstrate an emphasis on the doctrine of God as Warrior. It is God as Warrior who fights for Israel through the agency of his divinely authorized human warriors. During the conquest and monarchy periods, this warfare is justified on the basis that the land of Canaan was promised by God to the Hebrew nation (Genesis 12:19, Joshua 1:1-6). It is then this holy war justification that gives the Israelites the right to dispossess the people living in the land. I personally define a true "holy war" as where God himself commands the taking of life. In the Biblical account, this is a one-time event during the conquest of Canaan by General Joshua (Joshua 1:1-4, 6:21).

During the Revolt period, the warrior motif is rooted more in defensive war concepts than offensive holy war. With the possible extinction of the Jewish way of life on the line, warriors like Judas Maccabeus looked upon their violence as the divinely authorized ethic of protecting the Jewish nation and fighting in the name of their Warrior God. The War of Independence to establish Israel's national sovereignty in 1947 was for the most part not claimed as a holy war, and its fighters looked not to God as their Warrior. If anything they found their protection more in conventional air power and gun powder than trust in God!

Though Jesus did not present himself as a military warrior, warrior motifs and images are very strong in the New Testament. The research by Longman and Reid demonstrate the gospel accounts of Jesus' approach and final conflict in Jerusalem are under the divine warrior motif.[114] Likewise, the Apostle Paul viewed the second coming of Christ or *Parousia* as a specific term of divine warfare. These scholars note, "Just prior to the Day of the Lord, rebellion and hostility to God will dominate

---

114 Longman & Reid, p. 119.

and oppress the faithful. On the Day of the Lord's appearing, he will descend from Heaven as an approaching deliverer."[115]

Concerning the book of Revelation they say, "The book of Revelation presents the divine warrior tradition more boldly than any other New Testament writing. This is evident in the fact that the verb *nikao*, "to conquer," is used seventeen times out of a total of twenty-seven in the entire New Testament."[116] So, even though Jesus may not have revealed himself as a military figure, the theological motifs as presented in the Gospels, Letters, and Revelation all present a coming Jesus as the ultimate divine warrior deliverer. This is a crucial doctrine for those today wishing to justify violence against God's enemies in the name of Jesus the Deliverer, or in light of the coming Day of the Lord, a Day of Judgment.

Islam does not have the same Warrior motif as a character attribute of Allah. If anything Islam sees the warrior characteristics of Allah under the image of Allah as Judge of the earth. All believers will appear before Allah for judgment and be evaluated on the basis of how faithful they were to the five pillars of faith. Those dying in battle have already achieved Paradise! A more characteristic aspect of the warrior ethic in Allah is the emphasis on his divine will or fate. A Jihad is a holy war as declared by Allah's on-earth representatives (Imams and Caliphs). However, it is not Allah who fights as Warrior. It is his will that determines the outcome, or putting it more accurately, whatever happens is his will. When a Muslim is defeated in combat whose fault is it? The Koran says, "the defeat which you suffered when the two armies met was ordained by Allah, so that He might know the true believers and the hypocrites" (3:166). In other words, Allah is not a Warrior who wins or loses in battle, but Judge of the faithful in the conflict. In this sense, Muslims fight for the "causes" of Allah but do not necessarily see God as their Warrior. They are merely carrying out his will in the world.

Views of Human Life

Within Judaism there has always been the strongest defense of human life. Rooted in the Biblical concept of the "image of God," the *imago dei* (Genesis 1:26), the Jewish tradition is one of granting sacredness to all human life. However, during the Biblical period it is this sacredness that justifies the concept of capital

---

115 Ibid., p. 179.
116 Ibid., p. 180.

punishment for many crimes (Genesis 9:6, Deuteronomy 17:6-7). In addition, outside the community of Israel, all life does not seem equal. The "people of the land" (Canaanites, Amorites, Midianites, and Philistines) can be killed in holy war often without discriminating among noncombatants, women or children. These illustrations are set in direct contrast with the specific command from God to not kill or murder (In Exodus 20: 13, the Hebrew verb, *qatal*, is better translated "murder"). Therefore, it is better translated, "Thou shall not murder."

During the Rabbinic period the value of human life took on more importance. The only justified killing was in defensive warfare where Judaism or human life was threatened. This view of human life seemed to be the same as during the earlier Jewish revolt periods. Here, all human life was viewed as sacred, but when faced with the extinction of the Jewish people, killing the enemy was justified.

Christianity likewise, for most of its history, viewed life with the highest regard. Jesus extended compassion and value to those who were poor and disenfranchised in first century Jewish society. He protected, praised and blessed women, children and non-Jews alike. Still this high regard for humanity apparently was limited to the earthly state. He clearly taught that those who did not obey his words would be given "eternal punishment" (Matthew 25:46), and "could not escape the judgment of hell," and would "be cast into the outer darkness where there is weeping and gnashing of teeth" (Matthew 23:23; 24:51).

Later apostles affirmed the same teaching. Paul encouraged respecting and being at peace with all men (Romans 12:17-18) while also teaching that fornicators, idolaters, adulterers, homosexuals, thieves, drunks and swindlers will not inherit the kingdom of God unless sanctified and justified by God (I Corinthians 6:10-11). Likewise, when Christ judges all mankind, those not found in the book of life will be cast into the lake of fire (Revelation 20:ll-15). As will be seen later, these doctrines provide powerful raw material for fueling militancy among certain American groups. In short, Christians have high regard for human life, but it is not unlimited or uncritical. Christians view the world in two categories: those who believe in Christ and those who do not. This becomes the basis for how people are viewed, and ultimately how the divine last judgment will be made. Christians are cautioned by Jesus' words about those who claim to know him when he says, "depart from me for I never knew you" (Matthew 7:23). In other words there will be surprises in Jesus' kingdom!

Islam likewise, has the same world-view with reference to human life as does Judaism and Christianity. As shown before, Islam views the world in two categories: "Dar-al-Islam," that of believers, and "Dar-al-Harb," that of warfare, which is the entire non-Muslim world. Those in non-Muslim religions will be lost as the Koran states: "he that chooses a religion other than Islam, it will not be accepted from him and in the world to come he will be one of the lost" (3:85).

This dichotomy provides rich justification for violence among some of the terrorist groups to be studied later. In fact, the strict dichotomy in how the world and human life is viewed is one of the most powerful defining characteristics in predicting terrorist attitudes.

The Vision of a New World Order

In contrast to most Eastern religions, both Christianity and Islam have a universal world concern. Current Judaism lacks a universal impetus to extend the Jewish faith to the world, even though Israel was called to be a "light to the Gentiles" (Isaiah 49:6). Today, a person who wants to convert to Judaism must go to it. Even if some believe their religion to be superior or the only true religion, I have never heard this expressed. Judaism today is not thought of as a proselytizing religion.

Christianity and Islam, by contrast, both operate under the command of their founders to take the religion to the world. Jesus proclaimed to his disciples, "Go therefore, and make disciples of all nations" (Matthew 28:19). Mark records, "this gospel is to be preached to every creature (Mark 16:15), and the preaching must be accomplished *before* the end of times can come (Mark 13:10-23). This provides a very powerful motive for the gospel evangelist. Jesus cannot come back until the gospel is preached to every human being. This places a tremendous amount of human agency upon the end times and Jesus' return. There is an obvious clash here with Islam, because Islam teaches the same thing.

Author Exposito observes, "Islam constitutes the most pervasive and powerful transnational force in the world with one billion adherents spread out across the globe."[117] Continuing, he illumines, "Since Islam is God's command, implementation must be immediate, not gradual, and the obligation to do so is incumbent on all true Muslims. Therefore, individuals and governments who hesitate, remain apolitical, or resist are no longer to be regarded as Muslim. They

---

117 Exposito, p. 4.

are atheists or unbelievers, enemies of God against whom all Muslims must wage Jihad (holy war).[118] Allah's kingdom is the entire world as the Koran affirms, "For those that disbelieve in Allah and His apostle, we have prepared a blazing Fire. Allah's is the kingdom of the heavens and the earth"(48:14).

In short, both Islam and Christianity have a radical, all controlling vision for the world. Both faiths are universal and exclusive.[119] Both visions, in the hands of certain visionary leaders, can become lethal rallying points for those desiring to be obedient to their faith.

Good/Evil Polarization

Most of the Eastern religions lack clear categories and distinctions. Some might characterize Eastern thinking as more mystical, intuitive, and feeling oriented. As such, it lacks the logical, precise rationality of the west. However, Middle East religions have absolute distinctions found especially in regard to the concepts of good and evil. In Judaism, the Jews are God's chosen people bound together in a divine covenantal bond. Non-Jews are considered the "goyim," the nations or gentiles. In other words, there exists the nation of Israel who finds God's favor, while all other people for the most of history have been a thorn in the side of these "chosen" people. After all, for most of Israel's history they have been dominated and controlled by the "bad guys," beginning with the Egyptians, then the Canaanites, Philistines, Assyrians, Babylonians, Persians, Greeks, Romans, and now the United States, the United Nations and Palestinian violence. From this history it is easy to conclude the enemies of the Jews are the rest of the world, and especially those who do not support the legitimacy of Israel as a sovereign State.

Likewise, from the New Testament, it is an easy step to conclude the world is divided into only two groups of people: Those who know Christ and are Christians, and those who are not. For Christians, the ultimate blessing of their confession of faith in Christ is the privilege of spending eternity with Christ in Heaven. Non-Christians will receive eternal damnation and punishment in accordance with the magnitude of their earthly sins. To be a Christian is the ultimate good in the world, while to be outside the favor of Christ is to stand in condemnation and in consort with the forces of evil. Therefore, those who oppose the Christian faith

---

118 Ibid., p.19.
119 Lewis, *Faith and Politics*, p. 172.

can be viewed as enemies of the faith and subject to criticism, condemnation, and rejection by those who hold to the true faith.

Islam conceives the world in the same fashion. The world of Islam (Dar-al-Islam) is the place of Allah's favor and blessing, while the world of the infidel (Dar-al-Harb) is the place where all the enemies of Islam consort and conspire against the faithful of Mohammad. When taken seriously, these doctrines provide a powerful theological basis for extending and protecting the purity of Islamic devotion. In this sense, each of the Middle Eastern religions share a similar attitude and conception about the world. Each is pitted against a somewhat polarized enemy of the "outsider" or non-adherent. The result leads easily to placing the nonbeliever in a category of the "evil person," who as an enemy can therefore be inflicted with violence simply because he or she is "the enemy."

From this survey of the religions, perhaps we are now in a better position to understand how specific religious terrorist groups justify and carry out their lethal actions.

CHAPTER SIX

The Jewish Fist:
Sanctification of the Name

Israeli Right-Wing Religious Extremism

"If there's any place in the world where belief in the End is a powerful force in real-life events, it's in the Holy Land."
—Gerson Gorenberg

"A Jewish fist in the face of the Gentiles."
—Rabbi Meir Kahane

Qiryat Arba, the tomb of Dr. Baruch Goldstein, used to be a place of pilgrimage for many Jews. Lying just outside ancient Hebron on Israel's West Bank, many came to pray, light candles, and place stones on the physician's grave. However, on December 29, 1999, the Israeli army moved in with bulldozers and razed the makeshift shrine, acting on parliamentary legislation outlawing monuments to terrorists. The army was careful however, not to touch the actual gravesite and tombstone reading, "*Dr. Goldstein, A martyr with clean hands and a pure heart. He gave his life for the people of Israel, its Torah and land.*" The site had become a source of serious and often violent contention between Israelis and Palestinians.

Goldstein, a Brooklyn-born physician, immigrated to Israel and settled in Qiryat Arba. After the signing of the Oslo Peace Accords that allowed talks about removing Jewish settlements from the West Bank, Dr. Goldstein loaded his Glilon short assault rifle and donned his army uniform. He proceeded to the local mosque and killed twenty-nine Muslims while they were kneeling in prayer at the ancient Tomb of the Patriarchs. Another one hundred were wounded. When his gun jammed, surviving Muslim worshippers beat him to death. To non-religious Israelis, Goldstein was just another militant madman. Even Prime Minister Yitzak Rabin offered the single crazed madman theory for the act. Palestinians often tried to vandalize the grave, creating unrest for both the settlers and the local Arab residents. Goldstein's father, present at the razing, said "he gave his life to sanctify God's name; what are they doing here? What a shame, please forgive us."

It is only fitting that Goldstein's grave is located in a park named after Rabbi Meir Kahane.[120] Goldstein's friends and colleagues felt the massacre he created was not just an act of political-military revenge, but as members and supporters of the radical fundamentalist Kach movement, established by the late Rabbi Meir Kahane, the act was a *sacred mission*.[121]

In the Knesset (Israel's Parliament) the Shas religious party at one time held seventeen seats and often exercised a determining majority by pushing for funding of its religious schools. When Yossi Sarid, the Minister of Education, opposed it, the party's spiritual leader, Rabbi Ovadiah Yosef, issued a *fatwa* or religious edict calling for his murder.[122] One Israelis journalist commented, "the real problem is not Yosef's words but the fact that seventeen members of the Knesset, almost a sixth

---

120 Gershom Gorenberg, *The End of Days: Fundamentalism and the Struggle for the Temple Mount*, The Free Press, 2000, p. 3.
121 "Israel Destroys Shrine to Mosque Gunman," *The New York Times*, December 30, 1999.
122 Ehud Sprinzak, *Brother Against Brother*, The Free Press, 1999, p. 2.

of the parliament, unconditionally support him . . . If the rabbi is guilty of criminal incitement, they are, at the very least, his partners in crime."[123] The Shas spiritual guide died October 7, 2013. *The Times of Israel* reported, "The Rabbi's funeral was the largest in Israel's history attended between 300,000 and 800,000." In response to the question "Does Shas have a post-Yosef future?" *The Times* answered with a resounding "yes."[124]

What is going on here? Memorials to terrorists, and rabbis issuing death threats? For those who have been watching Israeli politics and culture for some time these developments are no surprise. They are symptoms of a climate that has been developing in Israel since before the signing of the Camp David peace accord. Camp David, and later the Olso Accords, viewed as a triumph by both Westerners and Palestinians, only radicalized religious Jewish settlers who deemed the giving away of "God's land" as acts of betrayal to the Jewish people and an offense to God. To Rabbi Meir Kahane it constituted "desecration of the Name" (Hillul Hashem), a serious crime against the Jewish people.

Early Roots of Israeli Radicalism

To understand the current environment in which terrorism on both sides of the Green Line (the line dividing Israel from the Palestinian West Bank) has become common, it is necessary to put current events into a historical perspective. As noted earlier, the Roman army destroyed the Jewish Temple in Jerusalem in 70 AD. For several decades after the destruction, Jewish defenders made periodic attempts to expel the Roman *desecraters* from Jewish soil. In a final climactic victory, the Roman armies isolated the remaining Jewish defenders at Masada where they committed suicide rather than surrender to their Gentile captors. The 120 AD capitulation of Masada is burned severely into the mindset of almost every Jewish person. "No More Masadas," as a motto, is equaled only by the Passover benediction of "Next Year in Jerusalem." After this final Jewish revolt, the Jewish people scattered

---

123 In 2011, Shas held eleven seats in the Knesset, and supported the Netanyahu government. Shas also held four posts on the cabinet; one being the Deputy Prime Minister, Eli Yishai. In 2013, the more right-wing coalition parties Likud-Yisrael-Beiteinu took 31 seats, with Labor 15 and Shas 11. Including the United Torah Judaism party with 7 seats it makes for a very powerful voice for religious parties. "Dump Shas Now," Ze'ev Chafets, *The Jerusalem Report*, April 10, 2000, p. 20.

124 Haviv Rettig Gur, "Shas tries to get back on its feet," *The Times of Israel*, October 5, 2014, www.timesofisrael.com.

throughout the world, but left with the longing and yearning to return to what they considered a divinely given land.

Until the late eighteen hundreds, the Jewish longing to return to their lost real estate was just that . . . a longing. A small Jewish community was always present in "Palestine," but most of the Jewish world population was dispersed throughout the *goyim* or gentile nations.[125] During the late 1800s, a Jewish political visionary named Theodore Herzl wrote his classic treatise on the *Jewish Problem*. In *The Jewish State* (Der Judein Stat), he argued the only solution to the Jews' longstanding history of pogroms (persecutions, property confiscations, and denial of national rights) and expulsions from country to country, was for the Jews to again have their own homeland. Herzl did not necessarily have in mind the land of Palestine and was not a religiously observant Jew. His conclusions were based more on his own political and historical experience and mere pragmatism.[126] He even suggested land in South America or Africa as possible places where a Jewish State might be built. Today Herzl is considered the father of modern Zionism.

Orthodox Judaism however, did not accept Herzl's political Zionism. In fact, during my first visit to Mea Shearim, an ultra-orthodox community in Jerusalem, I was surprised by graffiti scribbled on one house. Painted on a wall in the midst of this community was the statement, "Zionism is not Judaism!" In other words, the Zionism of Herzl was not considered Biblical or Talmudic Judaism. In spite of the lack of support from the ultraorthodox, political Zionism was the philosophy that mobilized and solicited support for the founding of the Jewish State. Israel declared itself a State in 1948 and was recognized by the United Nations. When the Arabs rejected the UN offer of a divided Palestine and simultaneously attacked the new state, Israel fought back and secured a surprising victory.

Following statehood, an increasing number of Jews from all over the world began *aliyah* or return to what they considered their restored homeland. When they arrived what they found was not the messianic community promised by the Biblical prophets, or even a community that honored religious traditions. Sprinzak observes, "Government officials believed it was their obligation to free the

---

125 See Roth, *A History of the Jews*, pp. 258-260 on the Jewish center of life in Upper Galilee (Safed) which in the second century AD became a "perpetual revivalist camp" for Jewish thought.

126 See Michael Karpin and Ina Friedman, *Murder in the Name of God*, Metropolitan Books, 1998, pp. 29-37, for a complete and concise overview of this early Zionist history.

newcomers' children of the old and decadent Diaspora mentality that comprised, among other things, *obsolete religiosity*. They accomplished this aim by establishing secular state schools in all immigration absorption centers."[127] Karpin and Friedman note that the Zionist goal was to "not only take Jews out of the Diaspora, but equally and perhaps primarily a spiritual, psychological and cultural mission of taking the Diaspora out of the Jews."[128] To the religious, this amounted to a *forced conversion* to secularism.[129] One writer suggests "Most Orthodox rabbis of the time despised Zionists as pork-eating secularists who defied God by trying to establish a Jewish state before the arrival of the Messiah."[130] Thus, from the very founding of the State of Israel a certain tension and division existed between the political leadership and the observant religious communities.

During the 1950s, the conflict led to the establishment of two religious underground militant groups. Consisting mostly of yeshiva (seminary) students, the *Hamachane* and *B'rith Hakana'im* saw their purpose in "establishing Torah life in the country by *all means necessary*." Their initiation ceremony consisted of a swearing in over a Bible and gun! These militants acted out of a belief that the secular state was determined to destroy Orthodox Judaism. They plotted actions such as planting bombs in the Knesset, and were granted rabbinic approval for their actions.

These early religious underground groups grew out the milieu of the *haredim* or the ultra-Orthodox communities who did not accept the legitimacy of Israel's secular government. Though having many disagreements among themselves, the *haredim* were united in their strict observance of the law and commandments (Torah & mitzvot), and their theological rejection of political Zionism. They believed only through a repentance of all Jews with strict observance of God's commands, would redemption and an earthly kingdom be established. This would come about through the arrival and intervention of a Messiah who redeems his people and removes their sufferings.[131]

---

127 *Brother Against Brother*, p. 62.
128 *Murder In the Name of God*, p. 35.
129 Many in the US today believe this is what is happening here with "political correctness." It is essentially a forced conversion to secularism.
130 Gershom Gorenburg, "Burning Gush," *The New Republic*, April 18, 1994, p. 22.
131 See Ehud Sprinzak's excellent chapter on the "haredim" in *Brother Against Brother*, Chapter 3, pp. 87-112.

As such, the *haredim* find most of their conflict with the Israeli secular government and its liberal modern culture. Their "violence" is seen mostly in demonstrating against Sabbath violations, movies, obscene advertisements, archaeological excavations (which disrupt burial bones), improper dress, and sexual expressions in public and private. This violence is sometimes directed at single immodestly dressed women. They are known to harass violators by beatings, stoning and even firebombing houses.

Only a few deaths have been recorded as being directly traceable to their demonstrations. Sprinzak, one of the leading experts on Israeli radicalism, believes the *haredi* fundamentally honor the commandment of not killing, along with observing a prohibition on the bearing of arms.[132] He concludes, "What is striking about the ultra-Orthodox violence is . . . not their intensity but its restraint."[133] However, restraint among some of the Israeli religious would change significantly during the 1970s.

Gush Emunim and the Land of Israel Movement

During an Independence Day yeshiva reunion on May of 1967, Rabbi Zvi Yehuda Kook looked at some of his former students and bemoaned the division of Israel's historic land and the Arab occupation of Jerusalem. He is recorded as saying, "This cannot last." Three weeks later they found themselves at the Wailing Wall in Jerusalem having taken possession of many of the sacred Biblical sites, including Jerusalem and the Temple Mount. To those gathered, the words of the Rabbi were inspired prophetic words. The six-day war was viewed by many in the Orthodox community as a divine miracle whereby God had intervened and given victory to God's people. Some evangelical Christians also view the event similarly. Rabbi Kook and his disciples felt the new lands taken by the Israeli army should be immediately annexed into Israel either by strict military action or settlement . . . they constituted *Greater Israel*.

A new theology developed among the Kook followers that God had used the secular government and its army to bring about a greater Israel. Therefore, the secular government, though not embracing Torah life, could be used to usher in the messianic age by reclaiming all the Land of Israel. Kook noted, "Every Jew living

132 Ibid., p. 104.
133 Ibid., p. 111.

in Israel was holy; all phenomena, even the secular, were imbued with holiness."[134] Influenced by Kook's vision, his followers founded Gush Enumin (Fountain of the Faithful) at Kfar Etzion, on the West Bank in 1974. Supported by the Labor-led government of Yizhak Rabin, Gush Enumin set out to obstruct any compromise on giving back lands taken in the wars; they also set out to organize demonstrations in Biblical Judea and Samara (West Bank) to make claims to the land in front of the Arabs; and finally to establish actual settlements on appropriated-purchased West Bank lands.

In May of 1977, the first observant Orthodox Prime Minister was elected in Menacham Begin. His government gave Gush Enumin a green light in establishing new settlements and authorized government funds to carry them out. Likewise, his Minister of Agriculture, Ariel Sharon, was equally ecstatic and supportive of the settlements. For the non-religious Sharon, he saw the settlements as security buffer zones, but for Begin and Gush, they were *Eretz Israel*, or the Whole Land of Israel.

Kook's theology further explained that every grain of Israel's soil was holy, and Israel's final redemption could take place only in the context of greater Israel. Without the land, there would be no final redemption. To return this territory meant forfeiting redemption. Further, the Palestinians did not really constitute a nation and thus had no claim to the land. At most they were *resident aliens* likened to Biblical Canaanites who could be expelled unless they were willing to accept the Jewish kingdom and laws over them.[135]

However, on September 17, 1978, everything changed. Their hero and ideological friend, Prime Minister Begin, signed the Camp David Peace Accord

---

134 Quoted in David Rappoport's *Inside Terrorist Organizations,* 1988, Article by Ehud Sprinzak, "From Messianic Pioneering to Vigilante Terrorism: The Case of the Gush Emunim Underground," p. 202.

135 The "Palestinian Issue" is so politicized historical facts are often lost in the rhetoric. The question as to who owns the land has no simple answer. If one argues solely on the basis of history it is a mixed bag. The current geography now called "the West Bank" was once part of Jordan, which was considered by the British Mandate, the Palestinian State. However when Jordan lost the territory in the Six Day War, the land fell under Israeli control. Before the territory was called, "Jordan" it was part of the British Mandate resulting from World War I. Before that it was under Turkish rule and a Province of the Ottoman Empire called Syria. Prior to the Turks, the real estate was part of Christian Byzantium, and before that under Roman rule. Add to this, further dominations by the Greeks, Persians, Babylonians and Assyrians, and one finally gets back to Biblical times when Israel's kings ruled. However, before the Hebrew conquest of Canaan, "Palestine" was ruled by various Canaanite, Philistine and Egyptian rulers. So who owns the land? Almost any of the above named peoples could make a claim to the land based on history!

along with Egyptian President Anwar Sadat, making peace with Egypt. The accord agreed to return all of the Sinai (taken in the six-day war) and to initiate talks with the Palestinians concerning an Autonomy Plan. To the members of Gush, if acted upon, the inevitable process of divine redemption would be halted by this Accord and make their Prime Minister a traitor. Apart from the outright shock and betrayal felt by the Gush Enumin membership, two individuals with Gush connections looked for deeper meaning in the Camp David Peace. Such a setback must be more than just the failings of a weak-willed, compromising Prime Minister. Ben Shoshan, a mystic in the Jewish Kabbalist tradition[136] and a zealot named Yehuda Etzion found an explanation in the Temple Mount.

When the Israelis took Jerusalem in 1967, the government cut a deal with the local Muslim Mufti of Jerusalem. If he would allow the Jews to pray at the Wailing Wall (the existing foundation or retaining wall of the Temple compound), then Muslim clergy could maintain control of the Temple Mount, including the al-Asqa mosque or Dome of the Rock. To Shoshan and Etzion, the Camp David Accord was a message from God that a national offense had been committed in the 1967 arrangement. Allowing the Muslims to maintain control of the place where the first and second Jewish Temples sat was an offense and sin against God.[137] The desecration of the mount, "the abomination" as the two underground Gushites called it, could only be sanctified by removing the mosque and rebuilding the Jewish third Temple. Only then would the holy site be cleansed of almost two millennia of Gentile abomination.

Etzion recruited a group of eight men with various areas of technical and military expertise to design a plan to blow up the mosque. However, the tone of the meetings also centered on Halakhic (issues of Biblical & Rabbinic interpretation) and Kabalistic mystical spirituality. When the group sought the blessing for their act from their mentor Rabbi Yehuda Kook, he refused. Without a rabbinic blessing, the idea was shelved. Being the mystics that they were, and without a benediction from their rabbi, they saw no reason to continue, but placed the issue in God's hands and His timetable. Sprinzak notes,

---

136 "All Jewish mystical practice falls under the heading of 'Kabalah' . . . for the mystic community and religious observance are one. The mystic cannot isolate himself from his fellow men even in his esoteric practices, for the core of his faith, the divine revelation at Sinai, appeared not to one man, but to a community." Perle Epstein, *Kabbalah: The Way of the Jewish Mystic,* Shambhala-Random House, 1988, p. xv-xvi.

137 Details were revealed in an interview with Etzion in prison by Ehud Sprinzak, May 18, 1985.

The rabbinical backing to the terrorism of the underground gets its full meaning in view of the rabbinical refusal to support the operation on the Temple Mount and the resulting cancellation of that operation. Both approval and disapproval indicate how critical was the rabbinical authorization. We learn, in fact, that despite the rather spontaneous organization of the group and its relative marginality, its terrorism could never have taken place without the participation of key Gush Emunim leaders.[138]

As Sprinzak clarifies, it was never the intent of the organization Gush Enumin to blow up the Dome of the Rock. It was only two of their fringe associates who proceeded with the planning. Most Gush members still viewed the Israeli government as God's agent and though disappointed with Camp David, they could live with the paradox.[139]

While the underground Gush fringe group was planning Operation Temple Mount they did however, carry out other terrorist events. On May 3, 1980 six yeshiva students returning from their Sabbath prayers were shot and killed by West Bank Arabs in Hebron. In response, Etzion designed a plan to blow up simultaneously the cars of five Arab mayors. In the attack the legs of two mayors (Nablus and Ramallah) were blown off.[140] In two others the demolition devices failed. Likewise, Etzion and Shoshan conducted an attack on the Islamic College in Hebron killing three and wounding thirty-three. Other attacks were planned but never carried out because Israeli security had become aware of their underground network. What is interesting about these attacks is that for each of these attacks rabbinic approval and blessing was apparently given. Surprisingly, the attacks were not opposed by the rabbis. Sprinzak notes that "Rabbi Eliezer, a prominent Gush rabbi and since 1981 a Knesset member, even volunteered . . . to participate in the first operation (the West Bank mayor's attack)."[141]

---

138 From *Messianic Pioneering to Vigilante Terrorism*, p. 215.
139 *Brother Against Brother*, p.161.
140 The author happened to be in Hebron at the time. Israeli soldiers prevented our entry into the city because they had received reports that terrorist acts were imminent. Our guide, having spoken with them in Hebrew, was then allowed to pass and have lunch there! Fortunately (for us), the attacks were elsewhere.
141 Ibid., p. 171.

Where Etzion differed with Gush theology was over his understanding of *active* versus *passive redemption.* Etzion, had read and been influenced by a little known thinker Shabtai Ben Dov. Dov believed that there was no need to wait for another miracle in order to establish the kingdom of Israel. All conditions for redemption were present. All that needed to be done was for the faithful to act. Following Doationalist School" of thought, Etzion believed obedient Jews needed to act on the vision of establishing a theocratic government on the Temple Mount. This is why the removal of the Dome of the Rock was so critical to Etzion. The redemption of the nation had stopped at the Temple Mount! The argument is still alive and well. Yisrael Ariel, founder of the Temple Institute in Jerusalem interprets, "If you see failures, if everything we do doesn't bear blessings, it's a sign . . . we aren't doing enough to build the Temple . . . We will remove the abominations that sully our holy mountain."[142]

As a result of the Camp David Accords, the Gush Enumin settlements in the Sinai had to be removed. The settler's logic on the Sinai proved to be surprisingly correct. They believed that if the Israeli government would remove them from the Sinai, then it was just a matter of time until they would do the same in Gaza, Judea and Samaria (West Bank). Daily news casts reported the issue of how to remove the some 150,000 settlers living on the West Bank. In spite of protests, and massive civil disobedience, the settlers in Yamit in the Sinai were removed by force of arms of the Israeli army. The settlers gave up their land only after a special envoy was send to Yamit by Prime Minister Begin. The envoy who convinced the settlers to surrender was none other than Rabbi Meir Kahane.[143]

Rabbi Kahane and the Kach Movement

If Etzion and Shoshan took radical religious Orthodoxy underground, it was the rabbi from Brooklyn who brought it out in the open. Meir Kahane was born Martin David in 1932 in New York City. As a youth he was attracted to the Zionist Youth Organization, Betar, and as a child remembers when his family hosted in their home Zionist leader Vladimir Jabotinsky, the aging Betar member. His father, Charles Kahane, was a rabbi and active in the American Jewish Revisionist

---

142 Quoted in Gorenberg, *The End of Days,* p.179.
143 "Collective Political Action and Media Research Report," Gadi Wolsfeld, *Jerusalem Quarterly,* No. 31. (Spring 1984), pp. 141.

movement. One of Kahane's early heroes was Menachem Begin, long before he was Prime Minister. As the Irgun's illustrious commander and freedom fighter, Begin was a legend to the young Kahane. The Irgun was an underground group of Jewish militants who fought against the British and the Arabs before Statehood.

Kahane attended Jewish Talmudic School and was ordained a rabbi. As a restless young Orthodox rabbi, Kahane founded the Jewish Defense League in 1968 to defend the lower middle class Jewish neighborhoods of New York City against crime in the streets and black anti-Semitism.[144] A dynamic speaker, he often spoke against the Jewish establishment, blaming them for their passivity during the Nazi years. "Never again" became the official slogan of the JDL, with the clenched fist against a Star of David as the organization's symbol. One of his favorite expressions was, "A Jewish fist in the face of Gentiles."

During the early seventies, the repression of Soviet Jews became Kahane's main obsession. Through his organization, he had Soviet diplomats attacked both in the United States and Europe. Demonstrations were made in front of Soviet Embassies, and Russian organizations. Through his outspoken in-your-face tactics during the seventies the numbers of his sympathizers and admirers grew and became significant social forces in the United States, Europe and Israel.[145] Some of his members we sent to jail after a JDL bombing of an anti-Semitic radio station. Assaults and bombings were also made against the Soviet airline *Aeroflot*, the Russian *Intourist Travel Agency*, and several Soviet cultural centers. American businesses doing business with any of these were also targeted.

Biographer Robert Friedman notes in late 1969, Kahane was contacted by a Knesset member and asked to forge a secret semiofficial support group in Israel endorsed by the future Prime Minister Yitzhak Shamir.[146] A *Muslim International* source records Kahane being jailed in the United States in 1971 (for firearms violations and conspiracy), and then being contacted by "Yitshak Shamir, then head of the Israeli secret service Mossad, to do dirty operations in Paris." The source also claims the Mossad planned and financed many of JDL's militant actions against Soviet targets in the US and Europe.[147] Whether true or not, to US charges, Kahane

---

144 Janet Dolgin, *Jewish Identity and JDL*, Princeton University Press, 1977, p. 16.
145 Robert I. Friedman, *The False Prophet: Rabbi Meir Kahane*, 1972, p. 108.
146 Ibid., p. 107.
147 "Kahane and His Kach Movement," Zafarul Islam Khan, *MuslimMedia International*, Taken off the Internet, June 10, 1996.

was fined $5,000 and given a suspended sentence. Kahane's US "rap sheet" also included a 1972 probation violation when he distributed literature about weapons.

In September of 1971 Rabbi Kahane immigrated to Israel. His critics claim it was to avoid prosecution in the United States, or because his JDL movement was in decline even though his organization numbered around 19,000 members. The public in Israel would hear Kahane's name when the JDL became fully operational in Jerusalem in 1972. Kahane and a handful of American followers took to the streets, attacking predominately American Christian missionary activities and a sect of African Americans who claimed to be Jewish.

Kahane quickly gained attention by planning a sabotage mission against the Libyan consulate in Rome. However, Israeli authorities did not arrest him for conceiving the plan. In April of 1973 however, he was arrested for sedition, followed by a June arrest for conspiracy against the US by planning to blow up the Iraqi embassy, assassinate Russian diplomats and attack the Russian embassy. For these he was given a suspended sentence.

In 1973, the firebrand rabbi ran for a Knesset seat and almost won indicating the degree to which the populace was finding in him a hero. After the Yom Kippur War, a wake-up call to Israel's security and self-identity, Kahane became even more radical. He intentionally set out to polarize the Jews against the Palestinians. Following the success of Gush Enumin settlements, Kahane and his followers moved to the Kiryat Arba settlement and changed their name from the JDL to *Kach*, Hebrew for *thus* (as in "Thus sayeth the Lord"). The name had also been an old Irgun slogan of defiance rich in significance for those who had lived during the early Zionist period.

Like Gush Enumin, the Camp David Peace Accord shocked Kahane. After all, Prime Minister Begin had been his childhood hero; his Irgun exploits had shaped much of his thinking about radical Jewishness. To Kahane, his hero Begin had become an extreme traitor who not only betrayed the Jewish people but defamed God's name. Kahane writes:

The heart of the Begin tragedy is that a man who was a symbol for half a century of Jewish pride and strength surrendered Jewish rights, sovereignty and land out of fear of Gentile persecution. It is, in a word, "Hillul Hashem," the humiliation and the desecration of the name of G-d by substituting fear of the finite Gentile for Jewish faith in the G-d of creation and history.[148]

After Camp David, Kahane became more radical both in speech and action. He made a number of attempts to demolish the Dome of the Rock, send out hit squads to beat Arabs in their houses, smash their cars and shops, and stage illegal "document checks" on Arabs. His organization distributed name-calling leaflets calling for the expulsion and extermination of the Arabs. In Hebron, he forcibly took over the Mosque of the Prophet Abraham and turned part of it into a Jewish synagogue. This is the same Mosque where Dr. Baruch Goldstein, a Kahane devotee, would enter with his rifle in hand and machine-gun twenty-nine Muslim worshippers. In October of 1978, members of Kach would even attack Israeli soldiers who were keeping the Hebron synagogue closed. In March of 1979 Kach members were arrested for insults, trespassing and attacks on the Temple Mount.

Rabbi Kahane next set out to attack the very heart of the Israeli government, by going after its most sacred document, the Declaration of Independence. This first document of the state assured equal rights to all inhabitants of the Jewish state regardless of race, religion or nationality. Kahane called the document "the most damaging statement ever made in the history of Zionism." He believed it was impossible to have equal Arab existence in a Jewish state. Besides, when the document was written there were only about 150,000 Palestinian Arabs who still lived in the land. The rest had fled to other Arab countries like Jordan and Lebanon. But in 1978, Arabs numbered around 500,000 and had higher birth rates than Jews. Kahane's solution to the "Arab problem" was to expel the Arabs to other Arab countries lest they eventually vote Israel out of existence by their superior numbers.[149] Where other radical religionists were not clear about the Palestinian issue, Kahane was uncompromisingly clear. He foresaw early on an increasing Arab Palestinian nationalism that would culminate in trying to be a state within a state. But in 1979 his call for Arab removal would fall on deaf ears.

The 1980s in Israel would turn out to be far different than the seventies. The decade opened with Kahane being put into "detention" for six months for stockpiling ammunition at the Hacotel Yeshiva. In 1981, the rabbi lost another

---

148 "The Activist Column: The Second Revolution," *Jewish Press,* June 3, 1977, p. 20.
149 *Brother Against Brother,* p. 195.

bid for a Knesset seat. In 1982 Prime Minister Begin, in outright desperation, called upon Kahane to moderate and put an end to the Yamit settlement dispute in the Sinai. For his "peaceful" resolution" of a volatile situation, Kahane gained popular support. By this time, two trends were converging. First, the radical ideas of Kahane were gaining more popularity on the streets, and among some high leadership. Secondly, the war in Lebanon had split the country between *Peaceniks* and Defense Minister Sharon's *Hawks*. Then in 1983 the Begin government collapsed. With it came a serious disillusionment of the government in general. The stage was then set for a broader based Kahane acceptance. Sprinzak observes, "Thus in 1984, frustrated settlers, angry residents of developing towns, young soldiers, and insecure people all over the country, 25,906 of them in all, joined forces to lift a ten-year ban from the head of Kach and install Meir Kahane in the Knesset."[150]

Not only was Kahane elected but other Kach members won seats as well. Kahane's attraction was summarized by one voter who said, "He is the voice of everything you wanted to say but never dared to say in open." To the Israeli political elite, he was a dangerous threat. The new Prime Minister, Haim Herzog, excluded Kahane from his coalition government and openly stood against his ideas. A special Knesset resolution prevented Kahane from visiting Arab villages, and a further law was passed stipulating that members running for office could not incite or authorize racist and undemocratic practices. In the 1988 Knesset elections, polls predicted that Kach could win at least eight seats, but with the new Knesset law against incitement, Kahane and other Kach members were prevented from being candidates. Now, at the highest level Kahane was ostracized and marginalized by the political elite. On appeal, the Israeli Supreme Court banned the Kach party from the political process.

On November 2, 1990, Kahane publically called for the extermination of both Palestinians and liberal secular Jews holding power in Israel. Of the liberals he said, "Their evil threatens every Jew, their sins will sink the Jewish ship."[151] Three days later in New York City, a Muslim fundamentalist gunned down the Brooklyn born rabbi. The accused assassin Al-Sayyid Nusair, an Egyptian, was acquitted on December of 1991. Many believe Sheik Abdul Rachman, the blind Egyptian cleric, later indicted in the World Trade Center bombings, was behind

---

150 Ibid., p. 207.
151 Quoted in *Muslim Media International*, p. 3.

Kahane's murder. The newly elected (now deposed) Egyptian Muslim Brotherhood President, Mohammad Morsi, asked US President Barak Obama for the release of the blind cleric! Others believe the Israeli Mossad may have carried out the murder of Kahane.

The impact and influence of this American rabbi should not be underestimated. Though he passed from the scene in 1990, his legacy, thought and admirers are still very much a part of American and Israelis Jewish culture. In particular, his beliefs about the nature of the Jewish state, the Arabs, the land of Israel, and his political/religious militancy to the point of using violence to accomplish God's purposes, are still mainstream among the radical religious right.

On the State he says:

The State of Israel that arises in the Land of Israel is not a Western state or an Eastern one; it is not a "secular" state, it is not to be modeled after "the nations." It is a Jewish state with all the uniqueness that this implies. It is a state whose personality, character, behavior and structure must be the reflection of Jewishness and Judaism.

On the land of Israel he expounds:

The Land of Israel is the home of the Jewish people and of no one else; there has never been a Palestine or Palestinian people and never will be. The non-Jew is welcome to live in the Jewish state as an individual but not as a sovereign people, for the boundaries of Israel are those indicated in the Bible and Eretz Yisroel cannot be divided.[152]

On the subject of the secular state, Kahane came to the conclusion, "The government is either unwilling or unable to protect Jewish lives and property, yet it lays down rules for both security forces and civilians that make it impossible to protect themselves properly."[153] For this reason, he had concluded the secular state had lost its legitimacy. Departing from the Kook theology of Gush Enumin where the secular state could still be thought of as "in process" as moving from democracy

---

152 Rabbi Meir Kahane, *Our Challenge,* p.109.
153 Rabbi Meir Kahane, *Israel: Revolution or Referendum,* p. 50.

to theocracy, Kahane and his followers saw the state as having no "inherent sanctity." In the words of Sandler, "the State of Israel has no inherent sanctity unless it adheres in full to the role destined to it by the divine commands."[154] Though the Brooklyn rabbi is dead, his thought lives on.

Kahane Connections and Continuing Radicalism

Even though the death of Rabbi Kahane was a shock to the then outlawed Kach members, Kahane left a group of sympathetic settlers in Kiryat Arba. Sprinzak records, "They kept alive the key institutions of Kach as well as several of its operational arms."[155] Though Kach continued under Rabbi Abraham Toledano for a while, a small group of Kahane supporters broke off and started Kahane Chai (Kahane Lives) headed by Kahane's son, Benjamin. They centered their movement at the settlement in Kfar Tapuach in Samaria, an ancient Biblical location noted in Joshua 17:8 as having been conquered by Joshua himself. Kahane Chai continued terrorist attacks on the West Bank but for the most part was not successful in gaining support, at least until the Oslo Accords and the Hebron Goldstein massacre. Jewish teenagers in midtown Manhattan on the anniversary of Kahane's death in 1992 threw a hand grenade into an Arab shoemaker's shop, killing him and wounding ten others. They were later identified as being members of Kahane Chai and living in the West Bank settlement of Kfar Tapuach.[156]

When Muslim terrorism erupted at the end of 1993 and into 1994, the marginalized movements of Kach and Kahane Chai were moved to center stage.

The increase of Muslim terrorism and response from right wing religious groups were the result of the now infamous handshake on the White House lawn. The ratification of the Oslo Accord between Prime Minister Rabin and Palestinian Liberation Organization Chairman, Yassar Arafat (September 13, 1993), shocked both militant Muslims and Jews. On both sides of the Green Line, the Accord was viewed at the least as compromise, and at worst, betrayal. Muslim groups like Hamas and Islamic Jihad had hated and mistrusted Arafat for years. To them, he was a traitor for not continuing the call for the extermination of Israel, and as a more secularized and "feigned" Muslim, Arafat never carried a passion for an

---

154 Shmuel Sandler, "Religious Zionism and the State: Political Accommodation and Religious Radicalism in Israel," in *Terrorism and Political Violence,* Volume 8, Summer, 1996, p. 145.
155 *Brother Against Brother,* p.233.
156 Robert I. Friedman, "The Brooklyn Avengers," *The New York Review,* June 23, 1994, p. 41.

Islamic state.[157] To those with Gush and Kahane sentiments, the peace accord was the final nail in the coffin of the Labor government legitimacy.

Even though the majority of Israel had supported the peace movement, a demonstration of some 200,000 showed up at the Knesset to express their disapproval of the Accord. As outraged Muslim terrorists from Hamas and Islamic Jihad struck civilian targets in Israel, the radical elements of Gush Emunim, Kahane Chai, and the Yesha Council (Council of Salvation, composed of leading rabbis) went into action. Rabbinic opinion authorized the killing of Palestinian attackers and their collaborators. Social observer Sprinzak concluded the most significant effect of the Muslim terrorist attacks were to further delegitimize the Rabin government in the eyes of the settler community.[158] To the religious right, the Oslo Accords that promised giving autonomy to Palestinians, along with the removal of Israel security forces, was tantamount to national treason. The settlements again felt betrayed by the secular, godless government and worse, were about to see the sacred real estate that constituted the Biblical Land of Israel given back to the authority of gentiles.

The American Connection

The Jewish Community back in the United States was also mobilized around Kahane Chai and Gush ideology. A Kahane Chai youth camp was even set up in the Catskill mountains in New York and offered Kahane ideology and paramilitary training.[159] On February 9, 1994 a full-page ad appeared in the *New York Times* challenging the Rabin government and the Oslo accords. In one section the ad read:

American Jews and other friends of Israel are now confronted with a dilemma. In the past, they have supported the government of Israel, even when disagreeing with some its policies. They never anticipated that a government would arise in Israel that would be ready to lead the people of Israel over a cliff by giving away to Israel's enemies portions of the Land of

---

157 For an enlightening article on this perspective, see Israel Amrani, "Enemies: Israeli and Palestinian extremists have more in common than they think," *The Progressive*, March 1994, p. 28.

158 *Brother Against Brother*, p. 231.

159 *The Brooklyn Avengers*, p. 41.

Israel vital to Israel's defense and part of the national and religious heritage of the Jewish people since Biblical times.

For American Jews to support such a government, a government of national suicide, would be to actually work against the people of Israel. With Israel's survival at stake, Jews and others are morally obligated to speak out and demand that their leaders tell Rabin that his policies are endangering Israel's existence.

Finally, American Jews must reach out to help the gallant and courageous pioneers of Israel's heartland, Judea and Samaria, and Gaza and the Golan Heights, who are trying desperately to hold on to their homes and communities . . . At this time of mortal peril for the Jewish state, we call on all friends of Israel to act now and join PRO ISRAEL's efforts to help save the land of Israel.

Pro Israel at the time was a US public-based charity set up to weaken support for the Rabin government and undermine the peace process. Funds raised by the group were passed to YESHA, the Council of Jewish Communities in Judea, Samaria and Gaza. *Pro Israel* was set up by Gush Emunim and used to help finance the settlements.[160] After the Olso accords, money poured in. Friedman records $100,000 being raised at one speaking engagement at an American synagogue, with annual charitable funding of around 10 million dollars. Friedman also notes, "As Rabin cut back on funds for the settlements, donations from American Jews have become increasingly important for the settlers' economic survival."[161] People like Israel's Former Prime Minister, Ariel Sharon, former American Senator Alfonse D'Amato, and former Secretary of Housing and Vice-Presidential Candidate, the late Jack Kemp, all spoke at fund raising dinners for Pro Israel or The American Friends of Ateret Cohanim, another settlement support organization.

Reading between the lines of the *New York Times* ad, it is clear the writers were convinced Rabin's secular government was a serious threat to the survival of the nation of Israel. If he (Rabin) was sinking the "Jewish ship" in Kahane's words, he then qualified for Rabbinic consideration of a *din Rodef*, a sentence pronounced on a Jewish traitor.[162]

---

160 Ibid., p. 42.
161 Ibid., p. 42.
162 *Murder in the Name of God*, p. 4.

The Israeli Tipping Points

A Kahane admirer decided something must be done. Dr. Baruch Goldstein, Kiryat Arba's emergency physician, had seen several of his friends die in his arms as a result of Arab terrorism. Like many Israeli settlers he had been disillusioned with the secular government's betrayal of the settler communities and Oslo accords. As a devoted student of Kahane, he had also suffered significant grief as a result of the rabbi's death. Apparently, he slowly had come to the conclusion that only a supreme *kiddush hashem* or sanctification of the name could put the course of Israeli history back on the messianic track.[163] Therefore, taking his assault rifle and three clips of ammunition to the Hebron Mosque, he opened fire, bringing down twenty-nine innocent worshippers. The February 28, 1994, massacre was one of the worst in Israel's violent history.

Immediately, the Israeli government outlawed Kach and Kahane Chai. For many on the religious right, the massacre was more the result of Rabin's betrayal of the Land of Israel than his acceptance of the PLO.

The Temple Mount Movement

One ideological legacy of the Gush-Kahane years was the reborn Yehuda Etzion. Having been arrested in 1984 for his terrorist acts against the Arab mayors and plotting to blow up the Temple Mount, when released in 1991, he founded *Chai Vekayam* or *Alive and Existing*, an obvious statement that he was alive and back! Though holding to his basic Gush theology and having never apologized for his underground terrorist activities, he did moderate during his seven-year prison term. He no longer viewed violence as justified but gravitated to actions of more peaceful resistance. He rewrote a sample Israeli Declaration of Independence, which in his mind better reflected the distinctive of a truly Jewish state. In the document he eliminated the statements about democracy, human rights, and equality, and replaced them with the Bible and the Kingdom of Israel.

The group is still known for their efforts to pray *on* the Temple Mount, an act prohibited by law. In 2005, the group celebrated the eleventh Temple feast by making a "sacrifice of bread and crackers."[164] It is thought they continue to promote civil disobedience as a strategy by the settlers. Even though the former

---

163 *Brother Against Brother*, p. 242.
164 Temple Institute Website, www.templeinstitute.org.

Defense Minister Ariel Sharon was never considered overtly religious, his action in October of 2000 in attempting to pray on the Temple Mount certainly was a demonstration in the spirit of Chai Vekayam. This now famous initiative by Sharon set off a round of violence on both sides and basically shut down the peace process to this writing. Of course, every American president since Jimmy Carter has tried to pull off some grand peace agreement.[165]

Rabbi Kahane's wife, Libby, with Yisrael Ariel, was instrumental in founding the Temple Mount Religious Seminary, with its historical research arm, the *Temple Institute*. Along with them was former Kach leader Rabbi Abraham Toledano. (Toledano was once arrested at the Tel Aviv airport trying to smuggle bomb-making materials, weapon components, arms manuals and $40,000 cash on a return trip from the US.) The Temple Mount group is devoted to rebuilding the Jewish Temple on the site of the Dome of the Rock and doing all the necessary research in order to reintroduce the priesthood and all its ritual practices. There is a perplexing irony noted by Gorenberg that it is predominately American evangelical Christians that have made the Temple Institute so successful. He observes, "Tour guides specializing in evangelical groups say the exhibition is a high point of visits to the Holy Land . . . the bottom line: Ariel, Richman, and Co. would have a harder time staying in business were they not "a landmark in time" for Christian premillennialists."[166]

One source claims connections between the Temple Institute and Chai Vekaiyam, which is not surprising since they both have Kahane connections. Since the Temple Institute receives government funding for its educational research, its funding is questioned by some authorities. If the Institute's goal is to build the third Temple on top of the mount, then the Dome of the Rock must be removed. This goal is tantamount to Israeli legal incitement to violence.

On one of my visits to Jerusalem I took a tour of the Institute and saw all the Levitical ritual implements they have meticulously designed for use in a reconstructed Temple. Carefully woven priestly garments are also on display. When I asked the Institute guide about the problem with the Dome of the Rock being where the Temple is supposed to be, her answer was, "God will take care of that!"

---

165 A current update on this chapter has Secretary of State Kerry and President Obama again trying to restart the peace talks with Israel and the Palestinians. However at the present time the relationships are strained between Israel and the US.

166 Gorenberg, *The End of Days*, p. 174.

The group was charged with furthering incitement to violence when their chief rabbi, Rabbi Yisrael Ariel, gave the eulogy at Baruch Goldstein's funeral, calling him a "martyr."[167] Another group who viewed Goldstein as a martyr was a group of university students at Bar Elan University. The student group was called Eyal, an acronym for Israel Fighting Organization. One of its most dedicated, soft-spoken members was Yigal Amir, an admirer of both Kahane and Goldstein.

Killing a Prime Minister

The world of the religious right and the secular government collided violently on the evening of November 4, 1995. Prime Minister Rabin had just finished speaking at a peace rally at Kings of Israel Square in Tel Aviv when Yigal Amir walked up behind him. As Rabin was about to enter his car, Amir fired three shots point blank into his side. Rabin was pronounced dead an hour later. Amir was anything but a lone crazed assassin. That evening the twenty-five-year-old having said his evening prayers took his legally licensed Beretta pistol, loaded it with hollow point bullets made by his brother Haggai, and tucked the gun under his shirt. This night was the third time he had tried to get close enough to Rabin to carry out his own *kiddush hashem*, sanctification of the name.

Most Israeli commentators now realize Yigal Amir was only the tip of an iceberg in an ideological "religious swamp." Hebrew University professor, Moshe Halbertal says, "Yigal Amir was not a madman, as many wish to believe. This assassination wasn't incoherent or out of character . . . he was motivated by a core of religious ideology that lives on the fringes of Israeli society."[168] What made his act so "coherent" was critical events which led up to November 4, 1995.

Following the Hebron massacre by Dr. Goldstein, Prime Minister Rabin was seriously considering removing the settlers by force from the Tel Rumeida settlement in central Hebron. Kach leader, Baruch Marzel, who represented the aspirations of religious Jews to settle all of Israel, headed the settlement. The government's political and tactical discussions about how to carry out this action were met with utter horror by the settlements and competing religious authorities. Many prominent rabbis joined in giving a ruling against the possible evacuation, including former Chief Rabbi, Shlomo Goren. What was unique about this ruling

---

167 "The Temple Institute," *Shomron News Service,* translation of an article in *Ma'ariv* Newspaper, January 21, 1996.
168 Moshe Halbertal, "Swamp Man," *The New Republic,* November 27, 1995, p. 16.

was that it was addressed to Israeli soldiers. Three rabbis called for the IDF to disobey the order to remove Jewish settlers from Eretz Israel. Sprinzak observes, "The presence of highly regarded spiritual authorities who no longer respected the sanctity of the Israeli army was a new development."[169] For some time the IDF, especially its elite forces and officer corps, was becoming more religious in nature and holding views compatible with the settlers. Shahak notes,

> For some time it has been noted that a growing percentage of junior and middle-ranking officers was of the national-religious tendency, the "people who wear knitted skull-caps," many of them settlers. There is no doubt that the percentage of those people in elite units of the Israeli army and its officer groups is now significant and growing . . . many secular Jews don't want to become officers. A growing number of students and soldiers educated by the rabbis of the messianic tendency learn a "deep contempt for the secular regime" in Israel.[170]

The rabbinic ruling was seen as a serious threat to Rabin's consideration of removing the settlement, but Rabin was undeterred and furious. He polled his senior officers including the religious ones, but they felt their soldiers would not disobey orders. However, Rabin changed his mind and withdrew the Tel Rumeida consideration. What the consideration did for the religious community was unite the entire "Biblical" Zionist community some 400, 000 strong against the Prime Minister. Rabin, a committed secularist, had never liked the settlers or shared their messianic views. Just a few days before his murder, he had met with two rabbis about the supposed death threats from the rabbinic community. Rabin's chief of staff took them seriously and felt they should be listened to. Rabin's response was laughter, and then saying, "How naïve you are."[171] His disdain for the religious community was self-evident.

The Tel Rumeida incident, having brought the rabbinic community together against Rabin, kept them together in discussing some ancient Halakhic sources. With increasing violence from Hamas and Islamic Jihad taking 87 lives, and

---

169 *Brother Against Brother*, p. 249.
170 *Israel Shahak, "Yigal Amir: Tip of an Iceberg?" Middle East International, No. 519, 16 February 1996.*
171 *Murder in the Name of God*, p.130.

wounding another 202 in suicide attacks, the council of rabbis began considering putting the government on trial for a *din Rodef* and *din Moser*. *Rodefs* and *Mosers* are the worst kind of Jews who put the entire Jewish community in jeopardy. "They betray the community through acts that may result in the loss of innocent Jewish lives."[172] A din Rodef is the only case in halakha tradition that allows Jews to kill another Jew without a trial. A Moser is a Jew who is suspected of giving Gentiles information about Jews or illegally giving Jewish property to Gentiles. From the consideration of many rabbis, Rabin qualified as both a Rodef for putting Jewish lives at risk, and a Moser, for giving back Jewish property, the land of Israel.

During the months leading up to the assassination, in yeshivas and religious circles, these discussions were taking place. There has been testimony by students that their professors and rabbis had very clearly determined Rabin qualified for the most serious action a Jew can do to another Jew. But after the killing of Rabin many of the rabbis involved denied they ever gave a formal declaration of Rodef to their students.

The important point to these rabbinic discussions about *Rodef* and *Moser*[173] is not whether they did or did not offer a final judgment on Rabin, but the mere fact that these issues were seriously discussed in the religious communities in both Israel and America.[174] The widespread discussion and interaction on the basis on rabbinic law was enough to create a climate ready-made for any serious dedicated student like Yigal Amir to act upon. As Sprinzak alludes, "A retrospective examination suggests that it was just a question of time before a hot-headed student was ready to jump to conclusions on his own."[175] Both Amir and his brother maintain they had a rabbinic Rodef, and that they would not have carried out the murder without it.[176] In fact, Amir's brother told sources the murder was carried out "according to Halacha," suggesting even an exact prescription. Based on a Biblical passage in II Samuel 2:12-28, Abner kills a fellow Hebrew named Asahel who was threatening his life. Talmudic sages held

---

172 *Brother Against Brother,* p.253.
173 Based upon the use of the Hebrew term "Moser" in Numbers 31:16, implying an influence toward apostasy by one taking a stand against the Jewish people.
174 Karpin & Friedman in *Murder in the Name of God* offers one whole chapter on the American connection to the assassination. "The American Connection," pp. 131-164.
175 *Brother Against Brother,* p. 257.
176 *Murder in the Name of God,* p. 128.

Abner's sword was placed precisely underneath Asahel's fifth rib, the precise spot on Prime Minister Rabin where Amir aimed his shot.[177]

Another action contributing to the violent atmosphere leading up to Rabin's assassination was the placing of a *Pulsa da-Nura,* or Lashes of Fire, upon the Prime Minister. On October 6, 1995, a month before Rabin's murder, a group led by Kahanist Avigdor Eskin, a thirty-five-year-old businessman, wrapped themselves in prayer shawls and met in front of Yitzak Rabin's official residence. There they performed the mystical and ancient ceremony of Pulsa da-Nura, an Aramaic death curse that invokes a mystical punishment. To be legitimate, ten rabbis from the community must convene and fast for three days, and then make the curse at midnight. If the curse is made against an innocent person, then the curse is returned upon the heads of those who gave it. Therefore, the mystical Cabalist curse is rarely done, and when it is, it is taken very seriously. A neighbor passing by at the time recalls seeing Eskin rocking in prayer and saying, "Put to death the cursed Yitzak, son of Rosa Rabin, as quickly as possible because of his hatred for the Chosen People . . . May you be damned, damned, damned."[178] The curse quickly became popular knowledge.

Conclusion

In one sense, the territory covered in this chapter illustrates the fine line between worship and terrorism. Halbertal concludes, "A perverse reading of sacred texts is yet further proof that a thin line divides the righteous worship of God from idolatry. The religious swamps that nourished Baruch Goldstein have now sent us Yigal Amir, who no doubt also sees himself as loyal heir to the Jewish tradition. For such men, it is a tradition in which absolute truths justify murder."[179]

The swamps are still there. The Israeli army withdrew its troops from Southern Lebanon after what some call a stalemate and others call "fiasco." Later, they withdrew from the West Bank and allowed the Palestinians to form their own security forces. Likewise, the IDF withdrew from Gaza although forces have had to go back temporarily to stop continuing rocket attacks (And more recently in the summer of 2014). President Hafez Assad of Syria died, and his son Bashar followed in his father's tyrannical footsteps. Experts have claimed his regime could fall at

---

177 Ibid., p. 129.
178 Ibid., p. 91.
179 Moshe Halbertal, "Swamp Man," *The New Republic,* November 27, 1995, p. 16.

any moment to a collection of rebels mounting daily offensives against what is left of the Syrian army.[180] Into this mix, a remnant of Al Qaeda established itself as the Islamic Caliphate of Iraq and Syria. They have as of this writing taken territory in both Syria and Iraq. The war continues now with an American formed coalition of Arab and European forces.

Yassar Arafat is gone, but his legacy of Fatah recently has made agreements with Hamas, the offshoot of the Muslim Brotherhood in Gaza. In fact, after Israel removed all its settlements from the Gaza area and pulled out all its soldiers, rockets continued to fall on Israeli communities. Rabin's short-lived peace idea, "Land for Peace," did not work! Likewise American envoys' attempts to get both sides back to peace settlements have failed. Israelis have built a concrete wall separating themselves from the Palestinians plus establishing an *Iron Dome* missile defense system throughout the country. Meanwhile, Palestinians continue to threaten outright declaration of a Palestinian State and have recently taken the issue to the United Nations. This act only furthers the anxiety among West Bank Jewish settlers. An armed Palestinian police force along with rock-throwing teenagers still wage occasional demonstrations against Israeli gunships and tanks. Deaths continue to occur on both sides. As a result of the kidnapping of two Israeli teenagers, supposedly by Hamas, the IDF engaged in another war with Gaza. Also in response Israel laid claim to 1,000 more acres of West Bank land in a Jewish settlement near Bethlehem. This, in spite of Palestinian and President Obama's demands to halt settlement building. President Abbas of the Palestinian Authority called the response not only a violation of international law but a "further deterioration of the situation."[181]

Following Rabin's assassination 150,000 protesters gathered in what is now Rabin Square. Many of the protesters bused in from Jewish settlements on the West Bank held banners proclaiming, "Barak is dangerous to Jews."[182] Ehud Barak

---

180 These "rebels" are a collection of Syrian Free Army personnel; Al Qaeda affiliated groups mixed in with a few Syrian democrats, and foreign Jihadis from Iraq, Saudi Arabia, and Turkey, Europe, United Kingdom and the United States. Add to this the new movements of Al Nursa, ISIS, even a few Iranian 'advisors.'

181 Isabel Kershner, "Israel Claims Nearly 1,000 Acres of West Bank Land Near Bethlehem," *The New York Times*, August 31, 2014.

182 These "rebels" are a collection of Syrian Free Army personnel, Al Qaeda affiliated groups mixed in with a few Syrian democrats, and foreign Jihadis from Iraq, Saudi Arabia, and Turkey, Europe, United Kingdom and the United States. Add to this the new movements of Al Nursa, ISIS, even a few Iranian "advisors."

succeeded Prime Minister Rabin and at Camp David offered up a generous eighty percent of the settlements on the West Bank to make peace with the Palestinians! Of course, Arafat refused the offer, affirming the long standing quip that "Arafat never missed an opportunity to miss an opportunity!"

Barak's offer to give back eighty percent of West Bank territories and even put Jerusalem on the table for consideration sent the religious community into frenzy. Shimon Riklin, head of YESHA, the Council of Jewish Communities of Judea, Samaria and Gaza, told a group of settlers, "If Barak orders the clearing of settlements he will be murdered."[183] Rabbi Daniel Shilo, a settlement rabbi stated, "It is betrayal of Torah and national tradition to hand over Jewish land. The criminal who does this is the same criminal who allowed the Holocaust to happen."[184] The same language and rhetoric heard before the killing of Rabin is proclaimed openly in the streets and settlements. Colonel Moshe Hager-Lau, the "unofficial" security advisor to the settlements and Orthodox adherent, runs Yatir, pre-military training academy for Orthodox youth. Recently, he advised, "We must change the rules of engagement . . . We'll shoot everyone who crosses into settlements or into military bases near Jerusalem. Those settlements and bases are the shield of Jerusalem."[185]

And then there's the Temple Mount movement. As many have observed, the thirty-five acres of sacred ground to two faiths (Islam and Judaism), are always in the forefront of explosive news. Whenever a rock is moved or a new archeological site found around the Mount, all hell breaks loose. The long-standing agreement is still in effect that though the Old City of Jerusalem is under Israeli jurisdiction, the Muslim Mufti of Jerusalem has authority over the Temple Mount area (Called Haram al-Sharif by the Arabs). Mixed with this, previously it was the Jewish Rabbinic view that the Temple area would have to be fully "cleansed" in order for Jews to do any worship there. But in the last few years, the attitude is changing.

Temple Movement Guru Dr. Randal Price notes, "At one time, the rabbi's proposal would have been thought to be extreme, but perhaps no more. "The Muslim blockade against Israelis entering the Temple Mount area and systematic destruction of areas under the surface of the Mount prompted the rabbinical council of Judea and Samaria, a group that has influence over hundreds of thousands of

---

183 "Barak Hears from Israeli Right Wing," Associated Press article, *The Orlando Sentinel*, July 17, 2000.
184 "Threats against Barak," *World Press Review*, August 2000, p. 26.
185 Ibid., p.26.

Jewish people, to reconsider the halakhic ban on going to the Temple Mount."[186]
So what we have is the attempt by the Mufti to completely transform the Temple
Mount into one holy Islamic mosque that would prohibit all non-Muslims from
entering the compound. More recent is the Mugrabi bridge issue. This bridge is the
only access for non-Muslims to the Temple Mount. After an earthquake weakened
the hill that ascended to the Mugrabi gate, the Israelis built a "temporary" wooden
frame bridge. Now Israeli engineers say it is unsafe, and a more permanent bridge
needs to be built. The Muslim Waqf holds this act amounts to desecration of
Islamic holy ground. Islamic websites have called for a third "intifada" if Israeli
authorities begin any work on the bridge.[187] At the same time, the Temple Mount
Faithful view the same space as what is holding up the ultimate Jewish redemption.
Again, Gorenberg notices the Christian and Jewish right wing supporting this view.
For a small but growing group of Jews on the Israeli right, every day since 1967 has
been a missed opportunity to begin building the Third Temple . . . for conservative
Christians, building the Temple is an essential condition for the Second Coming."[188]
It is no wonder that the peace process has stalled!

Current Israeli Tensions

As this peace process bogged down, conditions on the ground were placing the
Israeli army against the settlers. When the late Yassar Arafat was to arrive in Gaza
and then motor to Bethlehem, Orthodox settlers blocked the road and had to be
forcibly removed by the Israeli army.[189] This put the soldiers in a position they
did not like and has created further problems to this day. To the surprise of many,
one Israeli religious columnist observed, "Contrary to numerous forecasts and
assessments, the settlement enterprise in Judea and Samaria is now experiencing
one of the best periods in its history . . . not only will the torch be carried on, it will
burn ever brighter until the goal is won and Judea and Samaria are annexed to the
State of Israel. The Jewish settlements in Judea and Samaria are firmly ensconced
in their third decade, and are feeling just fine, thank you."[190] So on one side is the

---

186 "The Armed Invaders will follow the unarmed Palestinian marchers," *The Jerusalem Report,*
    July 31, 2000, p. 6.
187 Randal Price, *Unholy War: American, Israel and Radical Islam*, Harvest House, 2001, p. 298.
188 See "Bridge Over Troubled City," *Jerusalem Report*, December 5, 2011, pp. 8-11.
189 Gorenberg, *The End of Days*, p. 14.
190 William Orme, "Israeli Army Removes Angry Settlers Blocking Gaza Road," *The New York
    Times,* December 5, 2000.

group of settlers who refuse to leave, and on the other side is the IDF who may be called upon to remove them by force.

More currently, Leslie Susser writes, "As the Israel Defense Forces refined plans to remove illegal Jewish outposts in the West Bank, there are increasingly ominous signs that large numbers of young soldiers, especially religiously Orthodox recruits, might defy orders to evacuate settlers."[191] She goes on to say that according to some estimates as many as thirty percent of soldiers serving in the West Bank might refuse orders to evacuate. Many of these soldiers come from these settlements and believe that their religious conscience must override the secular law or military orders.

More recently, a controversial book published in Israel entitled, *Torat Hamelekh*, or the "King's Law," is gaining more public support and criticism. The book written by learned scholars Rabbis Yitzak Shapira and Yosef Elizur from the settlement of Yitzhar on the West Bank, raises serious questions on the issue of "murder." One chapter deals with the question of when it is necessary and permissible to kill innocents. The *Jerusalem Report* discloses, "*Torat Hamelekh* was now receiving full attention, raising not only questions regarding a purported "Jewish morality" but also regarding the role of rabbis in society." The article concludes by saying, "Given the growing influence of rabbis over the growing number of religious soldiers, and the growth of the army-affiliated yeshivas, the question arises whether *Torah Hamelekh* and similar rabbinic literature will affect the way soldiers respond to events in the territories."[192]

If this is not enough, another writer alludes to the somewhat amazing parallel between these religious Zionists and Islamic Hamas; both desire a religious theocratic state . . . the former where Halakhic law (Jewish law) is observed and the latter where Sharia (Muslim law) is enforced.[193] Obviously these two cannot coexist.

The American connection is also very active. Money pours into Israel from American Jews who desire to see the fulfillment of Eretz Israel. Miami millionaire Irving Moskowitz continues to buy up properties in East Jerusalem in order to establish Hebrew study centers and yeshivas. One article reports

---

191 Emuna Elon, "Obituaries Greatly Exaggerated," *The Jerusalem Report*, November 22, 1999.

192 "Holy Orders," Leslie Susser, *The Jerusalem Report*, December 21, 2009, p.6.

193 Kamoun-Ben-Shomon, "The Murder Midrash," *The Jerusalem Report*, September, 27, 2010, p. 14, 15, 16.

his foundation funded $18 million worth of settlements.[194] But every new settlement and purchase further incites Arabs and thwarts the peace process. Connected to both Jewish and Christian neo-conservative causes, Moskowitz bought an East Jerusalem hotel and had it bulldozed to make space for Jewish settlements.[195]

Moskowitz also provides funding for Christian groups that support Israel, like the Battalion of Deborah (www.battalionofdeborah.org) In fact, this Christian-Jewish connection is fostered by Israeli politicians at the highest level. Prime Minister Benjamin Netanyahu has become the darling of the evangelical prophecy movement. This MIT and Harvard educated, probably secular leader of the Likud party is appealing to conservative Christians even as he plays to orthodox Jews at home. Gorenberg reveals he most often displayed this "Netanyahu-evangelical alliance" in past meetings with the late Rev Jerry Falwell, Rev. Hagee and leaders of the Southern Baptist convention.[196] He goes on to say, "each side (Israeli right and conservative Christians), often assume that the other is playing a role it doesn't understand itself; each often regards the other as an unknowing instrument for reaching a higher goal."[197]

Kahane Chai remained alive and well in Brooklyn for while. 350 Jews attended a one hundred dollar a plate dinner to hear Kahane's son Benyamin speak,[198] though the political organization Kach is outlawed in both the United States and Israel. Kahane Chai (Kahane Lives!) established by the Rabbi's son, Benyamin, was reorganized in America as a nonprofit service organization, and continues to maintain the Kahane web site (www.kahane.org). Even though Benyamin and his wife were murdered returning to their West Bank home in 2000, still in Brooklyn, Israel, and the West Bank, posters, graffiti and bumper stickers abound proclaiming, "Kahane was right."[199] The posters were obviously printed and distributed by Kahanists. A *Jerusalem Report* article entitled, "Kahane is Back" claims "the followers

---

194 Israel Amrani, "Enemies," *The Progressive*, March 1994, p. 39.

195 Michael S. Serril, "The Power of Money," *Time*, September 1997, p.37.

196 "Irving Moskowitz Demolishes part of Jerusalem Hotel to Build Settler Housing," Guardian. co.uk. January 2011.

197 *The End of Days*, p. 166.

198 Ibid., p. 28.

199 Meir Ettinger, grandson of Meir Kahane, was recently arrested in Israel on suspicion of leading a series of violent attacks against Palestinians and being involved in a Jewish extremist organization.

of assassinated Rabbi Meir Kahane, whose anti-Arab party was outlawed 15 years ago, believe his ideas have prevailed."[200]

A group from Brooklyn even protested at the home of former US President Bill Clinton and his wife when they purchased it in Chappaqua, New York. They had still not forgiven President Clinton's role in offering up the settlement territories for the sake of peace at the Camp David talks with Barak and Arafat. Michael Guzofsky, a Kahane demonstrator said, "We operate openly and have nothing to hide." To the protestors, the message was the same. Biblical Israel includes the West Bank and it can never be given over to the Palestinians. Peace can only be accomplished by the expulsion of the Arabs.[201]

Perhaps the most important thing to be learned from this chapter is what I call the ongoing "Marginalization-Delegitimatization Dance." As Gorenberg notes, "It didn't take secret police to read the theological crisis on the religious right, and the delegitimization of secular authority."[202] From the beginning of the Jewish State a serious division has existed between the predominately secular governments and its religious populace. Over the years, as the government tried to marginalize the religious, the more the religious viewed the government as being illegitimate.

The assassination of Rabin was only the flash point of a very long historical development. Rabin was the first Prime Minister to not include the religious in his government, in retrospect now, a very serious tactical, political and theological mistake. Gorenberg accurately voices his take: "By ignoring the theological crisis set off by the Oslo Accord, Israeli authorities left themselves unprepared for Jewish terror. By regarding (Dr.) Goldstein as a madman, they avoided the urgent need to understand the religious rationale behind his action."[203] Prime Ministers Ehud Barak and Benjamin Netanyahu learned the lesson from this exclusion. To win and stay in power, a Prime Minister must form coalition governments that include the increasingly powerful religious parties. In particular, Israeli governments cannot stay in power without the Sephardic religious party, *Shas*. Goodman notes, "The electoral system has made *Shas* the holders of the balance of power in the Knesset,

---

200 Binyamin Kahane and his wife were assassinated by Arab gunmen while driving to their home on the West Bank, December 31, 2000. They were killed by three members of the Palestinian Liberation Organization.

201 Eatta Price-Gibson, "Kahane is Back," *The Jerusalem Report*, December 21, 2009, p.14.

202 Dean Murphy, "Terror Label No Hindrance to Anti-Arab Jewish Group," *The New York Times*, December 19, 2000.

203 Gorenberg, p. 238.

giving the ultra-Orthodox Sephardi party absolute say over virtually every decision the government may make. The real prime minister of Israel, therefore, has been cited publically as Rabbi Ovadiah Yosef[204] (the one who made the death threat on the Education Minister) and the real government, his council of sages.[205]

As of 2013, Shas held eleven seats in the Knesset and were a significant part of the Netanyahu government, although in the most recent election, he cut a compromise against the Orthodox settlers by proposing legislation requiring Orthodox youth to be drafted into the military like everyone else.[206] Netanyahu's argument was the government's support of the *Haredi* was unsustainable since among the tens of thousands who do not serve in the military (as required by all citizens) sixty percent live below the poverty line and are supported by the government. Susser comments about the dilemma, "The Zionist State is funding its own downfall."[207] At the time of this writing the Israeli Cabinet just approved limiting the number of seminary (yeshiva) students to only 1,800. This is down from 8,000 eligible for the draft each year.[208] Needless to say, the ultra-Orthodox are angered![209]

However, one Knesset member, Dr. Michael Ben-Ari, said in 2009, "I don't know how many times I've been in jail, but pretty soon the authorities will understand, we're the establishment now. Kahane was right, and everything he said has come true."[210] At that time, the *Shas* party held four cabinet posts and the Deputy Prime Minister of Israel, Eli Yishai was a *Shas* member! However, as noted above, the 2013 election forced Netanyahu to limit the *Shas* influence and at this time of writing, his inner circle is heavily weighted with Likud members, not *Shas*. In the March 2015 elections, the self-proclaimed "unapologetic extremist" Rabbi Baruch Marzel was predicted to win the election. However, just before the election, the Israeli Supreme Court banned him from the election saying, "he pushed the

204 Gorenberg, *The End of Days*, p. 207.
205 However, Rabbi Yosef passed away in October of 2013 with estimated funeral participants at anywhere between 300,000 and 800,000. If estimates are true, it would be the largest funeral in Israel's history. ("Shas tries to get back on its feet," *The Times of Israel*, October 5, 2014, www.timesofisrael.com). The same article asked the question, "Does Shas have a post-Yosef future?" The answer: a resounding yes!
206 The spiritual leader of the Shas party often called, "the most important living Halachic authority."
207 Hirsch Goodman, "An Easy Way Out," *The Jerusalem Report*, June 5, 2000, p. 14.
208 "Israel: Cabinet Approves Law Limiting Conscription Exemptions," Stratfor Global Intelligence, July 7, 2013.
209 See "Ultra-Orthodox Israelis protest proposed draft," *Orlando Sentinel*, May 17, 2013. P. 4.
210 Leslie Susser, "Bibi's Locust Years," *The Jerusalem Report*, August 13, 2012, p. 12.

limits of democracy to the extreme and abused freedom of speech." The court and many other members of the Knesset were concerned he would bring "Kahanism" back into the Knesset. Marzel lives in the Tel Rumeida settlement where PM Rabin tried to forcibly remove the West Bank settlers. Rabbi Marzel has remarked "All our diplomatic problems stem from the fact we don't believe this land belongs to us."[211]

For right or wrong, religious Israelis are there and are not going away. In fact, one University of Haifa study concluded, "Israel is on its way to becoming a religious state, a reality that would pose a threat to its survival."[212] Today, about 300,000 Israeli citizens reside in 121 settlements in the West Bank. This area is also home to 2.5 million Palestinians. Another 200,000 Israelis live in East Jerusalem, formerly a part of Jordan and the West Bank.[213] Though 9,000 settlers were evacuated from Gaza, peace was not secured between Israel and the Hamas government functioning in Gaza. The Hamas party won the first open election and then immediately launched missiles at Israel proper. In summer of 2014, Israeli troops again entered into Gaza in attempt to stop the constant barrage of rockets going deeper into Israel. So the conflict and the missiles continue.

As the year 2014 came to an end there were new tensions between the Palestinian Arabs, Jewish Israelis, and Arab Israelis (Arabs with Israeli citizenship). "Nationality bills have been proposed in the Knesset that define citizenship for Jews only, thus making the Arab Israelis second class citizens and denying any concept of equal rights.[214] To accomplish this, Israeli Foreign Minister Avigdor Liberman has proposed ceding the Arab majority areas in northern Israel to a future Palestinian State. The incentive to do this lies in Israel's funding Palestinians to leave the Israeli controlled areas and having them give up Israeli citizenship. In his own words, "The nation of Israel is more important than the land of Israel."[215] Mixed with these politically volatile issues is the renewed effort to allow Jews to pray on the Temple Mount. In other words, the Temple Mount for Israelis has become mainstream, as Yoel Cohen suggests, "Thirty years ago, Temple activism was perceived as the

211 "Extremist who could bring Kahanism back to the Knesset," *The Times of Israel,* February 18, 2015.
212 "Israel: Cabinet Approves Law Limiting Conscription Exemptions," Stratfor Global Intelligence, July 7, 2013.
213 Price-Gibson, "Kahane is Back," *The Jerusalem Report,* December 21, 2009 p. 15.
214 Jodi Rudoren, "Israel Struggles with its Identity," *The New York Times,* December 8, 2014.
215 "Lieberman 'peace plan' would pay Arabs to leave Israel," Times of Israel staff, *The Time of Israel,* www.timesofisrael.com, November 26, 2014.

concern of a couple of cranks. Today, leading modern orthodox rabbis favor Jews ascending the Temple Mount." He goes on to say, Prime Minister "Netanyahu fails to recognize the new reality on the Temple Mount."[216]

Add to this the statements by American Jewish billionaire Sheldon Adelson saying a 'big wall" should be put up around Israel, rejecting any possibility of a Palestinian state, and if Israel is no longer a democracy, "so what?"[217]

In addition, in October, 2014, two nations said they would support a United Nations resolution for a Palestinian State: Sweden and the United Kingdom. On the other side of the issue, a hard-line rabbi called for a complete "cleansing of Arabs" in Israel. Rabbi Dov Lior while speaking at a memorial for the two young boys kidnapped and killed by Palestinians, said, "Arabs are warmongers" and "incapable of grasping the concept of democracy . . . they are camel riders and wolves." He encouraged the Israeli government to encourage Palestinians to emigrate from the region, perhaps to Saudi Arabia. The Chief Rabbi of the Kiryat Arba settlement (where Goldstein was the physician) is affiliated with a hard right-wing faction.[218] Obviously, the continued expansion of settlements in what the Palestinians call "Occupied Territory," mixed with the above sentiments of Orthodox rabbis toward Palestinians does not make for peaceful relations. The situation of two peoples claiming the same territory has historically almost always led to war.

But this conflict is not only present in the Middle East. It is also at the heart of a considerable but little known conflict and policy debate here in America. Within the United States there are also groups who claim a certain kind of religious faith and feel alienated and marginalized from an increasing hostile American secular government. This one is more about Guns, sometimes Gold, the Government . . . and . . . lest I forget . . . Jesus.

---

216 Yoel Cohen, "The Temple Mount: Between Bibi & Moshe Dayan," *The Times of Israel*, www.timesofIsrael.com, November 5, 2014.

217 "Adelson: Palestinians an invented people out to destroy Israel," *The Times of Israel*, www.timesofisrael.com, November 10, 2014.

218 Israeli Staff, "Hardline Rabbi calls to 'cleanse' Israel of Arabs," *The Times of Israel*, October 1, 2014.

CHAPTER SEVEN
Guns and Jesus:
Christian Identity & the Patriot Movement

"Ninety nine percent of the people in the Christian patriot movement per se, would fit well in a Calvary Chapel or a Baptist Church."
—A Patriot Pastor[219]

Years ago, I was on my second cup of coffee at Kojays in Blowing Rock, North Carolina, when I overheard a conversation at the table next to me. To my surprise they were talking about Eric Rudolph, who had become a sort of local folk hero. I was surprised because it had been almost a year after the FBI had called off their manhunt for the suspect and gone home. At the time, one could find stores in the North Carolina mountains selling T-shirts that said "Run, Rudolph Run." The FBI had named Rudolph a suspect in four terrorist

---

219 Dean Compton, cofounder, National Alliance of Christian Militia, quoted in *Secrets, Plots & Hidden Agendas*, Paul T. Couglin, InterVarsity Press, 1999, p. 56.

bombings. The best remembered is the 1996 Atlanta Olympic bombing. He was also suspected in two other Atlanta bombings, one of an abortion clinic and the other a gay bar. However, he only became a suspect in these attacks after bombing an abortion clinic in Birmingham, Alabama. An eyewitness identified his truck as he sped off after the attack. Rudolph was on the most wanted list for years, until he was found digging around in a dumpster by a local police officer in Murphy, North Carolina in May 2003. At that time he plea bargained on his murder counts, receiving four consecutive life prison terms in exchange for information on where he had stockpiled his bomb making materials. He was sentenced in May of 2005 to his consecutive life terms without parole. He now spends twenty-two and a half hours a day alone in his concrete cell.

So who was this thirty-three-year-old murderer? Raised in a suburb of Miami, Eric Rudolph and his family moved to North Carolina after the death of his father, a prison chaplain. Settling in the Nantahala Forest near the old Appalachian Trail he made friends with a local neighbor and survivalist, Tom Branham. In school, he was remembered as being religious and a fundamentalist. His mother was extremely fundamentalist, with antigovernment sentiments. She had even lived for a while with a white separatist group in the Missouri Ozarks. Researcher Pedersen noted, "The mountains of North Carolina at the time were a hotbed of the Christian Identity movement, whose followers oppose abortion and homosexuality and sometimes preach that Jews are the spawn of Satan."[220]

Near Rudolph's home lived Nord Davis, a local leader of the Christian Identity movement.

At the time Rudolph became a suspect, he lived in a trailer in Murphy, N.C., had no credit cards, no bank account and no steady job. He worked periodically as a carpenter and always paid his rent in cash. After the last two bombings, police noticed similarities in the bomb material and received letters claiming the events as actions of The Army of God. The letters "lambasted *sodomites* and *abortionists* and threatened to strike again."[221]

In response, The FBI and ATF launched a massive manhunt, scouring the woods for this committed survivalist. Pedersen again observes, "The Feds offered a $1 million reward for Rudolph's capture, but more than a few locals were quietly

220 Daniel Pedersen, "A Mountain Manhunt," *Newsweek*, July 27, 1998, p. 18.
221 Ibid., p. 19.

rooting for Rudolph."[222] On December 14, 1999, after almost a year and a half of looking for Rudolph, the outgoing director of the ATF said, "My gut instinct is that he is still there, in a cave and he's dead."[223] To the people sitting next to me at Kojays, he was still very much alive and probably hidden out at one of the many Christian Patriot compounds around the country.[224] Today, Rudolph has his own web page from prison entitled glory2jesus@armyofgod.com. Though he quotes scripture regularly he claims he prefers the existentialist philosopher, Nietzsche.[225] For a full text of his views go to: www.armyofgod.com. It is also possible to download his book: *Between the Lines: The Memoirs of a Militant*, written in 2013.

Pedersen concludes, "He (Rudolph) is best understood as the product of a paranoid fringe of white supremacists, religious zealots, and government haters."[226] If this is the case, we need go no further in trying to understand this mindset. But perhaps there is another explanation. Perhaps, there are many more Eric Rudolphs out there who just happen to take their religious ideology seriously and believe the government is increasingly hostile to their faith and liberties.[227] To understand this perspective it is necessary to look into a little known and rarely discussed movement called the "Christian Identity" or "Christian Patriot" movement.

Who Are Christian Patriots and What is Christian Identity?

At the outset it must be admitted that much of what goes under the category of *hate groups* is very much just that. Many in the militia and supremacist movements are committed racists who hate African Americans, Hispanics, Asians and Jews. Some groups that claim to be religious or have church names are just fronts for neo-Nazi or KKK rhetoric. Groups like the Rev. Matt Hale's World Church of the Creator are mere "white supremacist organizations masquerading as religious organizations," trying to cover racist ideology with religious language. It was one

---

222 Ibid., p. 19.
223 "Investigator: Rudolph Probably Dead," Associated Press, *Charlotte Observer*, December 15, 1999, p. 4c.
224 See Morris Dees with James Curcorum, *Gathering Storm: America's Militia Threat,* Harper Collins, pp. 163-164 for McVeigh's connections to Elohim City.
225 He claimed to be a Catholic even though there is no evidence of him being a practicing Catholic as an adult.
226 "A Mountain Manhunt," p. 17.
227 There is also a view that Rudolph was hostile toward the government for not giving his veteran father proper treatment resulting in his death. His motive is then one of revenge and not necessarily ideologically driven.

of Hale's members, Benjamin Smith, who gunned down ten people during a two-weekend shooting spree in the Chicago area in July of 1999. Smith took his own life as police were closing in All those shot were Jewish and Asian, except for one Pentecostal pastor.[228] Hale says he does not even believe in God or have anything to do with organized religion. His title is probably purchased or self-proclaimed.

I would say the same thing about such groups as the Klan and the John Birch Society. They may attract some religious "Christian" followers, but their core beliefs are more about extreme right-wing politics than trying to present a coherent theology or religious statement of faith.

Among the patriot and identity groups that do claim to be Christian and try to interact with Biblical material, there are two camps: those that are not racist and those who are. Some racist views are hard to sift out because they are covert or hidden in various widespread conspiracy theories. It is very easy to start as a non-racist Christian Patriot and then move gradually toward more racist views. The analogy is often used that the militia movement is like a funnel that is very large at its opening but then narrows the further one goes into the system. One may enter because of sincere pro-life or gun rights beliefs and then later encounter the more racist elements of the movement.

The main thrust of this chapter has to do with those people and groups who, in the opinion of this writer, are in some way motivated by "Christian" doctrines that are used to justify or rationalize violence.

What Are the Beliefs of Christian Identity?

Christian Identity is a set of beliefs or doctrines that create a certain mindset about the world. The term *Christian Patriots* is sometimes used. Defining Christian Identity is like determining the contents of a moist sponge. To see what is in it, it must be squeezed! Christian Identity has no single leader or clear denominational statements.

Christian Identity is an amalgam of fairly mainstream Christian beliefs mixed with various extra-Biblical, pseudo-Christian and political doctrines. Abane's definition is more extreme: "Identity is a social, political and spiritual movement composed of religiously inclined racists from the ranks of the neo-Nazi community,

---

228 Susan Luke, "Gunman continues deadly spree," *The Wichita Eagle*, July 5, 1999.

the KKK, and other white supremacist organizations."[229] Hate group buster Morris Dees widens the "tent" a little further: "Christian Identity's worldview extends to the secular world of politics and provides a tent big enough to incorporate the views of extremist groups as well. It invites individuals who are extremely antigovernment, antilaw, antitax, antiabortion, antigay, antifeminist, anti-medical profession, antivaccination, pro-guns, pro-home schooling, pro-states' rights, and believers in an international one-world conspiracy that is about to take over America and the world."[230] Actual numbers of Identity members are difficult to obtain since there are no official membership records. However, some researchers estimate there are around 23,000 to 25,000 hard core members, with another 120,000 sympathizers who purchase literature and attend meetings, with another 450,000 who may not ever purchase literature but are interested and will read literature given to them.[231] However, four things serve as the unconscious glue that holds these various people together: an "excessive suspicion of the government, a belief in antigovernment conspiracy theories; a deep seated hatred of government officials; and an overall feeling that the United States Constitution has been disregarded if not discarded by Washington bureaucrats."[232]

Hardline Identity doctrines are not so obvious. They often get hidden among very fundamental or evangelical beliefs. In this sense, identity doctrines are not *in place of* the standard fundamentals of the faith but mere *add-ons* to mainstream Christianity. I have known people in my own church who would never dream of believing Identity doctrines (most don't even know what *identity doctrines* are), but in the context of a Bible study or conversation they pop out. My response is usually, "Where in the world did you get that?" More often than not, they don't even know.

British-Israelism

Core Identity beliefs center on conceptions of Israel, Armageddon, and race. This makes Identity beliefs more theological than political. With reference to understanding what they mean by *Israel*, some historical background is necessary. When the Assyrians and then the Babylonian empires took the nation of Israel captive, the Jewish people spent seventy years in captivity. During this time, two

---

229 Richard Abanes, *American Militias: Rebellion, Racism and Religion*, p. 155.
230 *Gathering Storm*, p. 18.
231 Raphael S. Ezekiel, *The Racist Mind*, p. xxi.
232 Abanes, *American Militias*, p.º 2.

southern tribes of Judah and Benjamin were better able to maintain their distinctive identity than the other ten tribes. The ten northern Hebrew tribes became more assimilated, and their fate was less certain. Throughout history, myths concerning the legacy of the *ten lost tribes of Israel* have emerged and inspired many theories. Today, many groups claim their lineage back to Israel.[233] However, the *ten lost tribes* are not that *lost* according to the Bible. See the evidence in II Chronicles 15:9, II Kings 15:29, II Chronicles 3:1-11, and I Kings 17:34. Also in the New Testament during the Jesus birth narrative Luke mentions a prophetess Anna who was of the tribe of Asher. Obviously she was not *lost* but was looking for final redemption of God in Jerusalem (Luke 2:36). So British-Israelism as a theory does not have sufficient Biblical authority to take seriously. But it has survived as Christian Identity doctrine.

The myth that took hold in Victorian England was that English Protestants (Caucasians) were related to the dispersed ten lost tribes of Israel. "Known as British-Israelism, this theory teaches *the Germanic kindred (white) people are the true descendants of Abraham, Isaac and Jacob.*"[234] When the doctrine was first developed in England, existing Jews were viewed as having descended from the southern kingdom and were on an equal basis with the British/Israeli northern tribes. Between 1840 and 1889, when the doctrine was transplanted to America, British-Israelism changed significantly. In 1887, Jews were viewed *as separated brethren*; by 1934 they did not "have blood pure enough to be considered legitimate descendants of the southern kingdom." By 1944, Jews had become in the literature "actual descendants of Edomites, Hittites, and Idumeans." In 1962, Jewish people in this Identity doctrinal development "had no direct link to Israelites." By 1989 they had become "a mongrelized race of Asian barbarians."[235] In the course of time, a spurious British-Israelism had become a rabid anti-Semitism. In another questionable historical sleight of hand, British-Israelism on American soil became rich fodder for anti-Semitic justification within Christian Identity whereby American Christians were considered God's chosen. American white Caucasians were now God's chosen people while Jews were a mixed race of barbarians! Therefore, Identity doctrine

---

233 See *Beyond the Sambatyon: The Myth of the Ten Lost Tribes of Israel*, Ariel Publications 1991 by Dr. Salva Weil, for an excellent development that tribes have been traced to places in Africa, the Caucasia, India, even China and Japan!

234 Abanes in *American Militias*, quoting Identity Pastor Pete Peters, p. 157.

235 Ibid., p. 161.

sees the white race and especially white Americans as God's chosen people or true Israel, the continuing legacy of the ten lost tribes of Israel. Having established the connection to the lost tribes, Identity proponents then go on to "explain" the origin of the Jewish people. Consequently, the theory of the Serpent Seed emerged.

Seed of Satan Theory

Without any Biblical support, Identity doctrine teaches Jews are the physical descendants of Eve and Satan. The Serpent, they believe, had sexual relations with Eve, and she gave birth to Cain who became the father of the Jewish race. Seth, the legitimate offspring of Adam and Eve, is the father of the white race. From this implausible Biblical reasoning, the entire history of the world is then viewed in terms of one big race war between the seed of Satan, the Jews, and the seed of Eve, the white race. Richard Butler, now deceased Aryan Nation founder, and pastor of the Church of Jesus Christ Christian, expressed this view: "There are literal children of Satan in the world today . . . the descendants of Cain, who was the result of Eve's original sin.[236]

What is amazing about this belief is that some Identity pastors are committed literalists on Biblical interpretation, but in this case there is virtually nothing to take literally. Look at any translation of the Biblical text and what is found is: "Now the man (Adam) had relations with his wife Eve, and she conceived and gave birth to Cain . . . and again she gave birth to his brother, Abel" (Genesis 4:1-2). No mention of Satan or the Serpent here! The only passage that might be twisted to fit the *two race theory* is an earlier one where God speaks to the Serpent and says, "I will put enmity (enemy) between you (Serpent/Satan figure) and the woman, and between your seed and her seed" (Genesis 3:15).

The standard interpretation for this passage within the Christian community is that the enemy of Satan is the promised Messiah who will stand between the seed of Satan and the seed of humanity and ultimately crush the head of the serpent. The passage does not explain or allude to who the *seed of the Serpent* is, but it is generally thought of as anyone who aligns himself with Satan.[237] To conclude that Satan's

---

236 Brad Knickernocker, "Followers See Validation for their Views in the Bible," *Christian Science Monitor*, April 20, 1995, p. 10.

237 Biblical Scholar Allen Ross states, "The offspring of the woman was Cain, then all humanity at large and then Christ and those collectively in Him. The offspring of the serpent includes demons and anyone serving his kingdom of darkness." *The Bible Knowledge Commentary*, Editors: John F. Walvoord, and Roy B, Zuck, Victor Books, Vol. 1, p. 33.

offspring is the result of sexual activity between Eve and Satan, producing the line of Cain, soundly rejects what is clearly taught when "Adam had relations with Eve." The belief is a complete fabrication and used to spawn a vitriolic anti-Semitism.

Pre-Millennial Apocalypticism

In terms of theological systems, Identity doctrine is a confusing amalgam of pre millennial apocalypticism and postmillennial activism. Premillennialism believes the current Church age will culminate in a thousand-year reign of Christ on earth beginning with his Second Coming. Hence, the current age is *pre* or before the *millennium.*

Part of this package is the understanding that certain *end time signs* will indicate when the end is near: "even so when you see all these things, recognize that He (Christ) is near, right at the door" (Matthew 24:33). The alert Christian is to look for these signs and prepare accordingly. The prophetic books in the fiction series *Left Behind* by Tim LaHaye, based on this theological understanding, are still best sellers. Likewise, one of the bestselling books of all time is Hal Lindsey's *Late Great Planet Earth.* For a hefty dose of this teaching tune in to Jack Van Impy's weekly television broadcast. More recently, radio teacher and retired engineer Howard Camping set the date of May 21, 2010 as the day of the *Rapture.* When we all went to church on May 22, everything was the same except for a tornado in Missouri and a volcano eruption in Iceland. He quickly changed the date to October 21, 2011, but he missed it again! Terrorism expert Michael Burkun confirms "religious conspiratorialists" are linked by two millenarian themes: "the final attempt by Satan/Lucifer to wrest power from God, and the sinister means employed by the forces of the Antichrist to secure and maintain world domination in the last days."[238]

Premillennialists are not in agreement as to when these events will take place. Some in the Christian community believe Christians will be taken out of the world or *raptured* before these signs and will return with Christ at the end of a great seven-year tribulation period. Others believe Christians will be exposed only to the first three and half years of the tribulation and then be raptured.[239]

---

238 Michael Barkun, "Religion, Militias and Oklahoma City: The Mind of Conspiratorialists," *Terrorism and Political Violence*, Vol. 8, Spring, 1996, Number 1, p. 58.

239 There is also a modification of the "Mid-Tribulation" view called the "Pre-Wrath Rapture of the Church." This view is espoused by Marvin Rosenthal and others who say Christians will enter the Great Tribulation period but be spared from the actual Wrath of God to take place

A third view believes Christians will be exposed to the full outpouring of God's wrath during this Great Tribulation period and must be prepared to still live faithfully for Christ. Identity doctrine emphasizes the fact that the true believers must be prepared for extreme persecution and violence against their beliefs.

The last great earthly conflict, called Armageddon, involves the emergence of a human *Antichrist,* called *the Beast,* based on the Revelation of John (Chapter 13). As a sequence to the appearance of this Antichrist is a certain alignment of world powers and nations centering into a ten-nation confederation (Psalm 2:2, Daniel 7:24, Revelation 17:16). Interpretations concerning these events and who the nations or *heads* are have spawned theories about who the Antichrist will be[240] and how he will bring together the nations of the world against God and His people. Paul Couglin explains that aspects unique to fundamentalism, fused to the certain belief that we are living in the end times, have produced a contemporary Christian world-view predisposed to conspiracy thinking. Fundamentalists identify the sources of evil unleashed during the last generation as the same evil forces they have hated and feared for decades: communism (former Soviet Union), advancing socialism (the United Nations), government (especially the FBI, CIA, Federal Reserve and IRS) and anything outside fundamentalism (the mainstream press, Hollywood, academia, psychology, Catholicism, Promise Keepers and so on).[241]

Fuller observes, "Conservative Christianity contains a strongly prophetic dimension. That is, it offers a source of revealed truth that can be brought to bear on the interpretation of society's moral and spiritual failings . . . Fundamentalist thought is anchored on millennialist beliefs that divide the world into two contrasting groups: the forces of Christ and the forces of Antichrist."[242] This system of theology is thus very attractive to and widely used among Christian Identity Patriots. The conclusion that the time is short, and the Antichrist is bringing about a worldwide conspiracy (often centered in the ungodly UN and American government) breeds a postmillennial activism.

---

later in the last three year period. See Marvin Rosenthal, *The Pre-Wrath Rapture of the Church,* Thomas Nelson, 1990.

240 See Robert Fuller's excellent and comprehensive study of various attempts to identify the Antichrist throughout history, *Naming the Antichrist: The History of an American Obsession.*

241 Paul T. Coughlin, *Secrets, Plots & Hidden Agendas,* p.173.

242 Robert Fuller, *Naming the Antichrist,* Oxford Univ. Press, 1996, pp.134-136.

Post-Millennial Activism

Post-millennialism believes Christ will return after a period of peaceful reign of righteousness. It is then up to true Christians to fight to bring about this state of righteousness. Some might say postmillennialism created early America. When the Puritans left England for the freedom and safety of New England, they saw themselves as carrying out a unique role in God's providential actions. Cotton Mather, a Puritan leader and pastor, saw New England as "the last conflict with Antichrist." In this scenario, the first Antichrists were the native savages who were thwarting the establishment of a righteous colony of Christians. After initial attempts to *Christianize* the savages, the colonies declared a "holy war" against them.[243]

Jonathan Edwards, one of the brightest and most prolific minds of Puritan America, coined the phrase that America was "the shining city on a hill." Edwards identified the greatest threat and Antichrist as the Catholic Pope, and maintained it was every Christian's duty "to participate in the Antichrist's defeat."[244] When King George III threatened the righteous colonies of New England, he too was viewed as the Antichrist. Fuller explains, "The notion that the church (Church of England) and the king of England were collectively the "beast from the sea" had been rampant in revolutionary England a century earlier,"[245] so it was easy for the American Christians to grasp at this identification. On the eve of the American Revolution, postmillennial activism was commonly preached in New England pulpits. One Presbyterian minister declared, "Bloodshed was needed to purify the earth in preparation for the millennium."[246] At a Sons of Liberty gathering in Boston in 1766, an orator reminded his audience, "The book of Revelation foretold the evil deeds that would be committed by the beasts from the sea and from the land (English Stamp Act) . . . beware as good Christians and lovers of your country, lest by touching any paper with this impression (King George's), you receive the mark of the beast."[247] All one needs to do in the above quotes is to change the names of King George, the Pope, and the Church of England, to

---

243 Ibid., p. 49.
244 Ibid., quoted on page 66.
245 Ibid., p. 69.
246 Robert Smith, *A Wheel in the Middle of a Wheel*, Original date, 1759, reprint: Hard Press Edition, 2012, p. 55.
247 Anonymous, "A Discourse Delivered to the Sons of Liberty," at a Solemn Assembly, near Liberty Tree, quoted in Ruth Bloch's *Visionary Republic*, Cambridge Univ. Press, 1985, p. 48.

Presidents Bill Clinton, George Bush, Barak Obama, the UN or the Council on Foreign Relations, and it would fit Christian Identity literature perfectly. Frankly, I am surprised Christian Identity thinkers haven't used this early American material to justify their views!

Influence of American Manifest Destiny[248]

Many historians have noted the link between theological post-millennialism and the political doctrine of American *Manifest Destiny*. Manifest destiny says that America has a certain *God-given destiny*. By virtue of having a vast domain of "unpopulated" land, it is the manifest destiny of Americans to spread the concepts of Republican liberties to the entire continent, even by force of arms. Illinois congressman John Wentworth said in 1845, "I do not believe the God of Heaven, when he crowned the American arms with success (in the Revolutionary war), designed that the original States should be the only abode of liberty on earth. On the contrary, he only designed them as the great center from which civilization, religion and liberty should radiate until the whole continent shall bask in their blessing.[249] In other words, because God granted the American victory and by providence had placed so much land before her people, God obviously desired the entire American continent to be both civilized and Christianized. Debates in Congress even argued that the "continent" should be thought of as "from the Arctic Circle to what is now Panama"!

From the above discussion, it doesn't take much of a leap for Christian Identity proponents to develop a conclusion about the use of force or violence. If the American government fails in its role of protecting what is considered God's providential role in American history, then it is up to the citizens, as true patriots, to rise up against the government and protect the sacred values upon which it was founded. So goes the logic. What is alarming is how often I hear this argument in many of the churches I visit!

---

248 Millet & Maslowski in their book on American military intervention root the doctrine of Manifest Destiny in Social Darwinism. Quoting them, "Manifest Destiny" proclaimed the white man's moral responsibility to spread 'civilization' and Social Darwinism gave Manifest Destiny a 'scientific' veneer, arguing that nations behaved like biological organisms." Allan R. Mallet and Peter Maslowski, *For the Common Defense*, Free Press, 1994 revised, p. 265.

249 Quoted in Frederick Merck, *Manifest Destiny and Mission in American History*, Harvard Univ. Press, 1995, p. 28.

What Created the Modern Patriot Movement?

Early roots of the patriot movement include the overt racism of the Ku Klux Klan; the anti-tax activities of Posse Comitatus (who believe there should be no government above the county sheriff); the illuminati conspiracy theories of the John Birch Society (named after a martyred Baptist preacher); the world-wide Zionist conspiracies of the Christian National Crusade lead by Rev. Gerald Smith, a fundamentalist radio minister in the 1930s; and the extreme violence of the Covenant, the Sword and Arm of the Lord, an Arkansas anti-Semitic paramilitary group known for firebombing synagogues and African American churches.[250] The Rev. Smith wrote, "the great covenant that God made with Abraham has been fulfilled not in the profane blasphemies of those who dishonestly call themselves *God's Chosen People* but in white Christians. If the covenant with Jews is a fraud, then of course the idea of Israel as the *promised land* is bogus. America, home of white Christians who are the lost Israelites, becomes the *promised land*."[251] Most of the above groups at one time or another spun off other groups, transitioned into something else, or saw their leaders jailed or killed. These groups have been around for years, however four critical events catapulted the ideas of these groups into more mainstream America.

FBI Raid on Randy Weaver

"Remember Ruby Ridge," in the patriot community is right there next to "Pearl Harbor" and "Remember the Alamo." It is a rallying point and proof of the government's sinister designs on peace-loving citizens who are trying to live a simple, godly life. Randy Weaver, a thirty-year-old former Green Beret, moved from Iowa to the Idaho mountains and built on a twenty acre property where he could raise his family away from the secular humanism that dominated the Iowa public school system. His wife, Vicki, home schooled their children.

In 1989, they started attending meetings and conferences at Richard Butler's Aryan Nations Hayden lake compound nearby, though Weaver claimed to have never been a member. Aryan Nations, at the time, was an extreme anti-Semitic Christian Identity compound. The Weavers were always short on cash, and Randy was convinced to deal guns by a biker named Gus. As it turned out, "Gus" was

---

250 See Kenneth S. Stern's chapter "Old Hatreds," pp. 42-57, in *A Force Upon the Plain*, Simon & Schuster, 1996, for a good overview of these groups.

251 Quoted in Stern, *A Force Upon the Plain*, p. 47.

an undercover FBI agent who was trying to mount a sting against Aryan Nations. Weaver refused to help the FBI, and was to appear in court on February 20, 1991, but he refused to show. For the next eighteen months he stayed in the family cabin. Vicki gave birth to a little girl and wrote a letter to the government saying, "My husband was set up for a fall because of his religious and political beliefs."[252]

On August 21, 1992, six deputies conducted a surveillance of the property, looking for an appropriate time to arrest Randy. Things went badly, shots were exchanged, and the end result was a long standoff with the ATF and FBI and the deaths of Weaver's nursing wife, his own son, and his dog. He and a friend were wounded. The siege ended through mediation of friend and fellow Green Beret, "Bo" Gritz, also a fellow Christian Identity adherent. Inside the cabin, near the door, was a sign with the phrase "New World Order" with a circle and line through it. To Randy Weaver, and many in the Christian Identity movement, their worst fears had come true through the New World Order government of President Clinton, Attorney General Janet Reno, and the FBI.

The trial of Randy Weaver was not a media circus like the O.J. Simpson trial, but for the Identity movement it was one of their finest hours. Cheyenne lawyer Gerry Spence defended Weaver. Spence successfully argued that Weaver had been entrapped in the gun violation to turn informant, and that the FBI had obstructed justice in destroying documents, tampering with evidence, and then trying to cover up their actions. The rules of engagement that allowed snipers to fire at will were seriously questioned. The sniper, an Asian American named Lon Horiuchi, later saw murder charges filed against him. The official FBI investigation found Horiuchi's killing of Vicki Weaver was accidental, and charges were dismissed. Randy Weaver was found guilty of failure to appear in court and given a short sentence, most of which he had already served awaiting trial. For a while, he returned to Iowa with his daughters in 1993. After receiving a wrongful death settlement from the government, he and his daughters moved to the mountains of Montana in 1996. He became a regular on the Christian Identity speaker circuit and sold a book about Ruby Ridge at gun shows. In a statement from 1999 he claimed he was not a racist or white supremacist, but a white separatist.[253] Today, he is described by his daughter Sara (who was in her mother's arms when the sniper shot Vicki) as

---

252 Ibid., p. 94.
253 *Secrets, Plots & Hidden Agendas*, p. 72.

a "doting grandfather." Randy lives with Sara and her husband still in Montana where they raise horses.[254]

Rudy Ridge can be summarized as a series of tragic mistakes on both sides. Randy Weaver was by all accounts a well-armed racist. Even Vicki carried a pistol at her waist all the time and was probably more outspoken about her views than Randy. On one occasion she had written, "the stink of lawless government had reached Yahweh (God) and Yeshua (Jesus) . . . whether we live or whether we die, we will not bow to your evil commandments."[255] She didn't!

An internal FBI investigation revealed serious operational problems within their "crack" Hostage Rescue Team. For the Christian Identity movement, it was the first of several "We told you so's." Stern concludes, "The FBI's errors, magnified artfully by Spence, gave ammunition to Weaver's supporters, white supremacists, and those who, shortly thereafter, would found the American militia movement."[256] In 2007, it was reported that Weaver was now an atheist. Even his bio on a web page lists his religion as "atheist."[257]

Rocky Mountain Rendezvous

Rev. Pete Peters, who died on July 7, 2011, was pastor of the Colorado Church of Christ in LaPorte, Colorado. At one time he was one of the most dynamic speakers on patriot themes. A self-proclaimed "cowboy wannabe preacher," his main impact was through his short wave radio programs and his internet messages. Besides speaking, he published the *Scriptures for America Newsletter,* still an enlightening mix of prophetic end-time observations with patriot themes. It can still be found at: scripturesforamerica.org, where readers can subscribe to a free newsletter called *The Dragon Slayer.* In a past issue, he expounded the devastating Japanese tsunami as a direct judgment from God. He called it "punishment" for their seventy years of not becoming a Christian nation after their ruthless treatment of American GIs in World War II. Though now departed from the scene he is still a factor because of what he engineered.

---

254 Ibid., p. 45.
255 *Kingsport Times News*, August 13, 1999 at www.sullivancounty.com.
256 *The Patriot News*, Associated Press article, "Ruby Ridge: 20 Years Later," August 20, 2012. After twenty years of depression and suffering from PTSD (Post Traumatic Disorder) Sara became a Christian through a friend and reading the Bible. In the article she says she has forgiven those involved in killing her mother and brother!
257 Ibid., p. 47.

Following the August 1992 shootings at Ruby Ridge, Peters gathered together with 175 "Christian men" in Estes Park, Colorado. It was October 22, 1992, and the purpose was to discuss what should be done about the Weaver killings.[258] The Estes Park meeting included neo-Nazis, Christian Identity adherents, anti-abortion activists, tax protesters, Ku Klux Klan members, and others who previously had seen each other as ideological and organizational adversaries and had little in common. Stern tells us it included "men . . . who in the past would normally not be caught together under the same roof, who would have worried about the effect on their "mainstream" credentials from participation in such a gathering.[259]

The consensus of the meeting was the need to form armed militias of volunteer soldiers in order to stand against government "terrorists." What emerged out of the meeting was a *Battle Plan for Future Conflicts*. They emphasized *leaderless resistance*, relying upon Aryan Nation leader Louis Beam's published article by that name, where individuals and groups operate independently of each other and never report to a central headquarters or single leader for direction and instruction. These "phantom cells" would be the only way to "defeat state tyranny."[260]

What is interesting about this conference is the standard racial element of white supremacy was missing (especially since so many Neo-Nazi and KKK leaders were present). The conference was "spun" in spiritual terms, thus appealing to a much wider base of concern. Larry Pratt, talking about the spiritual battle in America said, "This is not a political issue . . . it is something that comes first and foremost from the Scripture. What I see in the Scripture is not that we have a right to keep and bear arms, but that we have a responsibility to do so, for a man to refuse to provide for adequately for his family's defense would be to defy God."[261] Of course, Pratt is jumping from the clear Biblical principle of family provision (I Timothy 5:8) linking it to the more questionable means of gun ownership and joining a militia! Pastor Peters constantly referred to their meeting as one of "prayer and counsel" and even drafted a corporate letter to Randy Weaver's teenaged daughter

---

258 *A Force Upon the Plain*, 41.
259 www.nndb.com/people/700/000025625.
260 Quoted in *Gathering Storm*, p. 51.
261 The source for this information is Morris Dees' book, *Gathering Storm*. However, no source material is given in the book. However, it is commonly known among militia researchers that the Southern Poverty Law Center, Dees' organization, routinely has undercover contacts among the militia groups. If this information is correct, it is from a firsthand account from someone in attendance.

saying they were "led by the word of our heavenly Father." The letter also issued a call for "Divine Judgement upon wicked and guilty who shed the blood of Vicki and Samuel (Weaver)."[262] Many observers look to this Rocky Mountain conference as the birthplace of the modern American militia movement. It was here that a "fragmented group of pesky, and at times dangerous, gadflies (became) a serious, armed political challenge to the state itself."[263]

As a result of Rudy Ridge and the Rendezvous during the 90s, armed militia groups were formed around their own "leaderless resistance" cells and their unique anti-government agendas. The Coalition on Revival, a national Christian right networking organization, called for the creation of "countrywide *well-regulated militia*" according to the U.S. Constitution under the control of the county sheriff and Board of Supervisors."[264] This source may be overstating the case. But there is concern an organization such as this, which has produced so many mainstream evangelical documents and councils including the International Council on Inerrancy of the Bible, is calling for state militias to organize. It is common knowledge that the *well-regulated militia* clause in the constitution refers to the historical roots of our now National Guard.[265] These are organized under the governors of each state.

In the Midwest, Matthew Trewhella, leader of the Missionaries to the Preborn, a radical pro-life movement, organized paramilitary training for members of his church.[266] Anti-environmentalists also got into the act. A monthly newsletter of the National Federal Lands Conference featured in its lead article the need to form militias. Spokesman Jim Faulkner wrote: "At no time in our history since the colonies declared their independence from the long trains of King George has our country needed a network of active militias across America to protect us from the monster we have allowed our federal government to become. Long live the Militia! Long live freedom! Long live government that fear the people!"[267]

---

262 Information obtained by the "think tank" Coalition for Human Dignity," quoted in *A Force Upon the Plain*, p. 36.
263 Quoted in *Gathering Storm*, pp. 53-54.
264 Ibid., p. 65-66.
265 Ibid., p. 67.
266 Fred Clarkson, "HardCOR," *Church and State*, January 1991, p. 26.
267 My personal view is that the Second Amendment insures the right of all citizens to arm themselves, but this does not constitute the militia; that's why the two concepts are separated in the Constitution.

Apparently, the word that went out from the Rocky Mountain Rendezvous was heard, and new militia groups were formed across the country. By 1997, one political science researcher numbered "hard-core militia" membership at around 10,000, representing some forty states and still growing.[268] But the event that would rally the most marginal of sincerely religious people was the ATF-FBI attack on the Branch Davidians.

David Koresh and the Branch Davidians

If ever there was an "I told you so" in regard to the government's gun-happy use of violence against religious people, it occurred outside Waco, Texas on April 19, 1993.

Even passive churchgoers were shocked by the apparent display of federal force against this religious compound. Though many (including this author) viewed Koresh and his theology in cult terms, the force used did not seem proportional to the situation. Besides, wouldn't David Koresh eventually come out of the compound and go into town? It would have been easier to arrest him had there been no ATF surrounding his home, so go the arguments. But as it happened a fifty-one day siege that followed a botched assault ended in the fiery deaths of over one hundred men, women and children. Even to those unsympathetic toward militia patriot groups, this seemed like an extreme travesty of justice, civil rights, and religious freedom. To those in the militia groups, it was the classic illustration that their rhetoric was correct. The Justice Department, Janet Reno, and the combined forces of the FBI and ATF were just waiting to go after people of faith and their firearms. After Waco, militia growth exploded across the country.

David Koresh was certainly not a part of the patriot movement, but his conflict with government authorities would be used to the hilt by militia groups and their propaganda. Koresh's background was Seventh Day Adventist. After the leader of the Seventh Day Adventist Mt. Carmel retreat compound near Waco died, Koresh and the founder's son vied for leadership. When leadership went to the son, Koresh left town for east Texas but returned with semi-automatic assault weapons. Needless to say, Koresh won the day and took over leadership of the group even though he was tried and acquitted for attempted murder. By 1990, Koresh was the

---

268 John Goetz, "Missionaries' Leader Calls for Armed Militia," *Front Line Research*, August 1994, pp. 1, 3-4.

unchallenged leader of the Branch Davidians, named after the *branch of David,* a prophecy concerning the coming Messiah (Jeremiah 23: 5), but a title Koresh later claimed for himself. A self-trained student of the Bible, Koresh mixed orthodox Christian beliefs with spurious interpretations about the coming apocalypse. Over time, he became more extreme in his interpretations of scripture and his influence over cult members. At the core of his theology was the belief that there was an imminent confrontation between God's chosen (Branch Davidians) and the world forces of evil. Members of the group who left before the attack confessed Koresh believed strongly that a clash with the federal government was part of the fulfillment of end times prophecy.[269] One escaped member said, "There was never a time we didn't expect to be killed by the feds."

What moved the ATF to go operational against the Davidians was testimony by former members that Koresh had committed statutory rape with several young girls. In addition, a UPS delivery box addressed to the compound had accidentally opened revealing inert hand grenades. The driver told the local sheriff, who told the ATF. Koresh all but admitted his rapes of young women. Koresh wanted to talk scripture with a genuine Christian, so "born again" FBI agent Clint Van Zandt was put forward. Van Zandt says, "He was trying to persuade me that the Bible allowed him to have sex with young girls." He also said, "Brother Clint, do you know who I am? I am the Christ!"[270] No matter how justified the ATF and FBI may have been in the initial armed assault and then seeking to knock down the walls of the compound with an armored personnel carrier, the mythology of Waco is it was a government attack on people who just wanted to be left alone to pursue their own religious beliefs. Immediately following the attack, Indianapolis attorney Linda Thompson produced a video entitled, *Waco: The Big Lie* and later *Waco: The Big Lie Continues.* Thompson, a proponent of the "Unorganized Militia," claimed the ATF had set the fire themselves in order to get the people out of the compound.

The amateur movie immediately became a cult film for the far right. Many wanted to believe the ATF fired upon and razed the compound in payback for the four ATF agents killed and others wounded in the initial assault. No matter what the truth is about Waco (it is still being debated), the reality is that it galvanized the militia movement. One Florida militia member confessed, "Waco awakened the

269 Jim Faulkner, "Why There is a Need for the Militia in America," Update, National Federal Lands Conference, October 1994.
270 Daniel Junas, "Rise of the Militias," *The Christian Science Monitor*, October 8, 1997.

whole movement, it put the fear of God into us."[271] For those already in the militia movement, Waco was a call to arms equivalent to an ideological Pearl Harbor. April 19, to this day, is remembered as Militia Day both because it was the day that American colonists first fired upon the British at the Concord Bridge, and because of Waco. Two years later April 19 would again be placed in the annals of American history as one of the worst human tragedies. For many in the militia movement it is the day a true patriot struck back. Timothy McVeigh's favorite video was *Waco: The Big Lie*. In his car, literature was found about Waco along with a well-worn copy of *The Turner Diaries*.[272] But before looking into the Oklahoma City Bombing, a third mobilizing event must be considered.

Passage of the Brady Bill

Having been raised on the plains of Kansas, many of my childhood memories center on hunting with my father and going to my uncle's farm to hone our pistol and rifle marksmanship. We didn't collect tin cans then for recycling, but for targets! Guns were a way of life for me. My father bought me my first gun when I was nine. My dad was an avid member of the National Rifle Association and subscribed to the *Shotgun News*. He often joked about being able to hold off the government or the communists for at least a week. He had so many guns and so much ammunition in the house, I believed he could and would make his last stand against tyranny right in our own home. My dad was not a racist or a member of any organized militia. The only organizations he belonged to were the NRA and a local skeet shooting club. But my father, as I remember him, always lived with the thought that one day the government would come after our guns. I don't think my father was unique in this regard.

Those who live outside America's major cities on the plains, mountains and rural areas have a radically different view of firearms. This is why the passage of the Brady Bill took on such a significant meaning to many Americans. We are seeing the same dynamic today in the large-scale response to President Obama's and Congress's attempt to pass stricter gun legislation (limiting the sale of AR-15s and large capacity clips). The reaction at the street level was predictable and shocking: increased purchases of gun, ammunition, and concealed weapon permits. The

271 *Secrets, Plots & Hidden Agendas*, p. 75.
272 Ibid., p. 76

Brady Bill in 1993 imposed a five-day waiting period upon the purchase of any firearm with the gun show exemption in some states. It also required a computerized background check to see if the purchaser had a criminal record. The follow-on 1994 Crime Bill banned the purchase of nineteen types of assault weapons and limited gun clips to ten rounds. To some in Congress like Dianne Feinstein, (D-California) gun control was a necessity for a civilized society. "Even dogs have licenses," she argued. To people like Bo Gritz, militia defender and promoter, "gun control is hitting the target with every shot." Thus, a divide was created between the government and many gun-owning citizens. Stern comments, "Gun control legislation not only helped pull people into the militias funnel, it plunged those already in further down."[273] Morris Dees called this Bill the event that "ignited the militia movement into a national brushfire."[274]

After the passage of these bills, the militia movement again exploded. Audiences at meetings went up, and the message the government was now ready to disarm its citizens drew many that could care less about Identity doctrines or racial purity. They were frightened that the government was now breaching their clear right of the Constitution to bear arms and defend one's home and community. Gun owners suddenly became the first targets of who the government was going to come after. Militia rhetoric focused on the second amendment. NRA head, Wayne LaPierre (not necessarily an adherent of Identity doctrines) joined the fray by equating the federal agents of the Clinton administration with "Nazi storm troopers," and claiming that American gun owners were the vanguard of resistance. He wrote, "If we lose the right to keep and bear arms then the right to free speech, free practice of religion, and every other freedom in the Bill of Rights are sure to follow."[275] The more radical gun organization leader and Identity proponent went further. Larry Pratt, who had been at the Rocky Mountain Rendezvous, said, "It is time that the United States return to reliance on an armed people. There is no acceptable alternative."[276] This same language is common today in light of the current gun control debates even to the point that many are convinced that the ultimate goal of the administration is to confiscate all guns.

---

273 Stern, *A Force Upon the Plain*, p.64.
274 Ibid., p. 64.
275 Stern, p. 107.
276 *Gathering Storm*, p. 73.

What the Brady Bill did was cast the modern militia movement members as the preservers of America's freedoms. Gun ownership was a symbol of constitutional liberty and the only means to stand up to a tyrannical government. In this sense, by 1995, the conditions were ripe for some individual or group to act on the Christian Identity rhetoric. Enter a disenchanted, dedicated Gulf War veteran.

Oklahoma City: An Act of Patriotism or Terrorism?

To most reading the above heading, the answer is obvious. Of course, blowing up a federal building and killing 169 workers with another 500 wounded, including women and children, is an act of terrorism. But within the mindset of those in the militia movement the act carries a different meaning. It was payback for Ruby Ridge and Waco. Timothy McVeigh was then not a terrorist but a good soldier of the faith. So, what do we now know about this obscure figure who appeared out of nowhere in the front pages and prime time of our consciences? What is striking about Timothy McVeigh is that he was not a formal member of any militia or religious group.[277] He attended militia gatherings in several different states, and was an ardent embracer and disseminator of Identity doctrines. As such, his actions are part of the ideological "swamp" linked to militia rhetoric and Identity doctrine.

McVeigh was born in Pendleton, New York, a mostly white, middle-class community made of church-going Catholics and Protestants in the western part of the state. The McVeigh family was no exception. Early on they appeared to be the average American family. But by the time Timothy was ten, problems were coming to a head in his parents' marriage. His mother "Mickey" was quite a woman in the community who "turned men's heads." She prided herself in strutting around in high heels, shorts, and halter tops. One family acquaintance remembers her as "a very attractive lady, tall, long legged, well built and enjoying going out and dancing."[278] Timothy's father Bill liked to stay at home, so it was almost inevitable that the marriage was bound to come apart.

McVeigh's parents finally split when he was a teenager, with Timothy choosing to live with his father. An army buddy of McVeigh's later observed the only thing he ever said about his parents was referring to his mother as "that no-good whore and

---

277 Ibid., p. 111.
278 Ibid., p. 117.

slut."[279] It seemed common knowledge in the small community that Mickey was playing around.[280] After the divorce, Tim found solace in reading and guns. After finishing high school he worked several odd jobs and did a year of community college studying business and computer technology. But his love was guns. He often carried two or three guns at one time. In 1988, he enlisted in the Army where he met Terry Nichols, his later co-conspirator, during boot camp. After basic training he was assigned to Ft. Riley, Kansas, and a mechanized infantry group deploying the Bradley fighting vehicle.

McVeigh thrived in the military environment and was quickly promoted to sergeant. He took pride in his unit and especially his Bradley fighting vehicle. The only negative write-up in his military record was regarding his anti-racial comments and abuse of African Americans. He often called the blacks in his unit "niggers," and as a sergeant would give them demeaning jobs beyond what was required or what he ever required of whites. During this time, he didn't drink, date or socialize much. His reading consisted of *Soldier of Fortune, Elite Force, Sam's Military Catalogue, The Turner Diaries*, and war fiction. In 1991 his company was sent to the Middle East during the first Gulf War, Operation Desert Storm. His Bradley Company pushed into the liberation of Kuwait and it was here he obtained his *first kill*. Combat, it seemed, was a heady experience for him. He often boasted about killing an Iraqi soldier from a distance of 1100 meters with a perfect head shot that instantly severed the head from the soldier's body.[281] However, letters written to his aunt Jean reflect the reality that killing bothered him.[282] His sister Jennifer believes he may have been experiencing undiagnosed *post-traumatic stress disorder* that radically altered his personality.[283]

Following the war, McVeigh applied for and was accepted to Special Forces training (Green Berets). However, on the second day of training he dropped out, saying he had developed blisters that would not heal. According to a New York Times article he failed the psychological exam required of all Green Beret

---

279 Though raised Catholic he had left the church and there is no evidence he had any particular religious beliefs (other than Identify doctrines), or had ever joined any other kind of church or religious group.

280 Quoted in *All American Monster: The Unauthorized Biography of Timothy McVeigh*, by Brandon M. Strickney, Prometheus Books, 1996, p. 67.

281 *Gathering Storm*, p. 150.

282 *All American Monster*, p. 68.

283 *Force Upon the Plain*, p. 189.

candidates.[284] Since the Special Forces had always been his goal, when the first opportunity presented itself, McVeigh took an early out and left the army. He returned to upstate New York, joined an Army Guard unit and worked as a security guard in Tonowanda. During this time, he reconnected with his former army buddy Terry Nichols and visited him and his brother James at their Michigan farm in 1992.

In 1993, McVeigh moved to Kingman, Arizona, to stay with another former army buddy, Michael Fortier. Fortier had serious connections with the Arizona militia that had become infamous for its planning of attacks against synagogues, dams, and an actual attack on an Amtrak railroad. In Kingman, McVeigh worked various odd jobs, always wearing military fatigues and carrying a pistol. During the two years leading up to the Oklahoma City bombing McVeigh attended gun shows all over the country, and attended militia meetings in Michigan, Florida and Arizona. He always wanted to discuss Ruby Ridge, Waco, Janet Reno, the FBI, ATF, the Council on Foreign Relations, the Second Amendment, the United Nations, and One World Government.[285] He always had a copy of the *Turner Diaries* in his possession, and would often give copies away.

After the April 19 explosion at the Murrah Federal building the obvious became more clear. The attack was a striking parallel to what was depicted in the fictional *Turner Diaries*. In William Pierce's 1978 novel, a truck containing a little under 5,000 pounds of fuel oil and ammonium nitrate fertilizer is detonated at 9:15 a.m. in front of the FBI's Washington, D.C. headquarters. In Oklahoma City, a truck containing approximately 4,400 pounds of fuel oil and ammonium nitrate fertilizer is detonated at 9:05 a.m. in front of a federal building that housed the FBI and the ATF. The fictional bomb blows off the front of the building, causing the upper floors to collapse. In Oklahoma City, the bomb also caused the upper floors to collapse.[286] In Pierce's work, the attack is initiated in response to the passage of the Congressional Gun Control Act called the Cohen Act (notice the obvious Jewish illusion). McVeigh was reported to have been personally disturbed by the passage of the Brady Act, and the resultant Waco attack on those who bore arms.

When finally questioned by FBI agents, as a good soldier McVeigh would only give his name, rank and date of birth to the authorities. It's obvious how McVeigh

---

284 *American Monster*, p. 113.
285 Ibid., p. 117.
286 Parallel made by Morris Dees in *Gathering Storm*, p. 160.

saw himself. McVeigh was found guilty and given the death penalty. Rather than keep the appeal process moving in an attempt to save his life from the death penalty, against his attorney's desires, McVeigh asked to be put to death. The judge granted his request. When executed, on June 11, 2011, McVeigh was still unrepentant and as a good soldier willing to die for his cause. His own mother confessed to a friend, "It was like he traded one army for another."[287] He quoted the British poet, William Henley, for his last words, "I am the master of my fate; I am the captain of my soul." So he was!

How Do We Explain A Timothy McVeigh?

Simplistic explanations of Timothy McVeigh abound. The official government report about the bombing is it was not a conspiracy, but merely three former army buddies acting on their own.[288] Timothy's family felt he might have been suffering from *Gulf War Syndrome*. He never got treatment for this, though he applied for it. Some acquaintances of McVeigh during his stay in Kingman believe he was both using and selling drugs, especially methamphetamines and marijuana.[289] So the drug-induced explanation can be offered for his extreme actions. There is also the psychopath explanation that because McVeigh believed the government had implanted a microchip in his buttocks during his army time, he was just plain crazy. In reality, this microchip theory is a commonly held assumption by many in the militia movement. It is viewed as the *mark of the beast*, which keeps all citizens under surveillance.[290] Some of these explanations may be true to some extent (I doubt the microchip theory). However, what is clear and confirmed by several authorities is his connection with, and shared convictions with those in the most radical elements of the militia movement. He had contact with the Arizona Patriots through his friend Michael Fortier in Kingman. He was seen at a St. Lucie County, Florida, patriot meeting and assumed to be the bodyguard of well-known Michigan Militia leader, Mark Koernke. Likewise, personal accounts confirm McVeigh in attendance at Michigan Militia gatherings with Terry and James Nichols. Prior to the bombing, McVeigh had made calls to Bill Pierce, of *Turner Diary* fame (on

---

287 *Force Upon the Plain*, p. 194.
288 *All American Monster*, p. 244.
289 Ibid., p. 152.
290 Michael Barkun, "Religion, Militias, and Oklahoma City," *Terrorism and Political Violence*, Vol 8, #1, 1996, p. 56.

his personal line) and to Elohim City on the Arkansas/Oklahoma border. Elohim City, a Christian Identity compound, housed many former members of the radical Covenant, Sword and Arm of the Lord, an organization which had been busted up by the authorities after their killing of state troopers and other attempts.[291] In addition, McVeigh was an avid reader of Identity/Militia literature, and regularly listened to short wave militia radio programs.

So should McVeigh be classified as a *religious terrorist*? My own opinion in the matter is McVeigh was not motivated by any distinctive religious convictions. Though raised Catholic, there was nothing in testimony about him that shows any sincere religious beliefs or commonly accepted Christian practices. In this sense, McVeigh seems to have merely accepted the Identity doctrines and the need to act on them. However, to others in the movement, his act would become that of a patriot if not a martyr. The same day the Oklahoma City bombing took place, a gathering of pastors and members of the International Coalition of Covenant Communities was beginning a three day conference in Branson, Missouri. When it was learned that the attack may have been done by someone in the militia movement, Pastor Pete Peters rose and prayed not for the victims but for their own movement, "Keep us, your people Israel, safe from your enemy, the Antichrists, in Christ's name; Amen." One conferee stated, "They've been taking this country from us piece by piece for years, but we got a piece of it back in Oklahoma City." Speaker after speaker at the conference responded to questions about Oklahoma City with "what about the innocents at Waco?" A fiery East Texas pastor put it more bluntly, "this was God's retribution for the deaths at Waco. Look at the Old Testament, God did not mind killing a bunch of women and kids. Don't leave one suckling, don't leave no babies, don't leave nothing. Kill them, destroy them!" What also emerged out of the conference was the explanation it was the government who brought the Murrah building down. The government, it was explained, needed an event like this in order to pass its Comprehensive Terrorism Prevention Act of 1995, a measure designed to stop the militia growth. Louis Bean called the bombing an act of "unsung heroes." William Pierce himself delivered a speech saying, "When a government engages in terrorism against its own citizens, it should not be surprised when some of its citizens strike back and engage in terrorism against the government."[292]

---

291 *Force Upon the Plain*, p. 193.
292 This conference was attended by Southern Poverty Law Center researcher, Mike Reynolds, who gives us the account in Gathering Storm, pp.171-178.

Oklahoma City was both a climax and dividing line. It was definitely a terrorist criminal act carried out by one who acted on his own beliefs and the beliefs of others. His beliefs were nurtured through the subculture milieu of Christian Identity and patriot activism. In this sense, it was a culmination of forces that came to bear in one individual who acted but it was not rooted in sincere religious motives. The bombing was also a dividing line. After Oklahoma City, *leaderless resistance* was more important simply because militia groups were more than ever on the government's radar screen. Many left the movement, while others went underground and became more covert. I believe the more recent Boston Marathon bombing sends the same message to other would-be terrorists. To be successful it is better to not belong to any radical group and basically appear to be "leaderless"!

The Popular Patriot Umbrella

This section is difficult to write because I must include in the category some of my friends, my literary mentors, even some with whom I agree on many issues. So let me say at the outset, most of the individuals involved in the following organizations and groups are NOT IN ANY WAY TERRORISTS OR VIOLENT. But they happen to share some of the antigovernment sentiments and religious beliefs as those more hard line in the Identity/Patriot movement. One could find most of these people in the local Lions Clubs, mainstream denominational churches, and being pretty good next door neighbors. Unfortunately, some get wrongly labeled as belonging to *hate groups* or being guilty of *hate speech* when they are only expressing their sincere conservative and often religious beliefs.

Survivalists (Preppers)

The popular level of patriot sentiment is the grassroots of American society consisting of people who in one way or another really care about their country and community. But they often view their country through single issues as particularly threatening their values and security. These so-called *preppers* often include those who believe the economy is failing, a great depression is coming, and consequently they must be able to live off the land. This was uniquely popular during the years leading up to Y2K, but probably lost much of its punch after the Y2K fears were put to death. Today our downturned economy and world crises again foster a survival industry focused on stockpiling food, ammunition and the buying of gold.

Pro-Life Activists

I have friends in the pro-life movement who are sincere godly people, who have even consented to being arrested while blockading abortion clinics. I don't consider them terrorists even though terrorist acts have been committed by some in the movement: the most notorious, Rev. Paul Hill, an evangelical Presbyterian pastor completely motivated by his religious beliefs.[293] Most just believe (as I do) that abortion constitutes the killing of a human being and it should be called what it is, murder. However, many hate the government for making abortion legal and not protecting those most innocent among us . . . the unborn. Others are furious our government is unwilling to recognize the ongoing research showing *viability* of the fetus earlier and earlier and not granting legal protection to these children in the womb. Dr. Kermit Gosnel, the Philadelphia abortion doctor, was found guilty on three counts of first-degree murder. He was accused of killing several infants outside the womb in the name of *botched abortions*. This makes for a strange spectrum between Dr. Gosnel who is willing to kill babies outside the womb in the name of *abortion*, and Rev. Paul Hill who is willing to murder an abortion doctor outside the clinic!

Anti-Taxation and Internal Revenue

Everyone reading this book hates taxes and paying them. I am no exception. Some in my own circles are strongly anti-tax and IRS, and have opted out of Social Security. Others work to repeal the Sixteenth Amendment that gives Congress the right to "collect taxes on incomes from whatever sources." For various reasons they believe this amendment is unconstitutional and needs to be abolished. Some just refuse to pay them, and are even willing to go jail if need be. It's all within their rights, but what they have in common with patriots is their suspicion if not hatred of the IRS. Add to this the more recent outrage toward the IRS's apparent targeting of conservatives and Tea Party Patriots

---

293 For the full story see "Hill Defiant to the End: Urges on Activists," *Miami Herald*, Phil Long & Lesley Clark, September 4, 2003. Hill murdered with a shotgun Dr. John Britton, a Pensacola, Florida doctor, in front of his abortion clinic, August, 1994. Dr. Britton's security guard was also killed at the time. Hill received the Florida death penalty September 3, 2003. He believed his death would make him a martyr and that his actions were "justifiable homicide" because he saved the lives of babies in the womb.

Prayer in Public Schools and Other Places

Who would have thought years ago one could not say a prayer on a public school campus, graduation or football game? Yet across America today a student movement exists dedicated to *Praying at the Flagpole* before the school day begins as a protest against what is deemed as a spurious antireligious government regulation. When kids must be taught that "Susie Has Two Mommies or Daddies," or can obtain condoms at school, and then must allow Muslims to wear their distinctively religious dress, but they can't pray or have a Bible study club, something is wrong, they say. It makes many in the local communities raving mad with their only option to pull their kids out of the system and either home school or privately educate their children. Personally, as one who teaches history, I don't know how any teacher with an informed conscience could do justice to history without teaching religion. The result is not teaching a valid and complete history. So the Pilgrims at Plymouth Rock were not thanking God for their safe journey in escaping the religious persecution in England, but were merely thanking the Indians for teaching them how to plant corn! So at this point, I share the patriot sentiment of how off base our government is in seeking to make public education *religionless*. Especially when this coerced secularism is done without parental approval or political representation.

Home Schoolers

Many home schoolers are fundamentally antigovernment (public school) with commonly shared family values. Long term they have bred a very successful home school movement. Good parents care more about their children than anyone else . . . and much more than the government! In spite of hardship, self-sacrifice and money, many parents chose to stay at home and educate their own children. Early on, these parents fought huge battles with local and state authorities in order to gain the right to self-educate. Their memories of government bureaucracy and hostile interference have not faded. They still harbor mistrust and suspicion toward the institutionalization of learning as perpetuated by departments of education. Remember the Weavers just wanted to educate their children somewhere without interference and antagonism from government!

Antigovernment/Antienvironmentalists

In the great Northwest, many jobs, successful careers and support of families have been put in jeopardy by government regulations to ensure a better environment for bugs, flora, and endangered species. Many lumbermen and other hard working blue collar men feel *they* are the endangered species due to the federal government. It doesn't surprise anyone that the Northwest has become a haven for various militia and patriot groups. There's a lot of antigovernment sentiment out there!

Political Conservatives

I don't remember how many years ago it was a member of my church came up and asked, "Have you heard of Rush Limbaugh?" I hadn't. Now, that's quite humorous. He's probably America's most famous conservative radio talk show host, now joined by Sean Hannity and Glen Beck. When I finally listened to one of Rush's programs, I asked my friend if he thought Rush was a Christian. He looked at me rather strangely, and said, "I don't know, but I agree with him." To my friend it really didn't matter, he just agreed with Rush's conservative politics. Rush certainly is one among many who believe the federal government is the problem. Rush and the *ditto-heads* for the most part still believe government can be changed through the political process. But what Rushites have in common with patriots is a deep-seated suspicion about liberal government politics, to the point they sometimes view Rush as their political pope. Personally, I believe there was a time when being a Biblical Christian did not make one inherently politically liberal or conservative. There was a liberal/conservative spectrum in both parties. But times have changed. I do believe that my Christianity must critique all political systems on the basis of scripture without being bound to any. In this sense I am more a conservative Independent. But I have friends who believe otherwise. They hold to be a true Christian and *patriot* you must embrace conservative politics which today places you mostly into one party: Republican, or for some others, the Libertarian party.

Gold Standard Proponents

Whenever the economy goes south, Gold Standard Economist books sell well, and so do gold coins. I don't know how many times in my adult life I have seen this cycle. But to some like the late evangelical writer and talk show host Larry Burkett, many of our society's ills are due to going off the gold standard. Sometimes, this gets linked to a conspiracy theory that says Jewish bankers were responsible for this action through the establishment of the Federal Reserve System. Therefore, today some believe there is no longer any gold in Ft. Knox, and a cabal of powerful, wealthy internationalists control most of the gold. There are now several popular radio shows advertising the "fact" China is buying up all the gold. Libertarian Republican Ron Paul has gone so far as to threaten legislation to require an audit of both Fort Knox and the Federal Reserve Bank. He claimed their refusal to answer questions about amounts of gold on hand raises serious suspicions about its existence.[294] Federal Reserve chairmen, Allen Greenspan, who is Jewish, even made this a logical argument for many. I have my doubts about the theory, but I know many who share the anti-Federal Reserve sentiment. It doesn't make them terrorists but it can lead them to other antigovernment attitudes.

Anti-UN and International Organizations

When I was a student at the Air War College, the United Nations coalition of forces had failed miserably to stop the violence and ethnic cleansing in Bosnia. NATO then stepped up to the plate and put a coalition of forces together that stopped the killing. They have been there ever since to rebuild the country. What was debated at the War College was whether US forces should serve under UN commanders who were not American. It was a relief when NATO entered the fray and placed the unified command under an American commander.[295] What this illustrates is the amount of anti-UN and anti-Internationalist thinking there is in the country.[296] Americans have always been fundamentally isolationist in terms of foreign policy, and had to be pushed into intervening into someone's fight. As a result, a great deal of suspicion exists when the government seems to shove on American citizens international conventions and agreements like NAFTA, the World Trade Organization, or the current backdoor attempts to get rid of

---

294 Michael O'Brian, *The Hill's Briefing*, August 30, 2010.

295 When our country intervened into the country of Libya, after a unilateral intervention, the operation was turned over to NATO with our American air assets put under the command of a Canadian Admiral. Not one outcry was heard in this regard. So it seems for the time being our country is okay with this unique development.

296 The issue of whether US forces should serve under a foreign command is not new. It was an issue when the first expeditionary force was sent to Europe in World War I. The first troops served under British command, until the first all-American company was placed under a US Marine commander.

gun ownership through a UN treaty.[297] As I write, many are waiting on an UN Security Council authorization before punishing Bashar Al Assad for his use of chemical weapons!

Anti-Political Correctness & Affirmative Action

One day after I finished speaking at a military school, a woman officer came up to me and said, "I was offended by your talk today because you used profanity." I quickly thought back through my presentation trying to figure out where I might have used a bad word. I couldn't think of any. So I asked her what I had said that offended her. She blurted, "You used the world *man!*" To her, the word *man* instead of *person* was profanity. That's how extreme the political correctness movement has become and has influenced top leaders today. In response to initiatives promoted by certain feminist agendas (like the Equal Rights Amendment) or affirmative action for minorities, a growing number of people within mainstream popular culture are fed up with PC. These are viewed as government sponsored and funded agendas that many in the culture deem either a waste of taxpayer monies or frankly wrong. For example: Some local governments must now spend money for feet washing basins in public restrooms for Muslims, and the Federal government must accommodate new bathroom policies for transsexuals. Should they have separate ones, unisex ones or what?[298] No matter how right these decisions might appear to some, it must be granted there are many in this country who think it is not only wrong to do so, but a waste of their hard earned money. Antigovernment sentiment is the result.

Evangelical Prophecy Movement

During my last year of college, I heard Hal Lindsey speak on the subject of Biblical prophecy. The year was 1967. It was immediately following Israel's six-day war in which the Israeli army gained control of Jerusalem and the sacred Biblical sites on

---

297 See *Wall Street Journal*, "Obama's United Nations Backdoor to Gun Control," John Bolton, & John Yoo, April 14, 2013, where article 5 of the UN Arms Trade Treaty states, "to establish and maintain a national control system (of weapons).

298 One woman I spoke with in the Justice Department believes this is a radical violation of her personal space and civil rights. She exploded, "I not going in there with a man who thinks he's woman!"

the West Bank. Lindsey viewed this as a divine miracle and one of the first events that would bring about the last days. In his view, the *times of Gentile domination* had ended because Israel controlled all its land in accordance with the prophecy in Luke 21:24. He ended the message by saying, "Jesus could come back at any moment." Though there were other reasons (like feeling God called me), I went into full time Christian ministry under some of the influence of Lindsey. What this illustrates is the impact prophecy teaching has in evangelical circles. Today, there exists an entire industry of prophetic seminars, books, CDs, videos, radio, television programs and even cruises! Those who are seriously engaged in the prophecy movement share many of the same antigovernment, anti-UN, and anti-New World Order views that are at the heart of the patriot militia groups. The doctrines of Antichrist, an imminent end to the world, and a conspiracy by a confederation of nations and elites, also sells well among more radical groups.

Christian Reconstructionists

The prophetic camp of antigovernment adherents is usually premillennial in their theological orientation (whether they realize it or not). However, another group is predominately postmillennial. These are Christian *Theonomists* and *Reconstructionists*. This group believes in order to be the Christian society God desires, the Biblical Ten Commandments must be restored as the supreme law of the land, and God's law must take precedence over governmental laws. For this to be accomplished human activism must be recruited in building the righteous kingdom of Christ on earth. When this is finally accomplished, Christ will return. Therefore, it is up to Christians to work toward establishing righteous communities by reintroducing and enforcing the standards of the Ten Commandments and righteous, moral living. Whether getting the Commandments posted in schools, courthouses, or put back into local, state and national legislation, the goal is to change the course of government. The premise assumed about government is that it has become corrupt because it has departed from the righteous divine law as outlined in the scriptures. Again, any Patriot, Identity, or Militia member could agree with this sentiment. It was Paul Hill, the abortion doctor killer who went to his grave believing this doctrine and justified his killing of Dr. Britton on the basis that God's law of protecting innocents overrides the law granting legal abortion.

United States Military Personnel

When I began my research there was a growing concern especially within the United States Army that their Special Forces had been overly influenced by Identity doctrines. Many in the militia movement had military backgrounds or even Special Forces training, such as Col Bo Gritz, Randy Weaver, and Timothy McVeigh. Ft. Bragg, North Carolina, where McVeigh was trained, was for a while known for tolerating white racist views among its troops and where army personnel in an obvious skinhead initiation rite killed an African American couple. The Army finally outlawed racist affiliations, literature, visible racist tattoos, and language on base. A more recent Associated Press article revealed a murder case against four soldiers in Georgia who formed an anarchist militia and killed a former soldier and his girlfriend. They also had a plot to "take over" Ft. Stewart, Georgia and assassinate President Obama.[299] One former Marine who actively recruited people into Identity literature and beliefs now works at fighting the racism he once promoted. He confessed because the U. S. military is the best trained in the world it is where racist and militia groups send their people to get weapons and explosive training. They actively encourage young recruits to join National Guard units as well since that establishes them in the community while getting the same military training.[300] An irony lies in the numbers of active and reserve military members who disdain the federal government (particularly the Clinton and now the Obama administrations), while serving in it and being paid by it!

Good Ol' Boys

I have lived in Alabama several times and now I live in Florida, so I have come to know what the term *southern good 'ol boy* means. It may be thought of as a stereotype, but I have found the term to be fairly accurate. Who is a good 'ol boy? Well, he's a white male between the ages of twenty, forty or sixty, drives a truck with a rifle in the back or a pistol under the seat, is hard working, sometimes beer drinking, may or may not have the *stars and bars* on his bumper, loves his little woman and his kids, and attends church if for no other reason just to please his wife. But what he carries within him is a somewhat common sentiment: a sentiment that the system is rigged against him, and the way things are is not the

---

299 Russ Bynum, "Prosecutors: Murder case revealed terror plot by US soldiers operating militia inside Army," Associated Press, August 28, 2012.

300 Former Marine fights Racism for a Living," *Air Force Times*, September 11, 2000.

way they ought to be. He connects much of the way he feels with what he sees as an out of control abusive government. Just to go fishing or hunting he must have at least three or four different government licenses: one for the car, another if pulls a boat or trailer, another for his gun, and one to hunt and fish. At some point, it is very easy for him to view the government as something that only takes away his hard earned money and interferes with all the important areas of his life. As a result, he can be a real sympathizer to those who desire to take arms against the government. In short, what these people share is antigovernment suspicion and hostility mixed with a particular axe to grind on one or more issues listed above. For them, there is just too much government intervention in their lives. Add to this, an end time apocalyptic belief and a conspiratorial view of history, and what you end up with is a person very much on their way to embracing patriot ideology or militia activities. In the next chapter, both some hard line groups and what I call, soft ideologues will be examined.

CHAPTER EIGHT
Christian Patriots:
Serious Activists & Stolen Identity

Yes, we're gonna cleanse our land. We're gonna do it with a sword.[301]

—Rev. William Potter Gale

The bottom line is that at a certain point there is not only the right, but the duty, to disobey the state.[302]

—Dr. Francis Schaeffer

n one sense, there is nothing new about right wing groups or the ideology they profess. Coughlin notes, "The belief that elite, evil forces control the world has a long and varied history going back almost a thousand years."[303]

---

301 Quoted in *American Militias*, p. 166.
302 Francis Schaeffer, *A Christian Manifesto*, Crossway Books, 1981, p. 126.
303 *Secrets, Plots & Hidden Agendas*, p. 26.

In 1186 AD, prophecies of a New World Order were circulated during the Third Christian Crusade. Illuminati conspiracy theories go back to Bavarian and French sources in the eighteenth century. Even during the American Civil War conspiracy theories were popular, making Irish Catholics and Mormons the prime scapegoat conspirators. What is new about the current patriot or militia movement is not its doctrine but how mainstream some of the doctrines have become.

Over several decades, Identity ideology can be traced from groups committed to hard line racial violence to more mainstream "soft" acceptance. There is an important line to be drawn between the two. I use the term "hard line" to refer to those groups who have actually used violent actions to promote their cause or have called for the use of violence. "Soft ideologues" are those who share some, but not all, of the same beliefs as the hard line but so far have no history of encouraging or engaging in violent acts. Some of them would be appalled at the idea of using violence on behalf of their beliefs. The concern of this author is how the hard line teaching is tactically moving in the direction of softer ideologues in order to woo them to their own position; at the same time softer ideologues are calling for more radical action. This chapter will look at both groups.

The Southern Poverty Law Center's *Intelligence Report* for the year 2010 listed almost 1000 "hate groups." Militia researcher Mark Potok noted, "A dramatic resurgence in the patriot movement and its paramilitary wing." He observed an astonishing 363 new patriot groups in 2009, a 244 percent jump! The largest numbers of Identity groups are found in California, Idaho, Montana, Washington, Oklahoma, Arkansas and Virginia.[304] In 2012, the same report noted that for many extremists President Obama has been a "lightning rod and symbol of all that is wrong with our country . . . they claim he is a "Kenyan President" and secret Muslim." The report also noted the increase of "Sovereign Citizens" and their killing of six law enforcement members since 2000.[305] Recently in 2014, the standoff between rancher Cliven Bundy and the US Bureau of Land Management revealed Bundy's Sovereign Citizen ideology. Potok explained, "Bundy is obviously in tune with the message of the antigovernment militias in general and, more specifically, with the

---

304 *Intelligence Report*, Southern Poverty Law Center, Summer, 2010.
305 *SPLC Report*, "Radical-Right Movement Explodes," Spring, 2012, Southern Poverty Law Center Publication.

so-called "sovereign citizens" movement, which is composed of extreme right-wing radicals who believe the federal government has no legitimacy at all."[306]

A 2013 report showed an 813 percent growth rate since 2008 in patriot groups, of which 321 were listed as militias. The report claims "law enforcement officials in the last several years have uncovered numerous terrorism conspiracies born in the militia subculture: plots to spread poisonous ricin power, to attack federal installations, and to murder federal judges and other government officials."[307] In other words, the hard line Identity groups are concentrated in the Northwest and parts of the Bible belt. In a 2014 report the Southern Poverty Law Center reports an increase of 140 patriot groups in 2008 to over 1,000 in 2013. These included shooting incidents between antigovernment extremists and law enforcement. The article claims the increase is due to "the movement being emboldened by the initially successful defense of Clive Bundy against the Bureau of Land Management.[308] One of the early groups that seemingly influenced some in the patriot movement was Posse Comitatus.

Posse Comitatus

Posse Comitatus means "power of the county" and is a right-wing armed group founded in Portland, Oregon in 1969, and very active until the mid-1980s. National director James Wickstrom is quoted as saying, "Yahweh our father is at work setting the stage for the final act against the Christ-murdering Jews and their father, Satan. America is the Zion of Bible prophecy, but our nation is now completely under the control of the International Invisible government of World Jewry."[309] Posse members, like some patriot groups today, believe there should be no government beyond that of the county sheriff, and when organized these groups constitute sovereign citizens who are not bound to pay federal or state taxes or obey their laws. Therefore, they carry no driver's licenses and put no license plates on their cars. Some make up their own Sovereign Citizen driver's licenses and passports. Some have made death threats on government authorities that *harass* or

---

306 "Q & A with Mark Potok," SPLC Report, Summer 2014, p. 8.

307 *SPLC Report*, "Radical Right Groups See Explosive Growth," Spring, 2013, Southern Poverty Law Center Publication.

308 "SPLC warns of violence in wake of federal standoff with militias," *SPLC Report*, Fall, 2014, p.1, 3.

309 Quoted in *Force Upon the Plain*, p. 50.

violate their *sovereign citizen* rights. One of their leaders, the Rev. William Potter Gale, gave counter-insurgency seminars instructing people in the administration of poisons, night combat patrol and murder by ambush.

One member, South Dakotan Gordon Kahl, was wanted for tax evasion. When pulled over by federal authorities, he engaged in a firefight leaving his own son shot, one US Marshall dead and two others wounded. He fled, but was finally discovered hiding out in a house in the Ozarks. Rather than give himself up, he killed the county sheriff (so much for believing in the power of the county) who had come to arrest him and finally was killed in a fiery firefight with federal agents. Kahl quickly became a popular hero and martyr for the "Christian faith" and patriots. Over 200 attended his funeral where he was praised as a patriot and a committed churchgoer with a gun.[310] The founder Potter Gale died in 1989 while awaiting a prison sentence.

Aryan Nations

Richard Butler, a former aerospace engineer, established the Aryan Nations compound formerly located in Hayden Lake, Idaho. Butler moved to Idaho from California in the mid-70s to escape the "Jews, Blacks, and Hispanics" he saw taking over California. The vision he carried to Idaho was to establish an all-white nation in the Northwest. He believes Americans could only ensure their pure Christian culture by creating a new nation of all whites. Already established in Hayden Lake was Wesley Swift, a former associate of Rev. Gerald Smith, the fundamentalist pastor who founded the Christian Nationalist Crusade in the 1930s. Butler merged his Aryan Nations with Swift's Church of Jesus Christ Christian. Butler believed a race war was both imminent and necessary in order to save America as a Christian nation. Though his compound was filled with Nazi uniforms and images, he justified his views from Christian Identity theology.

Aryan Nations was prosecuted in 2000 when some of Butler's security guards chased and then assaulted a passerby mother and her son. The lawsuit bankrupted the organization with the compound being turned over to the Keenan family, the mother and son who were assaulted. Representation for the Keenans was provided by the Southern Poverty Law Center. Butler continued living in Butler, Idaho, but never really recovered from the loss. He died in 2004, but the organization lives on.

---

310 Ibid., pp. 50-53.

Also connected to Aryan Nations is Louis Beam, their *ambassador at large.* Some believe Beam was the heir apparent to succeed Butler.[311] Louis Beam is the one who first coined the phrase *leaderless resistance,* (now also taken up by Islamist groups) arguing this form of resistance is preferable because it prevents effective infiltration, and because it reduces the chances resistance plans will be foiled. Of course, *resistance* has become a code word in the movement for violent action.

It must be remembered that on August 10, 1999, a former Aryan Nation member and security guard for the compound, Buford Furrow, opened fire at a Jewish community center near Los Angeles, wounding three children and two adults. One of the children eventually died. From there, he murdered a Filipino-American postal worker who just happened across his path at the wrong time.[312] It should also be remembered the Aryan Nations compound was only sixty miles from Randy Weaver's home in Ruby Ridge. The Weavers often visited the compound and heard Butler speak. Many believed Richard Butler was one of the most dangerous men in the movement simply because of his persuasive ability and sincere commitment to racial purity in the guise of scriptural argument. But as dangerous as Butler was, his organization birthed an even more violent group.

The Order

Robert Matthews had been around for some time. He started out as a John Bircher, moved to William Pierce's National Alliance and then became active in Aryan Nations. After the death of Gordon Kahl in 1983, Matthews at a meeting of white supremacists in Hayden Lake voiced his concern the movement needed to move from mere *thinkers* to *doers.* He split from Aryan Nations, viewing them in the first category, and began the Order based on a resistance group in William Pierce's novel, *The Turner Diaries.* Rather than raise money for his organization he believed it was cheaper and easier to counterfeit money. After a member was caught passing phony fifty-dollar bills, Matthews moved to robbing banks. In 1984, members of the Order robbed a Seattle bank of $25,000, a Seattle armored vehicle of $43,000, followed by another for $230,000. In sum, the Order stole 3.8 million dollars and distributed the monies to other supremacist groups across the country. The money may still be funding various patriot activities.

---

311 Abanes in *America's Militias,* p.180.
312 *Intelligence Report,* SPLC, p. 28.

When a Jewish Denver talk show host invited members of the Order to call in and be interviewed, radio host Alan Berg ridiculed their beliefs on the air. After finishing his program on June 18, 1984, Order members followed him home and machined gunned him down. Members continued to counterfeit and rob in order to finance their organization. It would take the FBI two different shootouts with Matthews to finally put an end to the Order. Matthews died in a hail of bullets in 1994 at Puget Sound. He had successfully eluded agents for almost ten years.[313]

Militia of Montana

Many my age remember the FBI standoff with the Montana Freemen. It was potentially another Ruby Ridge fiasco in the making. But this time the FBI was more cautious. The FBI had evidence of firearm violations but rather than going in with guns blazing they called in not a FBI negotiator, but retired Lt. Colonel and fellow patriot, Bo Gritz. (Randy Weaver also accompanied Gritz.) After days of negotiating a peaceful settlement was accomplished. The Montana Freemen, a local county militia group, had their origins in John Trochmann and his Militia of Montana, commonly called MOM. Trochmann, a retired snowmobile repairman and a cross between Biblical prophet and cowboy, built a compound with his brother David and nephew Randy in Noxon, Montana, a booming town of 350 people. It has since declined.

What makes Trochmann unique in the militia movement is his emphasis on giving the United States Constitution a new twist. His argument was only American white males are *freemen*. Since he believed the US Constitution (along with the Bible) was divinely inspired when it was first written, then only the first ten amendments are valid. Since the early document granted God-given rights to white males in their respective sovereign states, then early American males were not citizens of a sovereign federal government. It was the Fourteenth and Fifteenth Amendments added later that granted federal equal rights to slaves, women, and minorities. Trochmann argues white males are then not federal citizens but *freemen* of sovereign states. The final punch line is that *resident aliens* (Jews, African Americans and other minorities) should pay federal taxes while "freemen" are exempt. Therefore, many in the Freemen movement have filed official documents

---

313 Summary taken from *Force Upon the Plain*, 54-55.

with the United States claiming they are not and have never been citizens of the United States.

Trochmann has a long history of racist views, but today he is keeping them more hidden. In the past he was a regular visitor and speaker at the Aryan Nations compound even though he denied any association. Even Richard Butler to his own defense admitted the Trochmanns had been at Hayden Lake several times.[314] Butler says Trochmann helped him write the Aryan Nations Platform for the Aryan Nations State. Trochmann may have been disavowing his racist views for two reasons. First, he is able to gather more people around the issues of anti-gun control or tax resistance by keeping race out of the initial exposure.

Secondly, after the Oklahoma City bombing he was one of several militia spokesmen who were subpoenaed to testify before the Senate Judiciary Subcommittee investigation on terrorism (July 1995). Before this committee, headed by Senator Arlan Specter (Jewish Republican from Pennsylvania), he flatly denied being a racist. However, a few months before appearing before the committee, Trochmann told a reporter, "I am following God's law . . . Blacks, Jews are welcome. But when America is the new Israel, they'll need to go back where they came from . . . It's just nature's law, kind should go unto kind."[315] According to a former close associate of Trochmann's, Mike Richter, Trochmann doesn't go along with the moral aspects of his "Christianity." He confessed how he and Trochmann visited a popular strip joint in Great Falls, Montana.[316]

From this obscure place in Montana, Trochmann's organization is a literal cottage industry for producing materials for the patriot movement. They publish manuals for structuring militia groups, fighting tax laws, even selling militia music with tunes such as "The Randy Weaver Ballad." Previous videotape titles available were one by militia defender former and late Congresswoman Helen Chenoweth of Idaho. Other audiotapes cover such titles as, "The Illuminati Today" and "The Bio-Chip Mark of the Beast." Books for purchase include: "Big Sister is Watching You," "Hillary's Hell-Cats," and "Gore's Whores." Listings also include books on the art of war and unconventional warfare devices and material on preparedness. Listed appearances for his members on his website are however out of date, showing schedules for 2008 gun shows in 2013. Specific meetings are only listed

---

314 *American Militias*, p.179.
315 Daniel Voll, "At Home with M.O.M," *Esquire*, July 1995, p. 48.
316 See endnote on page 264, *American Militias*, for personal confirmation.

for Montana, Oregon and Washington. His website (militiaofmontana.com) offers MOM's lengthy argument that the sovereign citizens of each state are the real constitutional militia, and not the National Guard.[317]

Though Trochmann may use code words to cover his anti-Semitism, the heart of his message is the same. His ideology is based on the spurious and known Russian forgery *The Protocols of the Elders of Zion*. His world Jewish conspiracy just gets recast as antigovernmentalism and the idea that "anonymous unseen hands" are pulling the strings of governments around the world with the goal of taking away American's freedoms.[318]

What is most sinister about Trochmann is how he poses as one who studies the Bible, quotes scripture and uses scripture to couch his real beliefs. This is not accidental. A former MOM member admits how "John spoke at length on the merits of "using" the Bible and God, not the swastika and Hitler, to advance his band of racism, bigotry and Christian Identity.[319] If true (and I believe it is), it makes Trochmann at the least an opportunist, and at worst, a dangerous deceiver who seeks to prey on religious people who are not educated enough in their faith to distinguish piety from racism. At this time of writing, he has morphed his Montana Militia into a more trendy sounding organization called The Sanders Natural Resource Council (www.snrcouncil.org). In an interview Trochmann explains how this new name keeps law enforcement more at bay by posing as an anti-environmental group. In an interview with State Senator Jennifer Fielder he states "the biggest threat the militia sees is from *globalist organizations and environmental wackos.*"[320]

The year 2014 saw another element of the Sovereign Citizen movement emerge. In a standoff between Nevada cattle rancher Cliven Bundy and the US Bureau of Land Management, the initial focus was on Bundy's right to pasture his cattle

---

317 This author refutes this on two counts. First, he is right that the Constitution never calls the militia the National Guard. This is later terminology. However, the Constitution never calls "Sovereign Citizens" the militia either. Secondly, the National Guard does not serve under the authority of the President of the United States (unless activated under USC Title 10), but under the authority of their respective states and the governor of each state. The militia (National Guard) are then citizens of their respective states and serve as paid volunteers for the protection of their states under the authority of their governors. When federalized to active duty under the President, they still retain their status as state guardsmen to which they will return after their tour of duty is completed.

318 *Force Upon the Plain*, 79.

319 Quoted in *Force*, p. 70.

320 The Cowgirl Blog: Montana's #1 Political Website, mtcowgirl.com. October 10, 2012.

versus the environmental protection of a threatened tortoise.[321] As the standoff proceeded, Fox New's Sean Hannity interviewed Bundy several times. Though I was somewhat concerned about the government's overreach, showing up with guns and SWAT teams, the more I listened to Bundy express his opinions, I noticed he referenced several times the term *sovereign citizen*. I finally told a law enforcement friend that this sounded like a common Christian Identity term. Soon afterward, it became very apparent Bundy held racist views, and quickly the Hannity interviews ceased and nothing has been in the news since. Strangely, no coverage was given to the sovereign citizen aspect of his beliefs, only the fact he made a racist remark. To this writer, the racism is rooted deeply in the Christian Identity movement of which the Sovereign Citizen movement is sometimes a part!

The Michigan Militia

Rev. Norm Olson, former pastor of Calvary Baptist Church, founded the Michigan Militia when a parishioner had taken on and lost a formal protest against the local school board. Ray Southwell, a real estate agent and father of three, was concerned about the *socialism* and *humanism* his kids were being exposed to in the school system. After losing the protest, he consulted his pastor, and as result Olson and Southwell formed "God's Army in Michigan," later to be called the Michigan Militia. Founded in 1994, they followed the model provided by the Militia of Montana. Like many in the militia movement, Olson and Southwell felt both Ruby Ridge and Waco were wake-up calls to God-fearing patriotic Americans. Olson also believed the passage of the Brady Bill left Americans "defenseless" from having the One World Government take over their lives.

Together they obtained a large plot of land for a compound and built a "fort" complete with ridges, trenches, and other defensive earthworks. The nearest road was several miles away. The only way in was to know ahead of time where the compound was located, making the compound inaccessible to outsiders except by helicopter. The stated goal of this militia was "to stand against tyranny, globalism, moral relativism, humanism and the New World Order."[322] By the fall of 1994, the Militia claimed to have units in between sixty-three and eighty-three counties in

---

321 Laura Zuckerman, "U.S. seizes cattle in rare fight over federal land use in Nevada," www.reuters.com, April 10, 2014.
322 *Force Upon the Plain*, 97.

Michigan. The number was probably exaggerated, but at least it was good business for Norm Olson's other job of running a gun store!

Like so many, Rev. Olson believed America was being invaded by International (UN) army personnel as recognized by their unmarked black helicopters and tanks with the inverted V on the side. Some of these beliefs are true! International officers have been attending US schools for many years. In my class at the USAF War College 50 out of 200 students were international officers. There is no conspiracy here. We also have many US officers who attend the schools of our allies. Yes, the US military does have black helicopters, (some are in fact called "Blackhawks") but they have "subdued markings" on the side making them unrecognizable from the ground. As for the inverted V's on tanks, they were put there during Desert Storm in order to identify the "friendlies" so we wouldn't fire on our own tanks. The evidence may still be out on whether Olson truly embraces the racist rhetoric so common in other groups. But Olson is important for no other reason than his confessed evangelical/fundamentalism commitment for over thirty years. In his Michigan gun store window he sold guns, survivalist equipment and Bibles! Olson even testified before the Senate Subcommittee on Terrorism. His testimony prompted Coughlin to conclude, "Perhaps for the first time America saw a clear connection between the militia and a unique Christian perspective."[323] Rev. Olson was a gun-toting pastor who still loved Jesus!

At a 1995 meeting of militiamen he told a reporter covering the meeting, "Hey, they need the Lord Jesus Christ, in fact one man received the Lord." Leading someone to Jesus Christ is considered among evangelicals one of the touchstones of a dynamic, spiritually alive faith. Olson also claims he is a dispensational-Calvinistic-evangelist who was once a member of the General Association of Regular Baptists. He also ran a Christian school serving as principal at one time.

Olson was the former head of the Northern Michigan Regional Militia. But in 2005, he moved to Alaska declaring Michigan "hopeless." He auctioned off his weapons and other memorabilia from his gun store and along with Ray Southwell relocated to Nikiski, Alaska. He now promotes the Alaska Citizens Militia (alaskacitizensmilitia.com). He is quoted saying "America is very, very ill and people across America are preparing themselves."[324] In his testimony before

323 *Secrets, Plots & Hidden Agendas*, 62.
324 *Intelligence Report*, Southern Poverty Law Center, Summer 2010, p. 22.

the subcommittee he didn't pull any punches (like Trochmann). He stated, "We're talking about a situation where armed conflict may be inevitable if the country does not turn around . . . where did we get this idea that we are supposed to sit down and let a corrupt government get worse and worse? Our Lord told us to contend for the faith and occupy until he comes."[325] On his current website he claims "dozens of militia with hundreds in each unit" and of course he is the Commander. The website further records his views saying, "We won't really act as a cohesive body until we are bloodied," and considers "any firearms restrictions an act of war."[326]

One of the main motivational speakers for the Michigan Militia was Mark Koernke, better known as "Mark from Michigan." Mark broke with Norm Olson, and started his own organization called *The Michigan Militia at Large*. As basically a conference and seminar speaker, Mark liked to pass himself off as a former Army Intelligence analyst.

This sells well in militia circles. However, his only military time was in the Army Reserve where he achieved the rank of Army Specialist, or E-4. He also likes people to think he teaches at the University of Michigan. He was an employee of the University of Michigan but the closest he got to the classroom was emptying the trash. He was a janitor! In 1993 he released a successful videotape entitled "America in Peril," which called upon Americans to defend themselves against such organizations as the National Organization for Women. Later, he claimed the Environmental Protection Agency was tracking vehicles by remote control and that *biochips* were going to be inserted into the populace by the Antichrist. It should also be remembered that Timothy McVeigh often listened to Koernke's shortwave radio program and reportedly traveled with him and six others to a militia meeting in St. Lucie, Florida.[327]

In spite of Mark from Michigan's exaggerations about his credentials, his religious motivation seems pure. A close friend and Koernke's best man confirms it is his end times interpretation of the Bible that fuels his belief in the New World Order as a fulfillment of Bible prophecy. His friend states, "Koernke believes that the book of Revelation showed him that he is living at the threshold of Armageddon."[328]

---

325 Testimony before the Senate Subcommittee on Terrorism, Technology and Government Information, June15, 1995.
326 Alaskacitizensmilitia.com. Website checked May, 2013.
327 *Force Upon the Plain*, p.102.
328 David Van Biema, "The Message from Mark Koernke," *Time Domestic*, June 26, 1995.

Like his fellow Michigan Militia members, Mark preaches that Christians must be ready to resist the mark of the beast even with force of arms; "If we do not accept the Mark of the Beast, we're going to have to take care of ourselves."[329] Mark, always looking for black helicopters, was finally done in by one. In 1998, he was wanted for skipping bail on an assault charge when a police helicopter on a routine marijuana mission noticed him. Later, in 2001 he was arrested for fleeing from the police and resisting arrest. Even in prison, Koernke continued his "broadcasts" to other patriots using prison pay phones. Released in 2007, he regularly airs his "Intelligence Report" broadcasts on his Liberty Tree Radio program, alerting his fellow militiamen to the coming violent exchange with the New World Order.[330] Training videos can also be found at libertytreeradio on YouTube.

So should Americans see these groups as armed and dangerous? In September of 1994, a policeman in Fowlerville, Michigan pulled over a car. When he observed a loaded 9mm in the seat he got a little concerned. Searching the car he found loaded semiautomatic weapons, gas masks, two-way radios, night vision glasses, and 700 hundred rounds of ammunition. Two of the three occupants of the car claimed to be bodyguards for Mark Koernke, wore army camouflage uniforms and had their faces blackened. They claimed they were on "night maneuvers." The men did not appear in court to face their charges. Instead around fifty protesters showed up burning a UN flag and calling the police names. The Chief of Police said one protester claimed "the next time one of them was stopped they'd shoot the cop."[331]

Before looking at the softer ideological proponents, I need to include some individuals who function as *bridge* resources between the hard line militia groups and the softer proponents of patriot ideas. Since all claim to be *born again* believers in the evangelical persuasion and have significant radio, literature or speaking *ministries*, they function somewhat as theological ideologues for the movement. Researcher Abanes contends, "A clear majority of patriots hold to some form of conservative Protestantism . . . in addition there is a huge overlap between militias and Christian fundamentalism."[332] Militia leader Dean Compton agrees saying, "Most of the people in the patriot movement are born-again believers."[333]

---

329 Quoted in *American Militias*, p.88.
330 *Intelligence Report*, SPLC, p. 20.
331 *Force Upon the Plain*, p.103.
332 *American Militias*, p. 87.
333 Personal interview with the leader by Abanes, in *Militias*, p. 87.

Moderate Identity Ideologues

Texe Marrs' Austin, Texas based Power of Prophecy Ministries, is a literature, radio and internet ministry where he publishes a monthly newsletter and does daily radio programs on the short wave American Voice Radio. Marrs believes the world is controlled by at least ten unseen, unknown men, who are members of the Council on Foreign Relations, the Tri-Lateral Commission, Freemasons and the Illuminati. He is equally suspicious of Roman Catholics, the Pope, Billy Graham, Democrats and Republicans, the UN, the Anti-Defamation League and Pat Robertson.[334] He claims the Oklahoma City bombing was part of Bill Clinton's agenda for the New World Order and has endorsed the clear racist views of Pete Peters and his *Scriptures for America* newsletter. In addition, Bo Gritz has been a radio guest several times, along with Linda Thompson, author of the video, "Waco: The Big Lie." His mix of Biblical prophecy and Identity interpretations should be of concern to any thinking person. On his website (www.texemarrs.com) he regularly advertises his own prefaced copy of the *Protocols of Zion,* and the current site has offerings entitled, *Conspiracy of the Six Pointed Star* and *Conspiracy World.* He believes the Jewish Rothschild family has a dark, secret plan for America including Wall Street bankers and social revolutionaries who will forge the New World Order. On his website positioned in a highlighted box runs a quote: "Scientific DNA proves Jews are not descendants of Israel but of King Bulan and the Khazars . . . Jews have no claim on the land" (Israel).[335] He wrongly named Newt Gingrich as the next Republican candidate for president being handpicked by the cabal of Jewish puppet masters. He also takes to task Mitt Romney and Glenn Beck as part of a larger Mormon conspiracy.

Pete Peters, mentioned several times in these chapters, also pops up speaking and promoting his ideas among evangelicals. He has hosted programs for the Pittsburg based *Keystone Inspiration Network,* an evangelical organization. Apparently, Reverend Peters is equally at home with militia groups and on evangelical television. He has categorically denied being a racist, but his associations and literature speak otherwise.

---

334 Claimed by Abanes, p. 205.
335 Website posted on May 10, 2013.

Abanes, when asked about being racist, just redefines his terms. In one response he uttered, "saying disparaging remarks about Jews and blacks is not racist or violent, it is simply the truth!"[336]

Lt. Colonel James "Bo" Gritz, US Army retired, is a highly decorated Vietnam War hero, supposedly the inspiration for the Rambo movie character played by Sylvester Stallone. In 1992 he was the Populist candidate for President and was on the ballot in twenty states. His platform was "God, Guns, and Gritz." For decades, he has devoted himself to denouncing the New World Order while conducting training seminars for militia groups on military tactics and revolutionary warfare techniques called S.P.I.K.E, (Specially Prepared Individuals for Key Events). He wrote a best seller among patriot groups, *Called to Serve*, has hosted a talk show, "Freedom Call," and publishes a newsletter, *Center for Action* from his compound in Sandy Valley, Nevada. In 1994, Gritz launched a project to develop a 900 acre tract of land in the Idaho wilderness as a *Covenant Community* (called Almost Heaven) where Christian patriots could find sanctuary from the coming tyranny and chaos. He called it "an Ark in the time of Noah." But the project was plagued with problems both within and without. The surrounding community had problems with his creating illegal common law trusts to manage property sales. Inside, a split occurred when some of his members did not think he was going far enough in his antigovernment activity.

"Almost Heaven" fell apart in 1998 when one of his members was accused of squandering $1 million in land sale funds, and finally Gritz's wife of twenty-four years left him. Deeply depressed, he attempted a nonsuccessful suicide gunshot to the head. After recovery, he left Idaho for Nevada. Gritz served as counsel and mediator at both Rudy Ridge and the Montana Freeman standoffs. He called the Oklahoma City bombing a "Rembrandt," but said, "If every American knew that every other American was equal under the law, including those who carry guns and wear badges, then it would put the militia back in the closet where it belongs."[337] This is a more moderate statement than those often made by others in the militia movement. Gritz's main emphasis in his writings and speaking is antigovernment, antigay, mixed with strong evangelical beliefs about the coming apocalypse. He

---

336 Abanes, p. 182.
337 James L. Pate, "Amateurs & Assassins," *Soldier of Fortune,* January 1996, p. 87.

claims to be a "born-again" Christian.[338] However, he embraces most of the Christian Identity doctrines, which makes him suspect about overt anti-Semitism although he denies being a racist. A quote from one his recruitment letters may sum up his views: "I can assure you that if I was ever convinced it was God's will for me to commit an act of violence against the laws of our land, I would hesitate only long enough to, like Gideon, be certain, I would then do all within my power to accomplish what I felt he required of me . . . If God does call me into the Phineas Priesthood . . . my defense will be the truth as inspired by the Messiah.[339]

So what do Biblical prophecy, the New World Order, even gold and silver coins have in common? These three elements create a perfect storm of fusion of end times expectation, fear of an impending evil world order, and the necessity of preparing to survive by stockpiling gold and silver, purchasing guns, and creating alternative food sources. These *preppers* are encouraged by a host of Christian popularizers, pastors, TV preachers, and "Insider Intelligence" reports. One does not have to watch or listen to Christian media very long to find these individuals marketing their views of economic collapse, impeding end-time doom, the return of Christ to this earth, mixed with cabal conspiratorial theories. One source coined a unique term for those being controlled by governmental forces. In one article the writer calls the majority of American people "sheeple."[340] This term may not seem significant but what is interesting about the term is that it is used commonly by white supremacists when referring to people who naively follow the Jewish inspired and controlled ZOG, or Zion Occupational Governments. Randy Weaver used the term "sheeple" as the "slaves of ZOG." The term was commonly voiced by the Montana Freeman and by Timothy McVeigh. [341] So as a code word it seems somewhat humorous to the naïve reader, while affirming in a more covert way an anti-Semitic philosophy at the same time. Many evangelical writers believe Christians will go through what is called "the Great Tribulation," a prophecy taken from the books of Daniel, Revelation, and Jesus' last discourse to his disciples (Daniel 9:24-27, Revelation 16, Matthew 24:15-28). Writers and preachers use this material to encourage

---

338 Information taken from briefing materials for the course, Terrorism, "Those Associated with Extremist Groups or Causes," USAF Air War College, Fall, 1996.

339 "Bo Gritz," www.splcenter.org/get-informed/intelligence-files/prolifes/bo-gritz.

340 Don McAlvany, "America at the Crossroads: Freedom or Slavery," *McAlvany Intelligence Advisor*, August 1994, p. 1-2.

341 Philip Weis, "They've Had Enough," *New York Times Magazine*, January 8, 1995, p. 48.

people to leave large cities, move to smaller communities, pull their children out of public schools and stockpile enough food for at least one year.[342] Survival products are regularly advertised along with strong recommendations for purchasing gold and silver. One militia busting online group calls one such source, "a conspiracy theorist who mixes stories of implanted biochips as the Mark of the Beast, with the predictions of impending economic collapse . . . He advises readers to buy gold and silver . . . interestingly enough he is also a dealer in gold and silver."[343] A Koinonia House email newsletter regularly promotes New World Order conspiracy theories, antigovernment charges and claims. Leading up to the year 2000, writer Chuck Missler promoted a large product line of survival merchandise of lectures, tapes, and books of Missler's Biblical prophecy studies. Speaking at a Y2K conference in 1998 where over 2000 people attended, a guestimate of $25,000 was raised from general admission charges.

Abanes and Couglin's concern about Missler is not so much about what he says but what his apparent sources are. Abanes claims "unfortunately, some of his sources are tied directly to the white supremacist movement . . . Missler not only quotes from but expresses thanks to and gives the address of the "American Patriot Fax Network . . . and The Spotlight."[344] The American Patriot Fax Network is a known source used by the Arizona Patriots, and several other Christian Identity groups. A Los Angeles Times article concluded "several racist organizations belong to the American Patriot Fax Network."[345] For one claiming to be Biblically based, and be quoting from or borrowing ideas from these kind of sources is questionable even though he denies any connection to racist or patriot material. As a fellow believer in Jesus, I want to give him the benefit of the doubt, but one should not be surprised by the concern.

Soft Evangelical Popularizers

This next group represents certain schools of theological thought. What they have in common is their scriptural-based teaching, concern about the prophetic end

---

342 Don McAlvany, "Toward Medical Self-Sufficiency: Understanding Alternate Medicine," *MIA*, August 1995, p.28.

343 Quoted in www.thenarrowwayministries.org. and www.skeptic.com.

344 Ibid.

345 Robin Wright and Josh Meyer, "Tradition-Rooted 'Patriot' Groups Strive to Curtail Modern Tyranny," *The Los Angeles Times*, April 24, 1995.

times, and in particular, where the United States fits into this future. They also share serious concerns about the moral and spiritual decline of America. Critical importance lies in the reality they have been successful in popularizing and mass marketing their ideas to very large audiences. In this regard, their ideas have found acceptance across a large spectrum of our society.

To some of my readers, the names that appear may seem strange to be included in a book on terrorism. So let me again affirm with great respect; the following leaders, speakers, and teachers, I consider fellow brothers and sisters in the Christian faith. I share their evangelical theological commitments, and with most embrace their system of theology (Dispensational-Premillennialism). Therefore, we together appreciate and embrace the same Lord, scriptures, and system of doing theological thinking about the future. Where I differ is in regard to saying that "this" (in the Bible) is the only authoritative "that" as connected to some current, past or future events. In other words, I can believe in a "ten-headed beast" in the book of Revelation, without saying it is the United Nations, a European Union or some Arab confederation. Observing a fact of scripture is one thing, while interpretation of the fact is another! The importance of including softer evangelical popularizers lies in seeing how easily their ideas can be used, misused or equated with ideas in harder line Identity camps. Equally, without distinguishing the differences between the soft and hard line, it is easy for patriot groups to enlist uninformed evangelicals to actions that are beyond the pale of the very scriptures they embrace.

Pre-Millennial Popularizers

Remember Randy and Vicky Weaver? The Weavers were lay Bible students in South Dakota, trying to live out their faith in Christ in the context of their own family and community. Randy claimed Hal Lindsey's book *The Late Great Planet Earth* was instrumental in their moving to Ruby Ridge and preparing for the Lord's return. Vicky said the enemies of God predicted by Lindsey were ready to strike at any moment. Make no mistake, in no way do I think Hal Lindsey's writings caused the Ruby Ridge shootout, but this case does illustrate how some in our Christian communities may take extreme actions while thinking they are preparing for the Lord's return. Coughlin affirms, they adhere to the contemporary interpretation of end times prophecy made popular by Hal Lindsey.[346]

---

346 Ibid., p. 144.

Abanes lists Lindsey as "America's number one prophet," not surprising since *Late Great Planet Earth* is one of the most popular best sellers in both the general and religious markets. Abanes says, "Patriots and militia members gravitate toward Lindsey's work because of his speculations about the nearness of the end."[347] I'm positive this is not Lindsey's intention, but the reality exists that hard line patriot members use Lindsey's apocalyptic interpretations for their own purposes in substantiating fears of the coming New World Order. Worse, they use it to promote Christians buying gold, AK-47s, and stockpiling food and ammunition.

Pro-Life Proponents

In response to the secular *Humanist Manifesto*, then popular Francis Schaeffer, a well-known Presbyterian pastor and founder of L'Abri ministry in Switzerland, had increasing concern in these "latter days" the Church and Christians had lost the *culture war* and were living in a post-Christian society characterized by godlessness, immorality and perversion.

At the same time, he believed the Church had lost its conscience and guts about standing against the atrocities of our age. His chief illustration of Church passivity was found in its quiet acceptance of the millions of unborn children being sacrificed since the Roe v. Wade verdict in 1973. He closed his *Christian Manifesto* publication with a call for Christian civil disobedience. He never said what Christians should do, but they should do something even to the point of breaking existing laws if need be. This was the only way a culture of murder (of children) legalized by the government could be changed.

At the time, this was a highly radical and questionable position for a conservative, evangelical Presbyterian pastor to take. What it did was give evangelicals and Catholics a popular theology of civil disobedience. Whether this was his specific purpose I don't know, but it had the long-term effect anyway.[348] Before Schaeffer, the American Church was viewed as passive and silently compliant to government on such issues. With Schaeffer providing the theological and ideological underpinnings, others could come along and show the way. One in particular was Randall Terry.

---

347 *American Militias*, p.94.
348 At an author dinner during a Christian Booksellers Association event, I had the opportunity to sit next to Edith Schaeffer, his wife. I asked her if she thought it was her husband's intent to give the evangelicals a "Theology of Civil Disobedience" which led to the abortion protest movement. She really couldn't say or didn't want to.

Randall Terry

Randall has been the most visible face in the aggressive pro-life movement. In1984 he founded Operation Rescue, as a direct-action anti-abortion rescue movement where civil disobedience methods of blocking entry to clinics would be used to "prevent the ungodly slaughter of innocent lives." Like Francis Schaeffer, Randall considered "child-killing the flash point in a broader cultural civil war . . . and the ultimate goal of the rescue movement as rescuing our society from the path of destruction it's on and effecting a reformation that will cause America to better reflect Judeo-Christian ethics."

A high school dropout from upstate New York, Randall became a Christian in 1976 and attended Elim Bible Institute in Lima, New York. He joined a Charismatic congregation and through his pastor was introduced to the writings of Francis Schaeffer. Terry considered Schaeffer "the greatest Christian modern philosopher," and considered *The Christian Manifesto* the charter document for his Operation Rescue, though Terry used the *Manifesto* illegitimately and out of context. After graduating from Bible school, Terry took a job in Binghamton, NY and started picketing local abortion clinics. Being willing to be arrested for the cause, especially after the passage of the Freedom of Access to Clinic Entrances Law, by 1990 Operation Rescue had mounted blockades at 683 sites, resulting in the jailing of approximately 41,000 people.

In 1990, Randall closed Operation Rescue and moved his financial operations underground in an attempt thwart government intervention. He started the Christian Defense Coalition where he sought "to teach Christian communities to defend themselves against police brutality, judicial tyranny and political harassment." This new organization was in response to the US Attorney's office in New York seizing the organization's bank accounts and levying a $50,000 judgment against Terry with another $100,000 fine for contempt. For refusing a judge's order to stay away from an abortion clinic by at least one hundred feet, Randall was sentenced to six months in jail. In total, Randall has been arrested more than forty times, most recently when President Obama spoke at the University of Notre Dame commencement in violation of the no-trespass order. Randall has unsuccessfully run for several political offices. In 1998, he ran for a New York US House of Representative seat, a run endorsed by Focus on the Family head, James Dobson. In 2006, he ran for a Florida State Senate seat but lost in the primary.

In 2003, he founded the Society for Truth and Justice and conducted programs called Operation Witness. After a divorce from his wife of nineteen years in 2000, he remarried and joined the Catholic Church in 2006. Questioned by many of his supporters, he disavowed his first marriage as an invalid sacrament.[349]

One can easily see how both the evangelical and Catholic communities, while also receiving praise by the most hard line militia, can view Randall as a hero. What they share is an increasing contempt for the federal government, its abuse of citizens and its own failure to create moral laws that protect children. To Randall, the "anti-abortion struggle is the fiercest battle in a war of ideologies and allegiances that must be waged on many fronts against those who are in the process of stamping out virtually every vestige of Christianity from our laws, morals, institutions and ultimately our families."[350]

What Randall represents is a sincere evangelical who has embraced a civil disobedience philosophy justified by the reasoning when a government has passed immoral laws its citizens are duty bound before God to stand against them. Religious people of several faith groups probably agree with this view. Even American father of the Declaration of Independence, Thomas Jefferson, would also adhere to the position. But so would those of patriot militia ideology who might not even care about the life of the unborn or even Jesus Christ. It is no wonder persons like Eric Rudolph, Rev Paul Hill, Michael Griffin and now Scott Roeder, who recently killed abortion provider George Tiller, have taken to the philosophy and action of bombing of abortion centers and murdering abortion doctors.[351]

To these and several others, their actions are not terrorist attacks but "justifiable homicide" in order to save lives. Scott Roeder pleaded guilty to killing the abortion doctor saying, "There was nothing being done and the legal process had been exhausted and these babies were dying every day. I did what I thought was needed to be done to protect the children." Randall Terry told reporters at his trial, it is "a railroad, a kangaroo court . . . had the prosecutors done a better job in prosecuting Tiller (the abortion doctor) he would be alive today."[352]

---

349 En.wikipedia.org/wiki/Randall Terry.
350 Taken from the 1994 Edition, *Current Biography Yearbook*, pp. 589-593.
351 Michael Griffin shot and killed Dr. Gunn, an abortion physician, in Pensacola, Florida March 10, 1993. For some in the Pro-life movement, like Rev. Paul Hill, it was considered a "justifiable homicide."
352 "Roeder: No regrets after Shooting Doctor," CNN Justice online, January 28, 2010.

As mentioned previously, one does not have to listen to radio or TV preachers very long until themes are expounded from the Bible of "black helicopters, UN troops on American soil, a conspiracy of elites leading to a One World Government, with persecution of Christians. For a person like myself who takes Biblical prophecy seriously without overly speculating about spurious details, what concerns me is how on the one hand prophetic teachers rightly state "no one can know the time of Christ's second coming" and then tell viewers when the event is "likely" to happen. One in particular, Jack Van Impe once "implied" the date of 1988 for the rapture of the Church (when true believers will be snatched from the earth to be present with the Lord). Later, he claimed the Tribulation would then begin in 1996. He then changed the "likely" time to 1992 for the Rapture with 1999 for the Great Tribulation. Next, the year 2000 was "likely" to be the termination of human history, as we know it. In a more recent video, 2001: Countdown to Eternity, he prepared the viewer for the end of the age, suggesting the millennial kingdom of Christ will be begin shortly after the year 2000.[353] Therefore, as he closes many of his programs, "The Lord is near" and as it says on his website, "Don't Miss it for the World" (www.jvim.com).

Is there any harm to teaching such ideas? Sure, some Christians may be so motivated by this teaching they sell homes, buy gold, move to the Northwest, and await the Lord's return. But there have always been groups of people who have done such things. What is disturbing is how close these teachings are to the standard Patriot/Identity doctrines. The only thing left out is the racial anti-Semitism so characteristic of patriot thinking. Unless one clarifies a belief in a coming One World Government is not a code word for ZOG (Zionist Occupational Government), then those who don't know the difference will think they are one and the same. When terms like *International* or *European Bankers* are used as the secret cabal desiring to take over America, obviously these get interpreted by some Christians and Jews as code words for a Jewish conspiracy. In this sense, most members in patriot Identity movements could offer a hearty "Amen" to the words. Morris Dees comments about one of Pat Robertson's on-air "700 Club" remarks: "they would make Louis Beam, Pete Peters, or William Pierce (author of *Turner*

---

353 The tracing of Van Impe's timetable changes are documented in Richard Abanes' book, *Defending the Faith*, Baker Book Group, 1998, pp. 189-191, where he calls teachers like Hal Lindsey and Van Impe "America's False Prophets."

Diaries) proud."[354] Stern says, "In the aftermath of the Oklahoma City bombing, an installment of Robertson's 700 Club, while condemning the carnage, virtually endorsed militia ideology." This should give us all some concern![355]

Coughlin observes, "Militia leaders have referred to Pat Robertson's book, *The New World Order,* as proof their conspiracy beliefs are true, and they may need to use violence in resisting the federal government."[356] Robertson's book functions like a formal benediction upon the militia movement. One former conspiracy buff said, "Pat Robertson's view of the New World Order was a huge influence on him. I placed all of my belief into what he was saying. How could he be wrong?"[357]

Conclusion

What these two chapters tried to demonstrate is here in America we may be breeding a unique brand of citizen who in some way justifies a kind of war in the name of God. Linked to this ideology, I believe, is a faulty understanding of the scriptures to affirm it. There exists a growing mindset among both the political and religious right that our country is in decline and being taken over by ungodly forces. All this may be true, but is the answer to take arms either defensively or offensively? Many in the patriot movement have already answered the question. Blowing up a federal building, killing abortion doctors, harassing and killing a racially mixed couple, with many attacks on local law enforcement are actions viewed by many in these movements as acts of extreme patriotism and godly defense. Fear often goes looking for justification for its actions. My concern is that evangelicals and other religious people do not go the way of what is happening in some circles in Europe. On July 22, 2011, an explosion ripped through the streets of Olso, Norway. A bomb planted in a van parked between the Prime Minister's office and the Energy Department damaged the buildings. It was a homemade ammonium nitrate bomb. The bomber was not Islamic but a member of a small little known group "Justiciar Knights," sometimes also known as Knights Templar. Following the bombing, Anders Breivik traveled to the island of Utoya where a youth camp was located belonging to Norway's ruling party. Armed in tactical gear he opened fire with a Mini-14 rifle and 9mm handgun. He killed 68 children and young

---

354 Morris Dees, *Gathering Storm*, p.116.
355 Stern, *Force Upon the Plain*, p.142.
356 *Secrets, Plots & Hidden Agendas*, p. 154.
357 Ibid., p. 142.

adults and wounded another 60. Breivik posted his own manifesto on the Internet expressing his anti-Marxist and anti-Muslim views. Stratfor reports, "he believed the Labor party was Marxist and responsible for the multi-culturalism allowing intolerant Muslim emigrants coming to Europe who did not want to be part of a tolerant liberal society."[358] Though not what I would call a religious terrorist, he was profoundly white supremacist, so committed to his ideology he used his trial to promote his beliefs.

Most who carry out acts like these are probably not crazed or drug-induced. These are the simple sound-bite explanations many grab in the absence of other understandings. Neither do certain violent ideas just pop into one's minds out of the blue. The perpetrators of these acts have been educated, inspired and made fearful by a host of communicational devices authored by serious theologies and ideologues. These ideologues do not pull the triggers but they are in many ways culpable for the transmission of their ideas and associations. So far, we do not have laws against incitement like other countries (Israel), even though *hate crimes* are gaining legal authority. Even racist views are protected by the first amendment, but this does not mean speech cannot cause conditions and actions that justify violence.

It is one thing to hold various views about getting out of debt, or buying gold in preparation for an economic depression or collapse. I would probably purchase some if I could afford it! It is another thing to foster ideas of a secret society's plan to start a world war and take control of the national government.[359] Ideas are important. So are sources. It seems many in my own evangelical community either do not want to take the time to do the hard work of verifying where their ideas come from or are merely capitalizing on the popularity of certain ideas for fame and fortune. Neither of these engenders academic virtue or trustworthy motivation.

---

358 Scott Stewart, "Norway: Lessons from a Successful Lone Wolf Attacker," July 28, 2011, Stratfor Global Intelligence.

359 Larry Burkett, *The Illuminati*, Thomas Nelson Publisher, 1991. In his acknowledgements, he writes, "It should not be assumed that this is prophetic in any regard. As best I know I have a gift for teaching, a talent for writing, and no prophetic abilities beyond that of any other Christian." To Burkett's caveat, I respond, from where does the concept of an Illuminati come, and why do so many popularizing prophetic speakers and Christian Identity teachers believe in an Illuminati? My answer: either they really believe it is true, or they have no idea as to the grossly Anti-Semitic nature of their assumption.

Abanes wisely cautions, "Evangelicals, fundamentalists, charismatics, and Pentecostals have allowed their frustration with liberal politics to be the key factor in determining who is a friend and who is a foe. Some conservative Christians now embrace virtually anyone who shares contempt for the liberal establishment. They take no time to discover other beliefs a person may hold."[360]

But in America today, another war is being waged. Some think it started on 9/11, but its roots are much deeper.

---

360 *American Militias*, p. 221.

CHAPTER NINE
Islamic Jihad:[361]
Holy or Unholy Warriors?

"From their point of view (the Islamists), the problem of the Islamic world went back to the Christian Crusades and the loss of the Caliphate."[362]

"As the Muslim fundamentalist sees it, the community of Islam has been led into error by foreign infidels and Muslim apostates."[363]

February 28, 1993 was a snowy day on Philadelphia's Main Line. Large flakes cascaded through most of the day slowing down the important *honey-do* list my wife left me in the morning. Brother-in-law Bill joined me in driving up

---

361 I am using the term "Islamic Jihad" in the generic sense of Islamic military warfare and not referring to the particular group by that name.
362 George Friedman, *America's Secret War*, Doubleday, 2004, p. 17.
363 Bernard Lewis, *Faith and Power: Religion and Politics in the Middle East*, Oxford Press, 2010, p.59.

and down Lancaster Avenue picking up various items for our daughter's evening wedding. Having hit several shops, we stopped for lunch at the historic Mile Post Inn. As soon as we entered we noticed a crowd gathered around a television in the bar area. The snowflakes falling outside were plainly visible coming down on the disastrous event being televised. As cameras rolled, we watched businessmen and women flowing out of the World Trade Center building. Some were escorted on stretchers, others walked around dazed, a man walked out bleeding from the head sans shirt. Many uttered, "What happened?"

Though the wedding went off without a hitch, my niece and her husband who worked in Manhattan arrived after the wedding was over. The Holland Tunnel had been closed for security reasons causing a nightmare in rerouting the Friday afternoon traffic. Reports circulated quickly that not only a bomb had exploded underneath the World Trade Center, but a second bomb had been placed in the Holland Tunnel. Though the World Trade Center explosion was not as destructive as some thought it could have been, the reality of Islamic terrorism on American soil alerted Americans and security officials to a new disturbing threat. What happened was an intentional attack upon the United States populace by an Islamic terrorist cell. The mastermind and spiritual director for the attack was a Muslim cleric! Little did we know at the time, this event was just a precursor to seeing the entire World Trade Center collapse.

At a military chaplain's conference, a few of us went out for dinner. At a table of eight I sat next to an active duty Air Force chaplain. Over the course of dinner our conversations ranged from ministry and family issues to various military deployments we had been on. As my friend detailed his assignments, I realized he had been in Saudi Arabia during the time of the Khobar Towers terrorist attack. I asked, "Were you near the Dhahran building when the explosion took place?" He attempted an answer: "I was right across the street and one of the first on the scene." That's all he got out. Before a lively group of men enjoying dinner, the Chaplain lowered his head and burst into tears. The two of us moved outside the restaurant and walked around the block several times. I listened as he detailed his experience of that tragic event. He had not spoken to anyone about what he had seen, done or felt. Afterward, my friend returned to his room, while I went back to the restaurant. A ranking officer commented as I sat down, "I didn't even know he was there!"

Such are the impacts and ripple effects of this new age of Islamic terrorism.[364] The officer manning NORAD's North East Air Defense Sector on that fateful 9/11 Tuesday blurted out "This is a new kind of war."[365] A different kind of war indeed, but unfortunately not the kind that captures our attention for very long. This officer was one of the first to call it what it was . . . war! Unfortunately, there are still many who refuse to call it such. Most of the previous paragraphs in this chapter were written in early 2001. Little did I know as I wrote what was being carefully planned by individuals living right under our noses. September 11, 2001, is now a new *day of infamy*, a day that will be etched in the minds of all who were old enough to watch the video of airplanes crashing into the World Trade Center. It woke us up, and made us believers . . . believers that we were no longer immune from such things. No longer could we hide behind our vast oceans and military dominance, thinking such things could never happen in America. Unfortunately, now over a decade later we have returned to normal lives: only interrupted by airport scanners and an occasional *lone wolf* terrorist who we like to think will never hit our own neighborhoods, schools, or businesses.[366] Even the *lone wolf* terrorist assassin, Major Nidal Hasan, an Army Muslim psychiatrist at Ft. Hood, has become a distant memory to most even though he killed thirteen fellow soldiers and wounded another twenty-nine. He was found guilty of all charges of murder and attempted murder. A jury of military officers was unanimous in their verdict. He is now on death row awaiting execution and has requested to be made a former citizen of the newly formed Islamic State (ISIS).[367]

Some politicians want to go back to the pre-9/11 approach and see terrorism as just another type of international or federal crime. This results in attempts to try terrorists as criminals rather than unlawful combatants. Because the death toll is normally not in the hundreds or thousands, most of us return to our routines fairly quickly. Now, over a decade after 9/11, I am amazed how many have forgotten what it felt like that first week after the simultaneous attacks. Children today will

---

364 The truck bomb explosion was set off across from a USAF dormitory, killing 19 Air Force personnel, and wounding another 372.

365 Quoted in *The 9/11 Commission Report, The Authorized Edition*, W.W. Norton & Co., 2005, p. 46.

366 The phrase "lone wolf" seems to provide a strange comfort to both citizens and politicians allowing them to think there is no real conspiracy here or a large network of e-connected people whose main ambition in life is to die killing us!

367 "Ft. Hood Shooter Nidal Hasan asks to be a citizen of Islamic State," *San Antonio News*, August 29, 2014.

never know the impact the event had on their parents unless the tale is told. But for those experiencing the attack or being painfully close to it, the impact is still significant. Even after 9/11 some Americans do not consider terrorism a kind of all-out military warfare. But to those within the mindset of Islamic Jihad, their violence is just that . . . warfare . . . holy warfare! Whether we realize it or not, groups of religious terrorists have declared holy war upon us, but few still want to call this a war. Even our own US President and Department of State it seems have struggled using word *war*. It's a none-war war, or a nameless Military Operation! For some time campaign ribbons were not going to be authorized for lack of an Operational name! This was finally remedied by the DOD. Therefore, considering the resistance from the highest agency officials to call it what it is, (war) it might be wise to understand these terrorists' motivation and intent. In this chapter, I will outline where this mindset began and look at the key players and events in this global Islamic movement.

What the Islamic Revolution is All About

In the early eighties, I attended a workshop in Washington, DC, on *Sovietology*. During one of our breaks, I spoke to an individual in the coffee line next to me, and found out he worked for the CIA. He was also surprised to see a chaplain at a non-religious workshop about the Soviet threat. As we spoke, we finally got to the subject of the recent Iranian revolution that had driven the Shah out and brought Ayatollah Khomeini into power. He openly acknowledged the role religion had played in the revolution and how the CIA was very ill prepared to deal with the subject of religion. He said, "We could have gotten better intelligence from the missionaries working there!" The point was well taken. At the grass roots level, everyone knew this was a religious revival and a serious revolution against the secular, modern, Western state the Shah had created with American aid. So what is this Islamic revolution all about and what is it that these terrorists want?

I've heard the question over and over again. The question itself is revealing. It implies if we give them what they want or cut some kind of deal, they will go away and we can get back to our safe, secure lives. Maybe we could even board a plane again without taking off half our clothes, both shoes and being patted down! But to answer the question as simply as I can, what the Islamic terrorists want is to please Allah! In their minds this means a global Islamic revival resulting in a global Islamic government with a restored Caliphate. Even Syrian-American Muslim Dr. Zuhdi Jasser agrees, "Islamism . . . is a belief system that holds Islam superior to all other world religions and political systems and seeks to dominate the world. They seek to establish Sharia law as a separate legal system for Muslims in the West."[368]

In other words, the goal of this Jihadist holy war is a worldwide, complete victory for Islam. But there are subcomponents and steps to achieving this goal. First, as noted in a previous chapter, the Koran divides the world into two spheres: Dar-al-Islam and Dar-al-Harb. Dar-al-Islam is the world of Islam or the area of the world where Islam rules. The other category, Dar-al-Harb is translated *the world of warfare*. Therefore, when someone says Islam is a religion of peace, they are correct. But the peace they are talking about is where Islam rules. There is no peace where Islam does not rule. In fact, the rest of the non-Islamic world exists in a state of warfare with Islam. This is the critical foundation upon which all other teaching rests. So the concept of Jihad is rooted in the Koran's teaching about the nature of the world. To bring true peace, harmony and unity to this world, Islam must rule. Ruling means Islam is to be the basis of all personal and political conduct because in Islam there is no distinction between the two. As Americans we would like to think there is some middle ground or a political or spiritual middle of tolerance and pluralism. If and where it does exist, it exists apart from the teaching of the Koran that says there are only two categories of people . . . people who are living under the authority of Islam and those who are not. Those in the second category are Dar-al Harb . . . in a sense, military combatants! Historically, some Muslim leaders allowed for a *Dar-al-Sulh* or *world of truce*. But this was only for a period of time (to gain strategic alliances or buy time to regroup before attack) and granted by the Muslim ruler.[369] In this sense, it is but a temporary cessation of hostility to gain an advantage, and not a doctrine of true tolerance as the West understands the term.

Part and parcel with this global Islamic movement is the goal of an Islamic Palestine with Jerusalem as its capital. Obviously, there is a problem here. From the chapter on the Kach movement, we saw this is the same goal the Jewish radical right envisions. This makes for a difficult if not impossible situation where two differing peoples want the same territory with the same geographical capital.

---

368 Dr. M. Zuhdi Jasser, *A Battle for the Soul of Islam*, Simon &Shuster, Inc. 2012, p. 17.
369 Christopher Catherwood, *Making War In the Name of God*, p. 16.

It's not just about the West Bank or Gaza but the whole area traditionally called Palestine. The only thing that stands in the way of achieving an Islamic Palestinian State is the existence of the Jewish State and the United States support of Israel. These two enemies, Osama Bin Laden called the "far enemy" (United States) and the "near enemy" (Israel). If Israel cannot be defeated militarily army to army, then strike at the far enemy that provides her support and military assistance, the US. Bin Laden's second fatwa (1998) clearly was a declaration of war on both Israel and the United States. At the time, few took it seriously in the United States. I happened to be teaching Religious Terrorism at the time, and many of my fellow professors thought it was just Arab rhetoric. They thought differently after the WTC fell down!

The Islamic revolution is also about establishing the rule of Islamic law or Sharia. In other words, non-Islamic civil laws are viewed as laws of the infidel and are not compatible with Islam. In fact, the ultimate sign that a country is truly Islamic is when Sharia is universally practiced . . . think Taliban Afghanistan! Also, look at Islamic enclaves in the UK and the US where Islamic clerics and leaders rule their own communities as if civil laws of the city or state did not exist. In some cases, local police do not want to go into those communities to perform local law enforcement duties for fear of confrontation with the entire community. This amounts to a type of Islamic America inside America or, as it's called in the United Kingdom, a "Londonstan." Dr. Jasser suggests their goal is an Islamic "State within a State" where Sharia law is "sneaked" in a little at a time.[370]

This phenomenon also raises the curious question posed by Princeton professor Emeritus, Bernard Lewis. He demonstrates there was always an Islamic consensus on whether a Muslim should live under the authority of a non-Islamic government. The consensus throughout history was it was not possible for a Muslim to live a good Muslim life in an infidel land. Should he find himself in one, he should leave his home and go to a Muslim country.[371] However, Koranic law would allow a Muslim to live in the infidel's country temporarily in order to find and return a runaway slave. Later jurists added that if the infidel government was tolerant, then a Muslim could stay while recognizing the danger of apostasy was far greater in doing so.

---

370 Battle for the Soul of Islam, p. 39.
371 See Bernard Lewis, *What Went Wrong*, The Modern Library, 2003, pp. 36-37.

Those of us who have made friendships with American Muslims know why they are here. They are here for the same reasons most of us want to live in this country . . . to have a better life, freedom to make money, schools for our kids, and pursue the American dream. The problem lies in that there is no Koranic justification for this purpose. Obviously, few in this country are trying to return runaway slaves. This leaves the average modern, Western-oriented Muslim in a position of having no real reason to live here from the perspective of jurist history. Consequently the American Muslim is set up to respond to a Koranic reason to stay . . . to do or support Jihad! According to many radical Islamic clerics, to do Jihad justifies staying under non-Islamic governments for a time until an Islamic government is formed. "To do Jihad" could be as simple as supporting the cause financially, giving aid and comfort to Jihadis, or becoming an active participant in a Jihad attack. It also gives a certain justification to adopting Western dress where formerly the admonition of "do not dress like the infidels lest you become like them" was a requirement for true Muslims.[372]

Another goal of the Islamists is to restore the Islamic Caliphate, or the single leader/spokesperson of Islam. Bin Laden called for this several times in his fatwas and for many in the radical communities, the loss of the Caliphate after World War I was a greater loss than the fall of the Islamic Ottoman Empire. Besides, many Arabs generally hated the "Turks." There has not been a clear, unified voice for all of Islam under a caliph since Ataturk abolished the old Ottoman Caliphate in 1924. Obviously, both Shia and the Sunnis would like to see one of their own re-establish the Caliphate, and a more likely scenario is that either group would not accept the authority of the other. Today, this has become largely a conflict between Sunni Saudi Arabia and Shia Iran. But it is in keeping with Islamic law that a Caliphate exist and give unified leadership to the world-nation of Islam.

Much has changed. In the summer of 2014, Abu Bakr al Baghdadi declared ISIS the Islamic State of Iraq and Syria with himself as Caliph. He holds a doctorate in theology, claims descent from the prophet Mohammad, and apparently sees himself as sort of soldier-Imam.[373]

The question then becomes, "Is this declaration of a Caliphate legitimate?" Stratfor Global Intelligence observes the change of name does not change anything:

---

372 Bernard Lewis, *The Middle East*, Scribners, 1995, p. 4.
373 Gary Anderson, "Abu Bakr al-Baghdadi and the Theory and Practice of Jihad," *Small Wars Journal*, August, 12, 2014.

"No amount of new monikers will change the fact that geography, political ideology and religious, cultural and ethnic differences will prevent the emergence of a singular polity capable of ruling the greater Middle East."[374] In short, they see this radical Islamist group's declaration as just a slogan that at most would only amount to an emirate and not a large geographical caliphate. In this sense it is more a propaganda move to gain a tactical advantage. The jailed Muslim Cleric Abu Qatada from his cell in Jordan quickly denounced the legitimacy of the State declaring it "void."[375] Likewise, Al Qaeda in the Islamic Maghreb said "they could not support the caliphate in its current form."[376] From a historical perspective, the Ottoman Caliphate was never really accepted as legitimate by the Arabs because the Turks had no direct succession to the Prophet Mohammad. They merely took over the caliphate by means of expansive warfare conquering "Christian" Constantinople in 1453, resulting in gaining them a Middle East and Balkan empire. Of course, this "illegitimate caliphate" lasted almost 500 years! After World War I, General Kemal Ataturk abolished the caliphate calling it "a historical relic." It was abolished March 3, 1924. In addition, caliphate scholar Bobrick observes, "most caliphs met *assisted fate* meaning their duration was rather short lived as aided by other would-be caliphs![377]

So time will tell whether most Muslims will accept this new ISIS caliphate. If this is what the Islamic revolution is about, then one has to ask from where this ideology came. Is this type of thinking a unique invention of Al Qaeda, Hamas, Hezbollah, or other radical groups, or are they merely twenty-first century warriors with ideological roots in the past?

Key Events in Islamic History

Most Americans don't care about history. As a history professor myself, I have been appalled by the ignorance of some of my students. I once (as a joke) asked on a final test "In what country did the Treaty of Paris take place?" One student answered: England! However, in the Middle East critical historical events are sometimes more important than they are in our educational system. Bernard

---

374 "Iraq: Examining the Professed Caliphate," Statfor Global Intelligence, July 1, 2014.
375 "Jordon: Cleric Says Militants Caliphate Declaration is Void," Stratfor Global Intelligence, July 15, 2014.
376 Stratfor Global Intelligence, July 15, 2014.
377 Benson Bobrick, *The Caliph's Splendor*, p. 212.

Lewis rightly observes, "The Muslim peoples, like everyone else in the world, are shaped by their history, but unlike some others, they are keenly aware of it."[378] 1099 AD is one of those dates.

Crusaders Take Jerusalem

What happened on that date is burned into the hearts and minds of radical Jihadists. It's the date the Christian Crusaders recaptured Jerusalem during the first Crusade. Yes, the Christians slaughtered the entire city of Muslims and Jews. I make no apology for this devastation except to say, most warfare at the time involved routine slaughter of combatants and noncombatants. There was no Geneva Convention then! Putting that aside for the moment, the importance of this event is that Islamists view it today as a forced intervention by Western Christians (called Franks or Greeks) into Muslim lands with the resultant slaughter of faithful martyrs. Notice I said, "is the view today by Islamists." Dr. Rodney Stark of Baylor University clarifies: Muslim antagonism with the West in fact did not begin with the Crusades but began with the founding of the nation of Israel in 1948.[379] Before the Crusades, Arab Muslims were very content to see the "Franks" going to war against their hated Turks. But after losing the Muslim Ottoman Empire with the founding of the modern State of Israel, the *intervention* doctrine of Western imperialism beginning with the Crusades became an increasing useful interpretation of medieval history.

A related point often missed is before the advent of Muhammad all these Middle East lands were part of the Christian Latin and Byzantine Empire. Yes, Christian! The Balkans, what is now Turkey, all of Palestine, Northern Arabia, North Africa including Egypt and Ethiopia were all part of the old Roman Byzantine Empire under the "Christian" authority of the Eastern Orthodox Church. But in Muslim theology a doctrine exists of "once Muslim, always Muslim."[380] When the train system in Madrid was blown up a couple of years ago, someone asked me "why did the terrorists to do this in Spain?" Answer: Because of this doctrine! Islam ruled Spain for almost three hundred years and to radical Islamists, it is still theirs!

---

378 Bernard Lewis, *The Crisis of Islam,* HarperOne, 2009, p. xix.
379 Rodney Stark, *God's Battalions*, p. 9.
380 Ibid., p. 16

Defeat of the Crusaders

One of the most exalted warriors of Islam is Saladin the Great. This Muslim Kurd defeated the Crusaders in 1187, killing most of the Knights Templar at the horns of Hittim near Galilee and then marching his army to Jerusalem putting it in siege until it surrendered. The movie "Kingdom of Heaven" celebrates his victory portraying Saladin as merciful to the Crusaders allowing them to vacate the city without being slaughtered. This of course, is true, but Saladin was anything but merciful throughout most of his career, and offering terms of surrender were common at the time. At the *horns of Hittim* Saladin ordered "I will purify the earth of these two impure races," speaking of the two orders of Templars and Hospitallers." Most were decapitated in a systematic manner while the remaining captives awaited their turn.[381] When Saladin finally took Jerusalem his "mercy" was extended to those remaining for a payment of 30,000 gold coins (dinars).[382]

Ibn Taymyya and the Sixth Pillar of Islam

Another important name to remember in this historical review is the name Sheik Ibn Taymyya (Sometimes spelled Taimia). This Islamic cleric emerges around 1269 and makes the claim Jihad should be the sixth pillar of Islam. Until his time, the five pillars of Islam had become institutionalized as the basic requirements for all Islamic faithful. However, with Taymyya, Jihad is argued as an equal, additional duty upon every believer. Though not mainstream at the time, his belief became critical to the formation of the belief system of Wahhabic Arabia and later Osama bin Laden. In the Al Qaeda Training Manual, Taymyya is quoted as saying, "the rest of what he (God) obligated us would not be accomplished except by force and lordship, be it Jihad, justice, pilgrimage, assembly, holidays, support of the oppressed or the establishment of boundaries."[383] This basically puts Jihad in the same category as the five pillars of pilgrimage, alms giving, prayer, fasting, and the confession. An editor's note in the Al Qaeda Manual follows saying "The manual regularly cites the writings of Sheikh Ibn Tamai as justification on the author's (probably Ayman al-Zawahiri, Deputy to Bin Laden) ideological formulations. So, modern Jihadists are significantly influenced by this thirteenth-century cleric!

---

381 Edward Burman, *The Templars: Knights of God,* Destiny Books, 1986, p. 107.
382 Ibid., p. 108.
383 *The Al-Qaeda Training Manual: Military Studies in the Jihad Against the Tyrants,* Jerrold M. Post, Editor, USAF Counterproliferation Center, Maxwell AFB, AL, 2004, p.21.

Golden Age of Islam

Some believe the Golden Age of Islam begins with the defeat of the Crusaders beginning in 1183 with the final fall of Christian Jerusalem in 1187. Roughly dated this would make the Golden Age run from the fall of Jerusalem to the invasion of the Levant by Napoleon in 1789. It was a time of continued Islamic expansion, consolidation, with the creation of academic centers fostering achievements in science, math, medicine, architecture, and philosophy. However, unknown to most Westerners, the Golden Age of Islam begins much earlier. The Abbasid Caliphate in Baghdad established one of the greatest centers of learning in the eighth century AD. This Caliphate extended to Persia, Mesopotamia, Arabia and North Africa. This "house of wisdom" (Bayt al-Hikma) under the Caliph al-Ma'mun collected the entire world's books under one roof and had them translated into Arabic. Al Ma'mun even sent men to Constantinople to obtain Greek texts from the Christian Emperor Leo V.[384] This radical "Translation Movement" included all previous works of astronomy, medical texts, and in particular the Greek works of Aristotle and Plato. Professor Rubenstein illumines the connection: "When Muslim invaders seized control of the Fertile Crescent and Persia in the seventh century, they asked Nestorian (Christians) to help them translate the famous books of wisdom into Arabic . . . and the learned *heretics* were quick to comply."[385] Famous scholars emerged out of this period including al-Kindi who translated Greek philosophy and introduced the Hindu decimal system into Islam.[386] Al-Khwarizmi wrote one of the first histories of science (800-850) plus a book on algebra from which we get the word *algorithm*. He is still known as the Father of Algebra. One other scholar was Hunayn ibn Ishaq (Arabic for Isaac), a never converted Nestorian Christian and expert on the Greek language. He translated all the medical works of Galen, who is often called the Father of Medical Practice. Some accounts name him as the overall director of the House of Wisdom. What made this center of learning so distinctive was the Islamic doctrine of "Mu'tazilism," where open inquiry of ideas was encouraged and Greek rationalism was fused with Islamic philosophy. Al-Khalili concludes, "It (the House of Wisdom) became the source from which sprouted all the subsequent achievements of the golden age of Arabic science, from Uzbekistan

384 Jim Al-Khalili, *The House of Wisdom*, Penguin Press, 2011, p. 71.
385 Richard Rubenstein, *Aristole's Children*, p. 78.
386 Al-Khalili, *The House of Wisdom*, p. 75.

in the East to Spain in the West."[387] Speaking of Spain, during the Umayyad Caliphate (929-1031), Cordoba, Spain, or Andalusia, rivaled the House of Wisdom as the center of Islamic learning during the height of this golden age. It was mainly from Andalusia Spain that Arabic science and learning got transmitted to Europe.[388] At one point, under the Caliph Abd al-Rahman III (929) the largest library in Europe was established with half a million books. The library located on the palace grounds in Cordoba was open to even Christian scholars from all over Europe.[389]

It was during this time the famous Ibn Rushd or Averroes integrated Christian theology with Islamic theology. Even Thomas Aquinas, the great Medieval Christian mind, thought Averroes was the master of Aristotle. The great Jewish scholar Moses Maimonides was also part of this community for a while until exiled to Egypt. Islamic scholar Ibn Sina would be heir of this scholarship and continue the Mu'tazilite movement until it would be shut down by a Muslim theologian Al-Ghazali (1058-1111). Khalili calls this event the "turning point in Islamic philosophy . . . that inflicts lasting damage to the spirit of Islamic rationalism."[390] Ghazali is called one of the most influential figures in Islamic intellectual history.[391] By the twelfth century, there was an increasing aversion to Aristotle and his concerns of natural law based upon cause and effect. To Ghazali, "God produces every effect, not nature." Rubenstein concludes about Ghazali's book, *The Incoherence of the Philosophers*, "it broke the back of rationalistic philosophy and in fact brought the career of philosophy . . . to an end in the Arabic part of the Islamic world."[392]

So from this perspective the Islamic Golden Age runs from the eighth century, peaking in the eleventh with its final collapse with the advent of Napoleon. Again, this means very little to us, but when Napoleon marched his troops into Tunisia, Egypt, and Palestine, it was viewed as Western intervention into Islamic lands. Though Napoleon did not stay very long, the memory of Western invasion, intervention, cultural re-education and modernization created shock waves to the

---

387 Ibid., p. 78. What is interesting about Professor Khalili is he is a nuclear physicist, born of a British mother and Sh'ia Muslim father. He now claims to be an atheist!

388 For an excellent full discussion of Islamic Andalusia Spain see Maria Rosa Menacal's *Ornament of the World*, Little, Brown & Company, 2002.

389 *The House of Wisdom*, p.193.

390 Ibid., p. 232.

391 Rubenstein, *Aristotle's Children*, p. 85.

392 Ibid., p. 85.

Islamic Ottoman Empire. Worse, it put Muslims in a position of being led astray, even possibly converting to Christianity. In the Islamic worldview, it is a sin for Europeans to conquer and rule, but to convert to Christianity for a Muslim is apostasy, a capital offense with the penalty of death.[393] Napoleon's intervention was viewed as Western infidels stealing the land of Islam and forcing Western ideals, religion, culture and customs upon them. A kind of society they did not want!

The Wahhabi Alliance

Another key event in this historical overview is the union of one brand of Islamic thought with the political and military power of one ruling sheik . . . a sheik that would become king. Muhammad ibn Abdul Wahhab (1703-1787), a theologian in Najd, Arabia, chose to dedicate his life to the study of the Koran, interpreting it the most literal way he could. He had been trained in the Hanibali School of Sunni Islam, and the branch of Salafists' interpretation of the Koran; the most radical right wing of the Hanibali school. As such, the Salafists based their authority on only the first three generations of the prophet. This meant a very literal interpretation of the prophets' teaching and tradition. Wahhab wanted to return Islam to its more pure and authentic form and in so doing purge Islam of all corruption, superstitions and false beliefs. Working as a village judge he used his position to destroy shrines and tombs to which pilgrimages where made. Finding a woman caught in adultery, he had her stoned in accordance with Sharia law.[394] Though this act disturbed the local elders, Sheik Wahhab found a protector in a recent convert, Muhammad ibn Sa'ud, the emir of Dar'iyya in the Najd. According to some sources, al-Wahhab instructed his converts in both his interpretation of Islam and the use of firearms. Thus, a great alliance was formed in 1744 between the house of al Saud and the Islam of al Wahhab. The Sheik fundamentally reformed the Islam of Arabia by banning smoking, dancing, music and anything that might distract from true obedience to the Allah. This change makes a radical departure from the previous Golden Age of Islam where in the bustling city of Baghdad existed many cabarets, taverns, game rooms, shadow theatre productions, concerts, and other kinds of entertainment. Christians and Jews were allowed to make and dispense liquor serving the Muslims of the city against the traditional ban on alcohol![395] Though Christianity still

393 Bernard Lewis, *The Crisis In Islam*, p. 55.
394 Recorded in Robert Lacy's *The Kingdom: Arabia and the House of Sa'ud*, p. 56.
395 See Benson Bobrick, *The Caliph's Splendor*, Simon & Schuster, 2012, pp. 71-72.

existed in Arabia, Christians were prohibited from holding services, alcohol was eventually banned and today the not-so-friendly persuasion of the Committees for the Propagation of Virtue and the Prevention of Vice patrol the streets, with canes in hand to swat offenders.[396] All this goes back to al-Wahhab and the alliance made with Ibn Saud in 1744. Bernard Lewis observes, "by the middle of the eighteenth century, these new warriors of the faith, led by military skill of Ibn Saud and inspired by the religious teachings of Ibn Abd al-Wahhab, conquered much of Arabia, and in time threatened the borderlands with Syria and Iraq."[397] Lewis goes on to note, this full Wahhabi doctrine and its religious revivalism influenced many Muslim countries and imbued them with a new militancy in their struggle against European invaders."[398]

Of course, the rest of the story is that the descendants of Ibn Saud conquered all the territory from the Red Sea to the Persian Gulf, and from Yemen to the deserts of Syria. When Abdul Aziz "recaptured" Riyadh in 1902, he inherited the proud Saudi/Wahhabi banner that took by force Mecca and Medina a century earlier. By 1932, Ibn Saud had unified the Hajiz, the Najd, and other Arabian regions, creating the Kingdom of Saudi Arabia, with him as King. From then on, Sa'udi Arabia would be the source of a virulent form of Islam . . . one that would produce the world's strictest interpretation of Islam and the world's most wanted terrorist!

Western Creation of the Modern Middle East

Another of the street-level complaints leveled against the Western powers concerns what happened in the aftermath of World War I. Even before the last bullet was fired creating our modern Armistice Day (November 11, 1918), the great powers of Russia, Britain, Italy, and France created a plan to carve up the Middle East when they were victorious. This plan, viewed by Arabs as a conspiracy, consisted of creating out of the fallen Ottoman Empire (Muslim) a four way territorial expansion for the victors. Northern Turkey would go to Russia, Southern Turkey to Italy, what is modern Syria and Lebanon to France, and everything else in the Middle East to Britain except Arabia, which would remain independent. Of course, the territory under British control would be what is now Iraq, Jordan and

---

396 Lacy, *The Kingdom*, p. 59.
397 Bernard Lewis, *The Middle East*, p. 333.
398 Ibid., p. 310.

Palestine.[399] In 1917, the Russian revolution took the Czar and his army out of the war so they never got their spoil, and Italy lost its bid for Turkey due to the Turkish revolution following the war. So that left Britain and France to share the remaining territories. The French/British details of the plan were worked out in February of 1916 between Sir Mark Sykes of England and French diplomat Georges Picot. The Sykes/Picot agreement was viewed by Arabs who supported the Allies in the war effort (remember Lawrence of Arabia) as betrayal. The promises made to Sharif Husain to make him "King of Arabia" ended in him the gaining the second-class territory of "Transjordan," or the territory across to the east of the Jordan River. Scholar Robert Lacy records, "The Sykes-Picot agreement delivered the most developed and educated areas of the Middle-East . . . into the hands of the colonial powers and sowed there hatred and mistrust of Western *friendship* that sour the area to this day."[400] Even this Transjordan area had to be specifically created by the British to appease Husain's son, Abdullah.

Little known to the Arabs who fought alongside the British and French against the Ottomans was the fact that another deal had been made in England promising territory to the Jews. In November of 1917, Lord Balfour, the British Foreign Minister, sent a letter to Lord Rothschild, President of the British Zionism Federation, that "His Majesty's Government views with favour the establishment in Palestine of a national home for the Jewish people." The declaration goes on to say, "Nothing shall be done which may prejudice the civil and religious rights of existing non-Jewish communities in Palestine," (Meaning Arabs). By the end of the war the Jewish community in Palestine was fairly sizeable, so the terms of the Balfour Declaration were worked into the League of Nations Mandate that allowed Britain to administer all of the area called Palestine.[401] In other words, the Jews were promised a homeland somewhere in this undefined territory (at the time) called Palestine, while at the same time, Major T. E. Lawrence under the authority of the British government was promising land, independence and recognized kingship to the supportive Arab leaders. Even Lawrence himself, years later admitted, "The promises to the Arabs were dead paper."[402] It is no wonder why this part of the Middle East is called the "Promised Land"!

399 Lacy, *The Kingdom*, p. 134.
400 Ibid., p.136.
401 Lewis, *The Middle East*, p. 348.
402 Quoted in *The Kingdom*, p. 134.

Consequently, to appease both groups the British in 1922 effectively separated Transjordan from the rest of the Palestine mandate creating an emirate or special territory for Abdullah, which would be enlarged after the British pulled out completely. When Israel declared its independence, war broke out between the Israel and the Arab nations and in the aftermath, Transjordan took over the West Bank area formerly controlled by the British. Abdullah then named his territory, "The Hashemite Kingdom of Jordan."[403] Another King Abdullah, son of King Hussein, now rules it.

The Great Powers were all-supportive of Zionism at the time and apparently were not all that concerned about the feelings of the Arab inhabitants. One House of Lords member said, "We do not want a United Arabia but a weak disunited Arabia, split into little principalities as far as possible under our suzerainty but incapable of coordinated action against us."[404] These tactics were also driven by British and French ambitions for carving up access to Middle East oil deposits.[405] Most Americans know nothing of this history and therefore are caught off guard when they listen to the street anger of the Muslim Middle East. It is part ideological, part religious, and part historical based upon this radical Western interventionism. Also, take note America had nothing to do with these secret agreements because at the time, the US still had plenty of its own oil. Though there was a large Zionist movement in the United States, most of the wheeling and dealing was taking place between the French and the British over the future of the Middle East.

Israel Becomes a State

Today many believe the entire Middle East crisis is the fault of the Western support of and the establishment of the modern state of Israel. Certainly, as seen above, the West favored its establishment over against the wishes of the Arabs. However, by now it can be seen that "Arab rage" has deeper and longer roots than just 1919, 1948 or 2011 when the Arab Spring began. In sum, the creation of the Jewish state in the heart of the Islamic Middle East can be viewed as the last straw in its dealing with the West. At the conclusion of World War II, where most of the Arab nations

---

403 See Dore Gold, *Hatred's Kingdom*, Regenery Publishing Co., 2003, for more details of the events, pp. 52-44.

404 Lacy, *The Kingdom*, p. 137.

405 See Edwin Black's detailed and well researched account into the West's secret pact to get Mideast oil: British Petroleum and the Redline Agreement, Dialogue Press, 2011.

had supported the Germans, world opinion held sympathy for the plight of the Jews during the Nazi regime. The horrors of Hitler's ovens gave momentum to both world opinion and desire among Jews for their own independence.

On April 2, 1947, the British government decided it had had enough of trying to administer the conflicts with both the Arabs and the Jews seeking independence. The government announced it would return the Palestinian Mandate under the defunct League of Nations to the United Nations. The date of termination would be May 15, 1948.

At the same time, the newly formed United Nations looked for a permanent solution to the "Jewish problem" of displaced Jewish survivors of the Holocaust. UN Resolution 181 in November 1947 then came up with the original "Two State Solution" to the Middle East. Member states voted to partition Palestine into two states, one Jewish and one Arab, with Jerusalem under international administration. The resolution failed with the Jewish representation voting for it, and the Arabs rejecting it.[406] Fighting then broke out between the two sides, and on May 14, 1948, the Zionist movement within Palestine declared the State of Israel. Several Arab armies invaded the land, but were defeated. Patrick Seale writes, "The brief, catastrophic war resulted in more bitterness than decades of semi-colonial occupation."[407] This war creating independence for Israel is called by many names in Arab countries, none too pleasing. In Arabic it is "Nakba" and often called "the Great Humiliation," "Catastrophe," "Disaster," or "Tragedy."

Ironically, it is sometimes called "holocaust."[408] As I write, several Arab nations are having Nakba demonstrations against Israel and the US. To radical groups like Hamas and Hezbollah, a nation by the name of "Israel" does not exist . . . the name does not even appear on their maps. It is merely labeled "Occupied Territory." But it was in this milieu of Israel becoming a nation that another critical event took place. A young man from Egypt left to study in the United States.

Sayyid Qutb (1906-66) and the Muslim Brotherhood

Back in the 1920s, a young man named Hasan al-Banna, after pursuing a degree in higher education in Egypt, became very disillusioned with Egyptian society. What he saw was Egyptian elites being so infatuated with secularism and Western

---

406 Peter G. Riddell & Peter Cotterell, *Islam in Context: Past, Present and Future*, pp.133-134.
407 Quoted in *Islam in Context*, p. 135.
408 See "Bitter Anniversary" in *The Jerusalem Report*, May 24, 2010, p. 16.

society that they had virtually left or betrayed their Islamic roots. To al-Banna, Western society was nothing but depraved with unbridled greed. Aslan observes about al-Banna, "Cairo had become a virtual apartheid state where small pockets of wealthy Europeans and Westernized Egyptians ruled over millions of impoverished peasants who labored and cared for their estates."[409] Al-Banna rejected the then common ideology of pan-Arabism and began preaching his vision for Egypt as a truly Islamic state in cafes, restaurants and to whomever would listen to him. His message was simple: "the problem is the West; Islam is the answer." In this regard, all Muslims are brothers, hence a Muslim brotherhood. As a community of Muslim brothers, his followers addressed the controversial issues of Zionism, Christian missionary activity and corrupt Arab monarchies. In 1949, al-Banna was assassinated, but this act only strengthened the resolve of his followers. Finally, in 1953, President Nasser outlawed the Muslim Brotherhood, and had most either executed or imprisoned with beatings and torture. It was during this time (1949), Sayyid Qutb as a member of Nasser's Ministry of Education traveled to the United States to do research at Colorado State Teachers College, now University of Northern Colorado. What Qutb says he found on the campus in Greeley, CO was what he called raw secularism, materialism, and drunken sexual debauchery.[410] His conclusion? This is not a society any sincere Muslim should aspire to live in. Qutb denounced American jazz, its support of Israel becoming a nation and in particular the "lustful ways of the American female." He stated, "The American girl is well acquainted with her body's seductive capacity . . . she knows seductiveness lies in the round breasts, the full buttocks and in the shapely thighs, sleek legs, and she shows all this and does not hide it." He added, "Even an innocent dance in a church basement is proof of animalistic American society."[411] What is interesting is Greeley, Colorado at the time was probably one of the most conservative, religious and peaceful communities in the 1950s.

In fact, alcohol was illegal and founders of Greeley were by all reports temperate, religious and peaceful. Poet/Journalist Sara Lippincott said of Greeley at the time, "You'll die of dullness in less than five hours . . . there is not a billiard or saloon in

---

409 Reza Aslan, *No god but God*, Stanford Univ. Press, 2006, p. 235.

410 Imagine for a moment what Qutb would have thought about our campuses today. This was "Father Knows Best" 1950s society, a society many Christian conservatives would like to get back to!

411 Quoted in "Sayyid Qutb's America," Robert Siegel, National Public Radio, www.nrp.org/ templates/story, 1253796.

the whole camp, nor a drink of whiskey to be had for love or money."[412] However, what Qutb saw was where he thought his own country was headed without an Islamic revival and revolution. When Qutb returned to Egypt he joined the Muslim Brotherhood and became active in the propaganda department. Though Nasser asked him to rejoin his government, Qutb refused and after an attempt on Nasser's life was arrested along with many other brothers, was tortured and left to die in prison. At this time, he put his thoughts and experiences into writing, penning *The America I Have Seen*, and *Milestones*. While in prison he came to the conclusion that preaching was not enough. He concluded in *Milestones*, "Those who have usurped the authority of Allah and are oppressing Allah's creatures are not going to give up their power merely thorough preaching."[413] From this position, he endorsed the use of violence to overthrow corrupt governments in order to create a true Islamic state. His radicalized vision completely transformed both the Arab street and some political elites. For this reason, it is said of him, "Sayyid Qutb is arguably the most important voice in the radical Islamism of the twentieth century."[414] Believing all secular governments (including Nasser's) should be replaced by force if necessary, Qutb becomes the ideological basis for many later Islamists, including Al Qaeda. Jasser's reading of Qutb convinced him "Qutb genuinely believed the West was out to undermine Islam and sought its destruction."[415]

Qutb was finally hanged in 1966 for treason, but his ideas were deeply planted in the remaining members of the Muslim Brotherhood who fled Egypt and found refuge in Saudi Arabia. Siegel reports "Qutb's writings would later become the theoretical basis for many radical Islamic groups . . . including al Qaeda."[416] Karen Armstrong goes further saying, "Every Sunni fundamentalist movement has been influenced by Qutb."[417] Here, the radical ideology and activism of Sayyid Qutb found a profound comfort and compatibility with their Wahhabic bedfellows![418]

412 "Sayyid Qutb's America," Siegel.
413 Quoted in David von Drehle, "A Lesson in Hate," *Smithsonian*, February 2006, p. 99.
414 Aslan, *No god but God*, p. 239.
415 Riddell &Cotterell, p. 116.
416 "Sayyid Qutb's America," Siegel.
417 Karen Armstrong, *Islam: A Short History*, Phoenix Press, 2005, p. 145.
418 A summary of Qutb's ideology is offered here by the author. I call it the Gospel According to Qutb: 1. Democracy is where the people are sovereign; Islam is where God is sovereign. 2. Democracy is where values are arbitrated by the financial market; Islam is where Allah is the determiner of all value. 3. Democracy values liberty as the right to determine one's destiny; In Islam, Allah determines one's destiny. 4. Democracy in the West is based on freedom that corrupts; Islam is based on virtue based on the Koran.

Two years later, the humiliation that began in 1948 would explode in a six-day war with Israel only reinforcing the "corruption" of Arab leaders, and the Islamic hatred toward the Jewish state.

Six Day War and Loss of Jerusalem

If the Arab nations consider Israel's independence a nakba, or tragedy, no term can describe what resulted in Israel's early dawn pre-emptive strike against Arab forces on Monday, June 5, 1967. On top of significant loss of life, military hardware and territory, the Arab nations lost control of the Holy city of Jerusalem. This event could be called a double nakba. The countdown begins in 1964 when at the Arab Summit Conference in Cairo, the heads of state decided to divert the waters of the Jordan River and create the Palestinian Liberation Organization (PLO). As Chaim Herzog notes "Jordan was in control of the West Bank (of the Jordan River), and Egypt was in control of Gaza, had they desired they could have established a Palestinian state in these areas."[419] Work on diverting the Jordan took place in both Lebanon and Syria combined with assault teams launching missions into Israel from both Syria and Jordan. In November of 1966, Israel began reprisal raids against these attacks. The Syrians then put pressure on Egypt to attack Israel from the South, while asking for military support from the Russians.

On May 22, President Nasser of Egypt closed the Straits of Tiran to Israeli shipping while also announcing his intent to destroy Israel.[420] Soon 250,000 Arab troops, 2,000 tanks and 700 fighter-bomber aircraft surrounded Israel. The Arab armies were mobilized and moved into positions to attack Israel. On June 5, 1967, Israel launched a pre-emptive attack, first attacking the Egyptian air bases and destroying aircraft before they could get off the ground. By the end of the day, Syrian and Jordanian aircraft were likewise destroyed on the ground or shot down in the air. The IDF ruled the skies and then moved their army against the Arab land forces.

Though not a major military objective, taking the Old City of Jerusalem held special significance for both the Arab nations and Israel. Israel had cut off the communication lines between Jordan and Jerusalem and encircled the city. On June 5-6, the historic battle for the centerpiece of the three monotheistic religions

---

419 Chaim Herzog, *The Arab-Israeli Wars,* Vintage Books/Random House, 2004, p. 147.
420 Ibid., p. 149.

began. By June 7, King Hussein of Jordan had lost half of his kingdom, his army had been pushed back across the Jordan River, and the West Bank of the Jordan River was then under the control of the IDF. The entire Jordan valley including Jerusalem was now in Jewish hands. The Jews wept for joy at the Wailing Wall after centuries of being denied access, while the Arabs wept in disgrace for what was lost.

In response to this loss, the next Arab Summit in Khartoun (September 1, 1967) passed their now famous "three noes" resolution: "No negotiations with Israel, no recognition of Israel, no peace with Israel."[421] The double nakba symbolized a massive failure and decline within the Muslim world of the Middle East, but this perception was about to end. The Arab summit signaled a hard line posture toward the West, and set in motion a series of events that would be viewed as Allah's sweet revenge!

---

421 Ibid., p. 191.

CHAPTER TEN
Allah's Sweet Revenge: Black Gold in the Ground

"The most frightening aspect of this new threat, however, was the fact that almost no one took it seriously. It was too bizarre, too primitive and exotic."[422]

"The Saudi committee responsible for transferring the donations to beneficiaries has been sending large amounts to radical committees and associations among which is the Islamic Society which belongs to Hamas."[423]

—**Abu Mazen**, delegate of the Palestinian National Authority to His Royal Highness Emir Salman bin Adbul Aziz, Saudia Arabia.

---

422 Lawrence Wright, *The Looming Tower: Al Qaeda and the Road to 9/11*, Vintage Books, 2006, p. 7.
423 Dore Gold, *Hatred's Kingdom*, Regenery Publishing, 2003, p. 245. Letters supporting Saudi financing of terrorist groups: the evidence. Salman bin Adbul Aziz Now king of Saudi Arabia.

U pon the invitation of Arabian king Abdul Aziz, an American by the name of Karl Twitchell arrived in the Arabian Desert community seeking the lost gold mines of King Solomon. He was also attempting to find new sources for water in the desert. The year was 1931. The British delegation stationed in Jeddah thought the enthusiastic geologist an interesting amusement and no more than a busybody.[424] Earlier in 1904, a British government surveyor had attached "no special significance" to the "bitumen" oozing from the ground near the hill of Burqan in Eastern Arabia. Irony of ironies, Standard Oil of New Jersey supplied once a year a kerosene shipment to burn in British stoves and lamps in Arabia! By 1932, with the successful find of Arab-D crude by the amusing geologist searching for Solomon's gold, everything changed. Twitchell was no longer an amusement, and the sticky stuff that oozed from the ground would remake the desert Bedouin nation into an international power broker.

Era of Petro Politics Begins: Allah's Good Gift in the Sand

On October 20, 1973, King Faisal of Saudi Arabia declared *Jihad* on Israel and on all the countries who supported her.[425] The result was an oil embargo on the United States creating the modern petro politics of using oil as a weapon. During the 1960s (when I was first driving), Western countries paid around $2 for a barrel of oil. After the oil embargo of 1973, prices shot up to $32 a barrel, a rise of 1500 percent. When I first wrote this piece it was over $100 a barrel. However, the summer of 2014 saw oil drop to around $50 a barrel. A nice vacation price! It doesn't take a genius to see how the petro power of the Saudis put most of the developed world literally over a barrel . . . theirs! Even American oil companies were alarmed, telling President Nixon American support for Israel would incite a reaction by the Arab oil producers creating serious oil shortages.[426] By itself, the inflation of crude prices might be negotiable as traded on the world commodities market, but since 1973, oil had become Allah's good gift for financing terrorism against the West. Almost every new conflict or threat of conflict in the Middle East changes the price of oil and gas at the pump. Early in 1973, my wife and two young children were in graduate school trying to eke out a living and make it through school. We had as our only form of transportation an un-air-conditioned standard

---

424 Robert Lacey, *The Kingdom: Arabia & the House of Sa'ud*, p. 231.
425 Robert Lacy, p. 9.
426 Raymound J. Learsy, *Over a Barrel*, Nelson Current, 2005, p. 96.

shift Ford Maverick, complete with crank windows. I still remember we were able to fill our gas tank for five dollars, and that usually lasted a month!

It was a lot of money at that time, but that changed drastically in October of 1973. On our black and white television we watched the events of the Yom Kippur war unfold in the Middle East. Being more consumed with fulfilling academic assignments, getting to class every day and making our schedules work with two children, daycare, and jobs, I did not pay much attention to the political realities about to explode. After the defeat of the Arab armies and the humiliation of losing the West Bank and Golan Heights to the Israeli army, the oil producing Arab nations gathered together and formed what we now know as OPEC (Organization of Petroleum Exporting Countries). OPEC initiated an economic boycott of the West (Europe and United States). Panic set in, and gas prices soared. My Maverick's tank full of gas went to $12-15 and we experienced long lines at gas stations. Fistfights broke out over people trying to crowd into lines before the station ran out of gas. In the words of Herzog, "From a global point of view, the 1973 war saw the first attempt by the Arab oil-producing nations to use oil as a weapon."

Though not very effective over the long term, it did send a very powerful psychological message to the West. "If you support and defend Israel against us, then you will pay at the pump!" Herzog continues, "It did have an effect of *sounding the alarm* for the free world. The volatility and instability of the Arab world, with its prodigious glut of wealth, only highlights the danger of this situation."[427] The Arab oil-producing nations now had a new weapon against the West . . . oil! The era of petro politics was birthed. Walid Phares noted, "The impact of the oil crisis in Western societies . . . showed the Achilles heel of powerful democracies: economic reliance on crude oil."[428] This newly found weapon had a certain irony to it. Of all the nations in the world, the petroleum deposits in the Middle East were almost exclusively in Muslim hands. To those of Muslim fundamentalist persuasion, they saw this reality as "Allah's good providential gift" to fight the West. Allah had placed this valuable resource in the desert sands to give the Arab nations a choke point on the Christian nations. It was the first step in a significant historical turnaround for the Muslim world.

---

427 *The Arab-Israeli Wars*, Chaim Herzog, p. 322.
428 Walid Phares, *The War of Ideas: Jihadism against Democracy*, Palgrave/MacMillan Publishing, 2007, p.128.

Iranian Islamic Revolution

In February of 1979, I first raised my hand and took my oath of allegiance to support and defend the Constitution of the United States of America against all enemies foreign and domestic. It was the same month hundreds of thousands Iranians took to the streets in celebration because the Shah of Iran had left the country ending his oppressive reign. These two events are still juxtaposed in my mind. My military career began the same month the modern Islamic revolution began. Since the early fifties popular movements within the country had been severely suppressed by the Shah with the support of the Russians, British, and Americans . . . all for the sake of access to their oil. By the 1970s, another revolution was almost inevitable. But on that February morning, along with the shouts of celebration, there were other voices. Not voices for democracy or a secular state, but voices crying out "God, Koran, and Khomeini." Others may have thought the *Hidden Imam* or Mahdi was about to appear. Aslan confesses about the return of Khomeini from his French exile: "Khomeini's guidance was, like the guidance of the Prophet and the twelve Imams, infallible and divinely inspired." It was no wonder he would be granted "absolute obedience from the people."[429] Like the Mahdis before him, he claimed descent from the seventh Imam and accepted the messianic title of *Imam*. Connecting his rise to power as the all-powerful Shia ruler of Iran, he immediately set out to avenge the historic massacre of Shia founder Husayn at the battle of Karbala in Iraq. In an eight-year war with Iraq, killing ten thousand children, he tried to right the wrong committed against Husayn. The children wore headbands with the word "Karbala" on them reminding them that this was not a war about territory but religion and revenge.[430]

Even though the *Islamic Republic* established by Khomeini replaced one tyranny with another, the impact of this event was felt around the world. It demonstrated that a deep seated religious sentiment fueled by a charismatic leader speaking with divine authority could throw off the Western powers and even humiliate an American President. President Jimmy Carter probably lost his presidency over the 444 days of "impotence." Not being able to get our American Embassy personnel and Marines released from Khomeini's revolutionary guards cost him the presidency.

---

429 Reza Aslan, *No god But God*, Random House, p 88.
430 Karbala, the town where Husayn was killed.

In short, a victorious Islam was back. Western powers were humiliated and now in retreat. But more victories were coming.

Withdrawal of American Forces from Lebanon

When King Hussein of Jordan kicked out the Palestinian Liberation Organization from their sanctuary in Jordan, they took refuge in Lebanon. From secure bases in southern Lebanon the PLO continued to carry out terrorist attacks against the northern villages of Israel. In 1975, civil war broke out setting the PLO, various Muslim factions, the Syrian Army and Christian elements all against each other. In response to continuing terrorist attacks, in August of 1982 Israel launched Operation Peace for Galilee and invaded Lebanon driving the PLO all the way to Beirut. When the ultimate defeat of Arafat's forces seemed imminent, President Ronald Reagan expressed concern. American pressure on Prime Minister Begin resulted in an announced cease-fire by the Israelis.

The Americans then negotiated an evacuation of the PLO and Syrian forces back to any Arab countries that would receive them. An American carrier received about 8,000 PLO fighters on board and took them to Tunis along with their leader Arafat. The morning of this event, my wife and I had a Marine Corps officer and his wife visiting in our home. When he read the paper that morning he was outraged. I still remember his words: "for all my career I have been trained that the PLO was my enemy and now we have helped them escape." His wife said she had never seen him so angry at his own country!

To stabilize the country, a Multi-National force of US Marines along with French and Italian troops remained. The Marines were stationed near the Beirut airport in a concrete multi-storied building. On October 23, 1983, two suicide bombers driving trucks hit both the American and French barracks in a simultaneous attack. The death toll was 299 French and American deaths. For the Americans, 220 Marines, 18 Navy and three Army soldiers lost their lives. It was the largest loss of life for the Marines in a single day since Iwo Jima. It was also the first use of suicide bombers later connected to Iranian backed fighters who became Hezbollah. The explosion at the Marine Corps barracks completely collapsed the building burying Marines under tons of rubble. For the French it was also its worst military loss since their Algerian war in 1962. They lost 58 soldiers.

American resolve was immediate. President Reagan called it "a despicable act" and pledged to keep the force in Lebanon. Secretary of Defense Casper Weinberger said there would not be any change in US foreign policy, and Vice President George H. W. Bush added, "the US would not be cowed by terrorists."[431] Reality was far removed from the rhetoric. There was no real retaliation for the Beirut bombing. The Marines were first moved off shore for protection and finally on February 7, 1984, President Reagan ordered a total withdrawal of all Marines from the country. The rest of the multinational force was out by April. Immediately, Hezbollah praised the two martyred Mujahidin who had defeated the American administration. Empowered by the successful attack, Hezbollah was now seen as the "spearhead of the sacred Muslim struggle against foreign occupation"[432] The message was clear, when attacked, and attacked hard, America withdraws and goes home even under the tough talking, standing-up-to-the-Soviets Republican President, Ronald Reagan. My Marine friends are still outraged by our country providing escape and salvation for the PLO after losing fellow Marines with the final humiliation of pulling out of Lebanon entirely. To the Islamic world it was the message that Allah was again victorious.

Defeat of the Soviet Army in Afghanistan

Step four in this historical turnaround was the shocking withdrawal of Soviet troops from Afghanistan after ten years of battling the Mujahidin. The year 1979 not only brought the Iranian Islamic revolution, it also saw the invasion of Afghanistan by the Russian military in December of that year. At the request of a crumbling communist regime, Soviet leader Leonid Brezhnev sent in troops numbering up to 100,000 to help maintain the Soviet-friendly communist government. Little did he know at the time resistance guerillas (mujahidin) would eventually launch missions from over 4,000 bases carrying out operations largely financed and equipped by American, Saudi, and Chinese intervention. It was the classic Cold War strategy. If the Soviets were there, the free West had to intervene to keep the balance of power. Numbered among the *Afghan Arab* freedom fighters was one Saudi named Osama bin Laden!

---

431 Robert McFarlane, "From Beirut to 9/11," *New York Times*, October 23, 2008, p.37.
432 Quote from FBIS, August 1994, quoted in Ranstorp, "Hizbollah in Lebanon," (1997) p. 38.

From 1985 to 1987 an average of more than 600 terrorist acts were recorded by the mujahidin against both combatant and noncombatant Soviet targets. The US supplied highly effective Stinger missiles to the resistance and other hand-held surface-to-air missiles. After eight years of increasing losses, the new Soviet leader Mikhail Gorbachev announced a plan to withdraw. When completed in February of 1989, over 14,000 soldiers had died, with 53,000 wounded, and 415,000 had fallen sick with serious illnesses.[433] Once gone, Afghanistan was plunged into a civil war that eventually led to long-standing tribal militia groups fighting each other, culminating in the rise to power by the Taliban. Once the Soviets retreated, America lost interest in the country and left it to the devices and designs of those left behind. For the US it had always been a war against communism and Soviet interventionism. But to the thirty-four Islamic nations who had signed a resolution condemning the Soviet invasion it was more about a fight against a godless atheism. To them, it was the unifying commitment to Islam that rallied the freedom fighters against the Soviets, and it was Allah who gave the victory. Little credit was given to the US or the West for supplying the weapons and training.[434]

The message was very clear to the Islamic world and especially the Arab street. Islam was back! The Mujahidin with Allah on their side had taken on one of the great military powers in the world and ground them down to a defeated foe. The feared Soviet troops had withdrawn in disgrace being unable to defeat a stone-age guerrilla army hiding in caves. But more was still to come.

US Forces withdraw from Somalia

The book and movie *Black Hawk Down* depicts the calamitous events for American soldiers in Somalia. What started out as a "humanitarian and peace keeping mission" under President Bill Clinton turned ugly and became another success story for Islamic fighters against American Imperialism. In September of 1991, severe fighting broke out in Somalia's capital city, Mogadishu. This was in response to many attempts by several factions to establish a stable legitimate government. What was perceived as "tribal warfare" by Western powers resulted in over 20,000 being killed and injured with complete destruction of agriculture with resultant starvation. A United Nations multi-national relief effort was initiated by then

433 *Russia and the USSR in wars XX century*. Moscow: OLMA Press, 2001, p. 537.
434 "Moslems Condemn Invasion of Afghanistan," *Pittsburgh Post-Gazette*, January 29, 1980.

US President George H. W. Bush to supply food for the nation. However, it was estimated that eighty percent of the food was being stolen and exchanged for weapons coming in from other countries. Between 1991 and 1992, it was estimated that 1.5 million people suffered under starvation and 300,000 people died. Most of the 1.5 million were eventually displaced to refugee camps.

In March of 1993, a mission shift occurred within the UN, when the UN Secretary-General authorized UNOSOM II to establish a secure environment throughout Somalia and create a democratic state: this in spite of the fact there was still no real effective government, police or national army! One key faction leader, General Mohammad Farrah Aidid, would not agree to the resolution and announced he would not cooperate with UN forces. On June 5, 1993, forces controlled by General Aidid killed twenty-four Pakistani troops. In response, the UN Security Council issued a resolution calling for his arrest.

On July 12, 1993, the United States under President Bill Clinton launched an operation to capture Aidid where he was known to be in hiding in a safe house. The US, in a seventeen-minute operation, fired TOW missiles and thousands of rounds of 20-millimeter cannon into the compound where he was supposedly hiding, but he was not there. Then on October 3, 1993, a second attempt to capture Aidid led to the infamous street fight between Delta Force Special Operators and a local collection of Somali citizens, militia and unknown fighters. The planned thirty-minute operation went badly from the start. After almost a day and a night of fighting with two helicopters being shot down, and dead American soldiers being dragged through the streets for the world to see, the failed mission ended. Nineteen US soldiers were killed in action and another eighty-three were wounded. Casualties on the Somali side ranged from American estimates at 2,000 to 315 voiced by Aidid, who had escaped unharmed.[435] Clinton's National Security advisor, Les Aspin, stepped down in the aftermath, and President Clinton instructed the Joint Chiefs Chairman, General David Jeremiah, to stop all actions against Aidid by US forces. He then announced all US forces would withdraw from Somalia by March 31, 1994. By late spring of 1994, all UN troops had been withdrawn and Somalia was viewed as a failed state controlled by local tribal warlords. In reality, it was a major shift in American foreign policy whereby

---

435 See Roger Sangvic, *Battle of Mogadishu: Anatomy of a Failure*, School of Advanced Military Studies, U.S. Army Command and General Staff College, 1998.

President Clinton became increasingly reluctant to use military intervention in Third World conflicts. But for Islamists, it was a victory of Allah over the forces of the West, especially America. In Peter Bergen's book *Holy War Inc.* based on interviews with Bin Laden before 9/11, he reveals Al-Qaeda was deeply involved in the training of Aidid's men.[436] Bin Laden had even made the same remarks in Arabic sources (Al-Quds Al Arabi).

Of course, most of this information was not available or deemed relevant prior to 9/11. But to the Arab street and dedicated Islamists it was the next sign that Allah was on their side, a sign signifying the demise of Western domination and the advance of the Islamic faith. Having defeated the Russians and Americans, the next victorious sign would focus on the Israelis.

Israeli Withdrawal from Lebanon (2000)

As mentioned earlier in the book, my first visit to Israel was profoundly eye-opening. Having gone there to study historical geography and culture, my wife and I were dropped in the middle of all the tensions of the Middle East. We were having lunch when car bombs went off in several West Bank towns. Then while at a kibbutz just south of the Lebanese border, a PLO rubber boat was blown out of the water by an IDF naval patrol, as mentioned in Chapter One. The year was 1980, and at this time the PLO had taken up residence in Lebanon and from the safe haven of that country launched terrorist missions into Israel, mostly targeting these northern "settlements."

As a result, in 1982 Israeli Defense Forces initiated an offensive into southern Lebanon in order to counter and destroy the PLO strongholds. The mission was successful and the IDF stayed in southern Lebanon to hold the ground they had captured. By June of 1985, President Shimon Peres ordered a unilateral withdrawal of troops leaving only a handful for a security zone along with Israeli trained Lebanese militias. However, the withdrawal did not end the hostilities between the Iranian supported Shiite militia in southern Lebanon and the remaining IDF forces in Lebanon. Besides, Israel experienced a relentless stream of casualties suffered at the hands of Hezbollah guerrilla attacks. As these attacks on both military and civilian targets inside Israel and on its northern border increased, popular support

---

436 Peter Bergen, *Holy War Inc.*, The Free Press, 2001 p. 82. Also see *Frontline* Interview "Hunting Bin Laden," Bergen's interview with Bin Laden.

for the IDF's military presence in Lebanon declined.[437] After almost fifteen years of constant military conflict in Lebanon, Prime Minister Ehud Barak made the decision for a final retreat. In May of 2000, all Israeli forces in Lebanon withdrew. Seventy percent of Israeli voters saw the retreat as the right thing to do after so many of their sons and daughters were sacrificed in what many saw as an unproductive security war in northern Israel.[438]

The IDF withdrawal from Lebanon left the southern border region in the hands of the Muslim group Hezbollah. From their perspective, it was a complete victory for Islam over the superior force of the invincible IDF.[439] A few months later, Katyusha rockets still rained down on northern Israel, and being empowered by the Hezbollah victory, Yasser Arafat initiated the al-Aqsa Intifada, a violent response motivated by the Israeli pullout. The tally on the Islamic scoreboard was now 5-0. Five victories for Islam, zero for the Christian and Jewish infidels! But the big one was still to come.

September 11, 2001 and Beyond

We all remember where we were on this September morning. I was in my office when someone said an airplane had hit the World Trade Center. Soon after that, I went into a staff meeting at our headquarters at Maxwell Air Force Base. Meeting in my boss's office, there was a TV on in the corner of the room. As about twelve of us gathered around a conference table, the live coverage flashed the second plane hitting the WTC. We all turned around and saw the second tower now inflamed.

I uttered, "It's bin Laden." Most looked at me and said, "Who's that?"

No, I didn't have any prior intelligence, I just knew who our enemy was, and that he was serious about his intents and plans. I did not know about the organization called *Al Qaeda* at the time, but I knew Bin Laden from my studies and teaching at the War College. He had made his views and intent very clear in his 1998 fatwah, *Declaration of the World Islamic Front for Jihad against the Jews and the Crusaders*. In the fatwah, he clearly states his goal: "To kill Americans and their allies, both civil and military, is the individual duty of every Muslim who is able, in any country where this is possible, until the Aqsa Mosque (in Jerusalem) and the Haram Mosque (in Mecca) are freed from their grip and until

---

437 Herzog, *The Arab and Israeli Wars*, p. 378.
438 *Palestine Facts: Israel 1991 to Present*, "Israel Leaves Lebanon," www.palestinefacts.org.
439 Herzog, p. 386.

their armies, shattered and broken-winged, depart from all the lands of Islam, incapable of threatening any Muslim."[440] His targets were clear: the United States, Israel (Jews) and the Saudi Royalty (who controls the Haram Mosque). Bin Laden knew the Arab street reflected a strong anti-Western sentiment (which I began to see back in the mid 1980s), but up to this time the same Arab street had not seen a powerful demonstration of Muslim power. As Friedman calls it, what was needed was a "sense of overwhelming power against the West, particularly America."[441] 9/11 gave them a clear signal that America the Great was not invincible. In fact, it was very *vulnerable*.

The response to 9/11 in America was one of *shock and awe* but not of the kind when we were the attackers. This shock and awe were rooted in the reality that America was no longer safe and secure. However, to the Islamic world, especially Arab countries, there was celebration.

People gathered in the streets firing weapons and exchanging gifts and candy. While America was grieving, the Islamic world was either celebrating or strangely silent. European nations chimed in with "We are all Americans," but in the predominately Muslim Middle East, the message was eerily different.

I agree with Friedman of Stratfor when he says (from Bin Laden's perspective) "The United States had to be struck by a blow that was both enormous, easily understandable by the Islamic masses, and against which there was no ready defense."[442] In this regard, 9/11 was not so much a message from Bin Laden to the United States, but a message to the Islamic world. The United States had been proven to be weak for some time (Vietnam, Lebanon, and Somalia). But the Arab street had not seen it this way. They still viewed America as all-powerful and invincible. In the 9/11 events, Bin Laden gave them a message they could no longer ignore or refute. Christian America was vulnerable. While our Military-Industrial Complex was developing gigantic bunker busting bombs called *daisy cutters*, we were defeated by a group of passengers armed only with *box cutters*!

Much has already been written about Osama bin Laden and how the Navy Seals and Delta Force eliminated him from the terrorist equation. Some believe Al Qaeda has lost its original leadership and strength, although ISIS was spawned

---

440 Quoted by Bernard Lewis, *Faith and Power*, Oxford Univ. Press, 2010, p. 3.
441 See *America's Secret War*, Doubleday, 2004, p. 33 for a detailed discussion of the concept.
442 George Friedman, *America's Secret War*, Doubleday, 2004, p. 34. Stratfor is an open source intelligence network providing intelligence commentary on international geopolitics.

from Al Qaeda. It is true key leadership was eliminated or captured, but as of this writing the organization is still alive, well, and expanding. Mullah Omar, the spiritual leader of the Taliban, was confirmed dead in summer 2015, but Dr. Ayman Zawahiri, the real ideologue of Al Qaeda, is still alive, and continues to have an influence. In addition, FBI chronicler Ronald Kessler says, "Al Qaeda has morphed into a sort of franchise operation, inspired by bin Laden."[443] Scott Steward of Stratfor concurs: "his (bin Laden's) death will likely have very little practical impact on the Jihadist movement . . . the phenomenon of Jihadism is far wider than just the Al Qaeda core leadership of bin Laden."[444] So the war goes on, from the Maghreb of Northern Africa, to Mali, Nigeria, Somalia, Yemen and of course Libya, Iraq and Syria, Al Qaeda inspired groups are not "on the run," as our President claimed, but thriving.

America has not seen successful follow-up terror events on its own soil with three exceptions: Major Hasan's shooting at Ft. Hood, the Boston Marathon bombing and the July 2015 shooting of four Marines and a sailor at military sites in Chattanooga, Tennessee. But there have been many attempts.[445] Two American journalists were beheaded by ISIS in Syria, and the American public outrage caused President Obama to launch counter strikes against the new caliphate. But hardly a month goes by without hearing of an attempt by someone trying to strike another blow to the American psyche in the name of Allah. In 2007, the FBI had 10,000 cases under investigation. These included such things as immigration violations, thefts and cigarette smuggling, all known to have some possible relationship to terrorist organizations or contacts.[446] Khalid Sheikh Mohammed, called the "Mastermind"[447] of both World Trade Center attacks, admitted to also planning attacks on the Sears Tower in Chicago, the Empire State Building, the New York Stock Exchange, the Panama Canal, Big Ben and the Heathrow Airport in

---

443 Ronald Kessler, *The Terrorist Watch: Inside the Desperate Race to Stop the New Attack*, Three Rivers Press, 2007, 217.

444 Scott Steward, "Bin Laden's Death and the Implications for Jihadism," www.stratfor.com.

445 The exception of course is one of our own; Major Nidal Hasan, the Army psychiatrist who shot 13 soldiers going through the mobilization line at Ft. Hood, Texas. He shouted "Allah Akbar" throughout the shootings. Since 9/11 the Department of Homeland Security records 32 terrorist plots have been attempted and failed due to good intelligence and vigilance by American citizens.

446 Ronald Kessler, *The Terrorist Watch*, p. 218.

447 Kessler, *The Terrorist Watch*, p. 57.

London. Plus, he planned the failed missile attack on an Israeli airline and claimed responsibility for the 2002 nightclub bombing in Bali, Indonesia, killing 202.

A 2007 Heritage Foundation report revealed United States law enforcement and intelligence agencies had thwarted nineteen actual attacks. Of the nineteen, only one was clearly not connected to any Islamic group or ideology.

Eight on the FBI's Top Ten terror attempts list were identified as Islamic terrorists. On January 7, Adis Medunjanin attempted a suicide attack on the Whitestone Bridge in New York City, attempting to destroy the suspension cables of the bridge that crosses the East River. Much publicity was given to the bombing attempt on Times Square, May 1, when a Pakistani tried to detonate homemade explosive devices in his vehicle. Nearby vendors reported the smoking vehicle and the failed attempt. Sami Samir Hassoun, a Lebanese citizen, attempted to use a weapon of mass destruction at Chicago's Wrigley Field. An FBI sting operation prevented the attack. In March, a switch in terrorist gender was observed.

"Jihad Jane," US citizen

Colleen LaRose was indicted in Philadelphia for her role in recruiting fighters to commit murder overseas. A month later a colleague in Colorado was also indicted.[448] An Orlando Sentinel article remarks on this new gender development. "A quarter of a million Pakistani students attended all-female madrassas . . . where legions of well-do-to women are experiencing an awakening of faith." The article goes on to point out "the number of all-female madrassas has boomed over the past decade. Some experts now say these female schools are just as dangerous simply because they are training more middle and upper classes of Pakistani society. Because of this, "female madrassas spread their ideas further into mainstream society through religious study groups held in member's homes."[449] Both in America and the United Kingdom, young women have sneaked out of their countries to become "Jihadi" wives . . . all to the surprise of their friends and parents.

A Somali-American, Mohamed Osman Mohamud, on November 26, attempted to ignite a car bomb at local Christmas Tree Lighting ceremony in Portland, Oregon. In December of the same year, Muhammad Hussain, an

---

448 "The Year in Review: FBI Cases, Part I," *FBI Stories*. www.fbi.gov/news/stories /2010/ December/cases-122710/cases_122710.

449 Rebecca Conway, "At Pakistan's Madrassas, Girls' Fanaticism Fanned," *Orlando Sentinel*, June 19, 2011, p. A18.

American convert to Islam, was arrested by FBI agents for his plot to blow up a military recruiting center in Maryland. On Christmas day of 2010, the "Underwear Bomber," Nigerian Umar Farouk Abdul Mjutallab, tried to ignite explosives hidden in his underwear on a Northwest flight over the Atlantic. The device failed, and he alone received severe burns.[450] Faisal Shatzad, a naturalized US citizen, attempted to set off a large vehicle-borne explosive device in Times Square on May 1, 2010. Jason Abdo, a US Army private, planned to attack a restaurant near Ft. Hood in Killeen, Texas. He was arrested while trying to buy materials for a pressure cooker explosive device[451] (like what was used in the Boston bombing). Finally, on June 22, 2011, Abu Khalid Abdul-Latif and a friend tried to fire loaded M-16 assault rifles at the Military Entrance Processing Station in downtown Seattle. Before they could carry out the attack FBI agents and local law enforcement arrested them.[452]

What these attempted and thwarted attacks say is the war on terrorism is not over and will not go away. Though few may call it war there are plenty of self-recruited Jihadis training and plotting to continue the bin Laden legacy. But there is some good news.

As of February of 2011, 161 Muslim American terrorist suspects and perpetrators had been arrested and reported since September 11, 2001.[453] Most of these suspects and perpetrators came to the attention of law enforcement from their own Muslim American communities. In fact, one community was so concerned about an extremist; they turned in someone who was an undercover informant![454] A report done by the Muslim Public Affairs Council reported that fourteen of the forty-one Islamist terrorist plots studied were in fact foiled through the efforts of the Muslim communities.[455] This is good news because these Muslim communities are really the first line of defense on American soil. A Rand report concluded: "Relatives and

---

450 "The Top 10 Attempted Terrorist Attacks of 2010," www.topsecretwriters.com/2011.
451 "Grassroots Militants after the Boston Bombings," Stratfor Global Intelligence, April 19, 2013.
452 Scott Stewart, "The Seattle Plot: Jihadists Shifting Away From Civilian Targets," Stratfor Global Intelligence, June 30, 2011.
453 Charles Kurzman, "Muslim-American Terrorism since 9/11: An Accounting," Department of Sociology, University of North Carolina, February 2, 2011. Triangle Center on Terrorism and Homeland Security, p. 1.
454 Ibid., p. 4.
455 Alejandro J. Beutal, "Data on Post 9/11 terrorism in the United States," Muslim Public Affairs Council, Washington D.C., updated version, November 2010.

friends are often more likely than the authorities to know when someone is turning dangerously radical and heading toward self-destruction."[456]

However, other countries have not been so lucky. One website keeps a running total of Islamic attacks worldwide. It now numbers 17,077 since 9/11! The day I counted the numbers for the year 2011, I found around 1760 attacks. These included attacks in the Philippines, Nigeria, Somalia, Israel, Iran, Sweden, Pakistan, Kenya, Egypt, Chechnya, Russia, Algeria, Dagestan, Tajikistan, Thailand, Sudan, Mali, Yemen, Kosovo, Bosnia, Canada, Jordan, Turkey, Germany, Liberia, United Kingdom, Bangladesh, India, France, and of course too many to really count in Afghanistan and Iraq.[457]

These statistics, if correct, illustrate the world is aflame with seriously motivated Jihadists willing to give their lives if necessary for the cause of Allah. As Phillip Mudd, a former CIA officer, described it, "this is not a conventional war and the adversary will keep coming . . . in this war, this adversary will not go home."[458] They won't go home simply because Islam is their nation, and the rest of the world is "Dar al-Harb," a place of warfare. The Rand report summarizes, "There are no frontiers, no front lines, no home fronts. The battlefield is everywhere . . . and there is no distinction between combatants and bystanders."[459]

My main concern in this chapter is not so much about specific groups or personalities, but money and mosques. The old adage of *follow the money* is only partly true. Money follows ideology. So this chapter will conclude by looking at the well-recognized money connections and how they have led to our own American mosques.

The Saudi Connection: Oil for Al Qaeda

As mentioned earlier, Middle East oil is viewed as *Allah's Good gift*. To put this reality into perspective consider one fact alone. Throughout the 1990s the Saudi actual cost of extracting oil out of the ground was around fifty *cents* a barrel. By 2005, that cost was estimated to have risen to a whopping $2 a barrel. Since the Saudi infrastructure was created almost fifty years ago (by Western oil companies), today the main cost of extraction is personnel and maintenance. When this desert

---

456 Brian Michael Jenkins, "Would Be Warriors," Rand, *Occasional Papers*, 2010, p. ix.

457 www.thereligionofpeace.com/attacks-2010.htm.

458 *The Terrorist Watch*, p. 113.

459 *Rand Report*, "Would be Warriors, p. 4.

country is earning around 350 million dollars a day in profits, there is a constant available source of funding for their global ideology.[460] As such, it is a commodity to be exploited and used mostly for the personal priorities of the Arab State's royal families . . . one of which is the promotion of Wahhabism.[461] Oil permeates the entire economy of Saudi Arabia. Their oil receipts account for ninety percent of their government revenues and forty percent of their gross domestic product.[462] OPEC and the estimated 7,000 Saudi princes have used this oil wealth to fund everything from extravagant life styles to the financing of mosques, Madrasses, and materials promoting the Wahhabi form of Islam.[463] Learsy notes, "Millions of dollars of Saudi Arabian and Kuwaiti money go to finance schools, mosques and supposedly charitable organizations that actively promote the virulent anti-Western Wahhabi strain of Islam and encourage Muslim citizens of Western nations to reject the principles upon which their governments were founded."[464]

Former CIA operative Robert Baer says, "no matter what country you buy your oil from, Saudi Arabia determines world price by how much oil it chooses to produce."[465] He records, "The United Nations Security Council indicated that Saudi Arabia transferred half a billion dollars to al Qaeda in the ten years beginning in 1992."[466] Dore Gold, former Israeli ambassador to the UN, believes the West has either conveniently overlooked or ignored this Saudi connection. He writes, "The West's campaign has overlooked a critical component of terrorism, that is, the precise source of the terror, the ideology that motivates individuals and groups to slaughter thousands of innocent people . . . the problem is Wahhabism as it has developed in the milieu of Saudi Arabia."[467]

In short, there is no real oil shortage, only the perception of such generated by OPEC and its two non-OPEC conspirators, Mexico and Russia.[468] In fact, the

---

460 Gerald Posner, *Secrets of the Kingdom: The Inside Story of the Saudi-U.S. Connection*, Random House, 2005, p. 16.
461 Raymond J. Learsy writes, "The Saudis consider it a sacred duty to propagate the faith because Islam began in their country." *Over a Barrel: Breaking the Middle East Oil Cartel*, Nelson Current, 2005, p. 63.
462 "Challenges for the Saudi Royal Family," Stratfor Global Intelligence, September 12, 2012.
463 Gerald Posner, *Secrets of the Kingdom: The Inside Story of the Saudi-U.S. Connection*, Random House, 2005, p. 172.
464 Learsy, *Over a Barrel*, p. 63.
465 Robert Baer, *Sleeping with the Devil*, Crown Publishers, 2003, p. xxiv.
466 Baer, page xxii.
467 Robert Baer, *Sleeping with the Devil*, Crown Publishers, 2003, p. xxiv.
468 Ibid., p. xxvii.

interruptions of our oil supply only happen when leaders of OPEC purposely close the spigots for personal or political reasons.[469] Some might think this is not such a big deal and the simple answer is to put up windmills and affix solar panels to our houses. What few realize is how tenuous this makes our world until such time alternatives to petroleum are created. Up to seventy-seven percent of all fuel used in aircraft, ground vehicles, ships and DOD weapon systems are fueled by petroleum. Our Armed Forces consume more than eighty percent of the entire federal government's energy needs. Ninety-four percent of our entire transportation system is petroleum based.[470]

So oil fundamentally funds the Western way of life. Factor in the reality that pipelines are easy fragile targets; it leaves the Saudis and oil producing states in a powerful position against America and the West. As the oil flows, so does the money.[471] It flows to finance the ideology of Jihad. Ralph Peters writes, "Saudis, Yemenis, Omanis, and oil-rich Gulf Arabs are every bit as determined to reassert Muslim domination of the lands Islam once ruled . . . Saudi madrassas never encourage young people to integrate into their host society."[472] *The Economist* alerts its readers, "This pernicious ideology, now aided by the failures of the Arab spring, continues to spread through madrassas and mosques and Jihadist websites and television channels. Money still flows from rich Gulf Arabs, supposedly the West's friends, to finance these activities and worse."[473] Even where Islam has never ruled like the United Kingdom there is a concerted effort with great success to establish an Islamic civilization. In the UK, it is a numbers and money game, primarily financed by Saudi Arabia.

Estimates show fifty percent of the 1.8 million UK Muslims are under age twenty-five. Of this number, it is said 18,000 would join up for Jihad under the right conditions. After the UK bus bombings, twenty-three percent of British Muslims

---

469 Learsy, pp. 214-15.

470 Learsy, *Over a Barrel*, where he says, "OPEC perpetuates the phony theory of scarcity and successfully manipulates the price of oil with the help of Mexico, Russia and other non-OPEC producers," p. 7. See also p. 203 for "scarcity as a mirage." John Nagl and Christine Parthemore, "Prepare for a post-petroleum era," *Armed Forces Journal*, November, 2010.

471 See Learsy's whole chapter "Hysteria Premium" for sourcing of these facts. UCLA Professor James Gelvin notes, "Oil exports account for 70% of Qatar's revenues, 90% of Saudi Arabia's, 94% of Kuwait's, and 95% of Abu Dhabi's, *The Arab Uprising: What Everyone Needs to Know*, Oxford Univ. Press, 2012, p. 126.

472 John Nagl and Christine Parthemore, "Prepare for a post-petroleum era," *Armed Forces Journal*, November, 2010.

473 "Al Qaeda Returns: The New Face of Terror," *The Economist*, September 27, 2013.

said the bombings were justified! Saudi funding has changed the nature of Islam. When communities are poor and without money, the Saudis come in and offer to build mosques and provide an Imam. Of course, the Imam is trained in the Wahhabi/ Saudi branch that preaches hatred of the West. Posner observes, "Saudi money that flows to Muslim organizations always comes with the implicit understanding that the institution or mosque receiving it has to promote Wahhabism.[474] The funding is also accepted because there exists an ideological vacuum in the communities, and this is filled by the "theology of a Muslim empire"[475] In total, the House of Saud has financed in Europe and America 210 Islamic centers, 1,500 mosques, 202 colleges, and 2,000 primary schools. Posner notes, "These Islamic centers recruit individuals and establish extreme organizations."[476] It is estimated that half of the mosques and Islamic schools in America have been built with Saudi funds.[477] More frightening is the fact the Institute of Islamic and Arabic Sciences in Fairfax, Virginia, funded by the Saudi embassy, trained at least seventy-five lay leaders to serve as U.S. military chaplains![478] Ambassador Madeleine Albright also confirms, "One cause for alarm is the extent to which private Saudi money has helped to finance terrorist operations . . . During my meetings before 9/11, the Saudis reacted indignantly to any suggestion that Muslim terror networks were gaining strength. They viewed such allegations as an attempt to discredit Islam."[479]

Evidence exists today that Saudi money has financed terrorism either directly or indirectly through shell organizations or "charities." Federal investigators identified more than 27 million dollars as "suspicious transactions" from Saudi embassy bank accounts to Muslim charities, clerics and Saudi students being scrutinized for links to terrorist activity.[480] The official response from the Saudi government (royal family) is that they disavow any connection to terrorism. However, before 9/11, a CIA report concluded that a startling one third of all Islamic charities were linked to terrorism. In 1999, under pressure from the CIA, FBI and NSA, the Saudi government conducted an audit of its own National Commercial Bank and found

---

474 Posner, *Secrets of the Kingdom*, p. 172-3.
475 Heidi Kingstone, "Foreign Bodies," *The Jerusalem Report*, October 30, 2006, p. 23.
476 Posner, *Secrets of the Kingdom*, p. 173-4.
477 Ibid., p. 24.
478 Posner, *Secrets of the Kingdom*, p. 173-4.
479 *The Mighty and the Almighty*, pp. 208, 209.
480 Blaine Harden, "Saudis Seek to Add U.S. Muslims to Their Sect," *New York Times*, October 20, 2001, p.Al.

at least 3 million dollars had been transferred to charitable organizations believed to be bin Laden fronts.[481] In 2005, a US Treasury Department investigation of Saudi terrorist financiers listed 10 million dollars supporting Hamas. This amounted to fifty percent of their operating budget.[482]

A 2007 Jerusalem Report article "Arming the Saudis" concludes: "Six years after 9/11, it's still impossible to speak about funding for terrorism without mentioning Saudi Arabia. According to both the U.S. State Department and the Government Accountability Office, wealthy Saudi donors and unregulated "charities" are a major source of funding not only for Hamas, which rejects Israel's right to exist but also . . . for other anti-Western groups that promote hate-filled extremist ideologies. In August of 2014, Saudi Arabia donated $100 million to the United Nations to fund a "counter-terrorism agency."[483] Called "half-in, half-out," Ed Husain of the New York Times said of the Saudis, "It is a reflection of the inner paralysis in dealing with Sunni Islamist radicalism. It wants to stop violence but will not address the Salafism (branch of Islam from which Wahhabism is a descendant) that helps justify it."[484]

Saudi Wahhabi clerics have preached and recruited for terrorism in Iraq, and Saudi money has sustained the Sunni insurgency there, and the majority of suicide bombers in Iraq have been . . . you guessed it . . . Saudi citizens."[485] Former CIA director James Woolsey adds, "Saudi Arabia earns about $160 billion from exporting oil, and a big share of that goes to the (ultra-fundamentalist) Wahhabi sect to set up madrassas in Pakistan and other places."[486] In addition, Saudi Arabia underwrites the development and dissemination of overtly biased social studies curricula for American public high schools! Dr. Jassar chides our top universities, "Universities such as Harvard, which so blithely take Wahhabi petrodollars and then in return have professors teach one-sided courses in Middle Eastern history that somehow conveniently blame Israel for all problems in that region, must be called out on their collusion with the Islamists."[487]

---

481 Glenn Simpson, "Saudis Cut Back Diplomatic Visas amid Policy Shift," *Wall Street Journal*, December 8, 2003, p. B2.
482 Michael Isikoff, "New Questions about Saudi Money and Bandar," *Newsweek*, April 12, 2004.
483 Robert Horenstein, "Arming the Saudis," *The Jerusalem Report*, October 1, 2007, p. 47.
484 Ed Husain, "Saudis Must Stop Exporting Extremism," *The New York Times*, August 22, 2014.
485 Press release from Senator Charles Schumer (D.N.Y), Senate Judiciary Subcommittee on Terrorism. September 10, 2003. www.senate.gov/schumer/SchumerWebsite/pressroom.
486 Ibid.
487 Jasser, *Battle for the Soul of Islam*, p.213.

The author was recently on a college campus and noticed a religious studies table in the Student Union. I went over to look at the literature and was amazed to find that the "religious material" was all about Islam. When I looked at where the literature was printed, guess what . . . it was in Saudi Arabia! In fact, one of the slick, multi-color brochures was entitled "Women's rights in Islam." The brochure extolled the virtues of women's rights within Islam . . . I wondered if the writer was ever in Saudi Arabia, or was this just a ruse to attract naïve young co-eds!

It has been known for some time that Saudi Arabia was funding "Middle East Studies" or "Islamic Studies" (which amounts to the same ideology) at major universities in America. To them this is considered missionary work![488] One Saudi prince donated $20 million to both Harvard and Georgetown Universities to fund chairs of Islamic studies. A 2008 *Newsmax* article reports "There's a possibility these campuses aren't getting gifts; they're getting investments."[489] Clifford May, President of the Foundation for the Defense of Democracies, cautions, "Departments of Middle Eastern Studies tend to be dominated by professors tuned to the concerns of Arab and Muslim rulers." In 2007, Mike McConnell, Director of National Intelligence, went on the record by saying, "there are still funds coming from Saudi Arabia . . . to help Sunni insurgents in Iraq." Saudi Arabia as a government is not providing funding to the Sunni insurgents, but they still do flow to some extent . . . funding comes from private individuals within Saudi Arabia and the Gulf States."[490]

Of course anyone basically familiar with Saudi Arabia and most of the Middle East knows there is no such distinction between what is "private" and what is "public" for these royal families. Oil profits are divided between the consortiums and the Royal Family, but where the money goes after that is largely unknown. The money is for the personal/public use of the royal family. One point of view on the Iraq war suggests the often-contradictory response of the Saudis as officially supporting the US military surge in Iraq while at the same time funding the Sunni insurgency against the Americans out the back door.[491] The same could be said of their support for anyone who shares the Wahhabi Salafist viewpoint. Again,

488 Posner, *Secrets of the Kingdom*. See whole chapter on funding terrorism.
489 "Are Rich Saudis Aiding our Schools," *Newsmax*, February 2008, p. 64.
490 Robert Horenstein, "Arming the Saudis," *The Jerusalem Report*, October 1, 2007, p. 47.
491 Robert Horenstein, "Arming the Saudis," *The Jerusalem Report*, October 1, 2007, p. 47.

follow the ideology![492] The Saudis can claim no connection to terrorism while their personal banks, friends, and shell companies fund the Wahhabi religion that in turn influences and trains terrorists. Horenstein warns in a 2011 article, "Nearly a decade after 9/11, when fifteen of the nineteen hijackers who attacked the US were Saudi citizens, Saudi donors remain the chief financiers of al-Qaeda and the Taliban. According to secret cables made public by WikiLeaks in November . . . even Secretary of State Hillary Clinton agreed, "These terrorist groups probably raise millions of dollars annually from Saudi sources.[493] In other words, America's ostensible allies are fueling the spread of radical Islam while posing a direct danger to U.S. national security.

Like it or not, the US and Saudi Arabia are joined at the hip or as CIA agent Robert Baer calls it "sleeping with the devil." The reality we face he claims is fourfold: 1) The industrial world is dependent on the oil that is largely in Islamic hands . . . and will be for some time to come. 2) Of the Islamic states none is more critical than Saudi Arabia because they have the largest oil reserves. 3) Of all the oil consuming states, none consumes more than the United States. 4) If Saudi Arabia goes under (or is taken over by the more radical Islamists) along with the other four dysfunctional families in the region, the industrial economies will go down with them, including the United States.[494]

Some today claim Islam was "hijacked" by al Qaeda and the likes of Osama bin Laden. Ambassador Gold disagrees. He states emphatically, "Osama bin Laden was preaching nothing new . . . An entire generation of Saudis was brainwashed with this hatred; bin Laden merely set out to mobilize predisposed Wahhabi Muslims for a war against the West. Of course, by employing its international Islamic charities and relying on private contributions to extreme Islamic groups, the Saudi government could distance itself from the terrorist organizations even while paying "protection money" to those who could cause the Saudis harm."[495] But for the newly elected George W. Bush administration this ideology was new.

The friendship between the US and Saudi Arabia that began in the fifties would be seriously strained by the events of 9/11. The "Security for Oil" agreement the

---

492 Dore Gold, *Hatred's Kingdom*, Regenery Publishing Inc., 2003, pp. 214-15.
493 Eric Rosenberg, "U.S. Intel Chief: Saudi, Iranian cash fuels sides in civil war," *Orlando Sentinel*, March 4, 2007, p. A14.
494 Baer, *Sleeping with the Devil*, p 206-7.
495 Gold, 184.

US had maintained and coveted for years looked different on September 12. "W" Bush was not his father, cozy with the House of Saud. In fact, the disturbing facts of this chapter began to emerge and caused a new rethinking of the relationship. The now infamous Rand Pentagon briefing by researcher Laurent Murawiec on July 10, 2002, did more than raise eyebrows. Though the White House immediately assured the Saudis the briefing did not represent administration policy (always a good cover story line), it did create quite a furor.[496]

The essence of the briefing as given by Murawiec characterized Saudi Arabia as "a kernel of evil, the prime mover, and the most dangerous opponent of the United States." Quoting directly, he stated, "The Saudis are active at every level of the terror chain, from planners to financiers, from cadre to foot-soldier, from ideologist to cheerleader . . . Saudi Arabia supports our enemies and attacks our allies."[497] More recently, an *Economist* article (Sept, 2013) says the Al Qaeda "network now holds more territory and is recruiting more fighters than at any time in its twenty-five year history." And from whom are they getting their funding? Answer: "money flows from rich Gulf State Arabs, supposedly the West's friends, to finance these activities and worse."[498] Husain affirms, "The Saudi government appointed emissaries to its embassies in Muslim countries who proselytize for Salafism."[499]

This by itself creates the perception that Wahhabic Salafism is the mainstream of Islam. However, this ideology makes up only about three percent of the world's Muslims, with Indonesia being the largest Muslim population in the world. Yet, for five decades Saudi Arabia has been the official sponsor of Sunni Salafism all around the globe.

With all the West's outrage over the decapitation of our journalists, James Foley and Allen Henning, Saudi Arabia has, since August 4, 2014, beheaded 19 people, nearly half for nonviolent crimes. Husain believes the Saudis created the monster of Salafist terrorism, and the slaying of this monster cannot be outsourced to the United Nations.[500] Follow the money and one finds the ideology: follow the ideology and one finds the money! The money also leads us to other Gulf States and in particular, our supposed friend in the war on terrorism, Qatar.

496 Peter Beinart, "The Devil We Know," *Time*, March 5, 2007, p.43.
497 Robert Horenstein, "Selling Arms to the Saudis," *The Jerusalem Report*, January 17, 2011, p. 47.
498 "Al Qaeda Returns: The New Face of Terror," *The Economist*, Sept. 28, 2013.
499 Ed Husain, "Saudis Must Stop Exporting Extremism," *The New York Times*, August 22, 2014.
500 Ibid.

The New York Times Editorial Board concluded, "Though Qatar hosts the largest American military base in the region, it has supported a range of Islamist groups (including Islamic radicals in Syria) with safe haven, financial aid and weapons.[501] Foreign Policy analyst Elizabeth Dickinson adds, "Qatar, as a tiny, oil-rich emirate, has pumped millions of dollars through funding networks to hard line Syrian rebels and extreme Salafists, building a foreign policy that punches above its weight." She reveals that the Qatari network of Islamic-leaning proxies includes former Syrian generals, Taliban insurgents, Somali Islamists, and Sudanese rebels. These so-called "Rolodex Middlemen" have played a major role in "destabilizing every trouble spot in the region and in accelerating the growth of radical and Jihadi factions."[502]

Another Gulf State that supports the radical Islamic State is Bahrain. Ala'a Shehabi, of Foreign Policy Journal, writes, "Not only is there a direct link between IS (Islamic State) and Bahrain's security services, but the Bahraini cohort in the Islamic State includes Turki al-Binali, one of the movement's most influential radical preachers." He is neither a funder nor fighter of Jihad but provides the ideological and moral support to the group as the spiritual leader of the Mosul-based mosque.[503] All this Sunni collaboration over oil could make one think Iran is off the hook. Yet, it may be that the Iranian Ayatollah loves the attention given to the Gulf State Arabs just to keep the focus off of what is going on in his own country. If they are in the "axis of evil" as claimed by President W. Bush, he certainly left someone out!

Resurgent Islam is alive and well. Through the course of writing this chapter, the "Arab Spring" arrived, became the Arab Summer, then Fall, then gone! It seems the Arab Spring was not a refreshing democratic uprising at all. American intervention in Libya produced the assassination of our Ambassador and three others, plus chaos and a failed state. Currently, they have a government in exile with various factions fighting over the country. Our influence to have Mubarak step aside in Egypt gave us the Muslim Brotherhood and repression of non-Muslims. Now the country is controlled by the military having removed the duly

---

501 The Editorial Board, *The New York Times*, "The Unlikeliest of Coalitions," September 21, 2014, p. S R10.

502 Elizabeth Dickinson, *Foreign Policy*, "The Case Against Qatar," September 30, 2014.

503 Ala'a Shehabi, "Why is Bahrain Outsourcing Extremism?" *Foreign Policy Journal*, www. foreignpolicy.com, October 10, 2014.

elected President Morsi being replaced by General Al-Sisi as President. Some stability has returned but it is anything but democratic. In Yemen, the royal family regime is fallen and gone with both Al Qaeda and Al Houthis vying for control. Despite prophecies of Syria's Al Assad's demise, he is still in power. So far no good options exist for Syria. The "rebels" opposing his rule are in all probability a consortium of Sunnis, Kurds, Saudi and Turkish Jihadis, and defected Syrian military, each with differing agendas for a post-Assad Syria. Getting most of the attention is the Islamic State (ISIS) due to their torturous videos and slaughter of innocent Christians and Jews.

In addition, no one seems to know what the long-term outcome is going to be in the countries of Tunisia, Egypt, Libya, Bahrain, Jordan or Syria. As Gelvin astutely says, "No one predicted the uprisings, but then no one could have done so. All rebellions, the Arab uprisings included, are by their nature unpredictable as to the course they take." But he goes on to say the moral of the story is not that the experts got it wrong; rather, it is that they thought they could get it right.[504] Stewart Scott of Stratfor Global Intelligence cautions, "Not all Jihadists are linked to Al Qaeda, and not all militant Islamists are Jihadists. Islamists are those who believe Islamic law or Sharia best governs society. Militant Islamists are those who advocate the use of force to establish Sharia."[505] Hence, the so-called Arab Spring drew from many differing groups with only an agreement to see a Syria without Assad. In January of 2013 it was reported how Saudi Arabia was still financing many of the most radical groups. Friedman notes, "Saudi Arabia is channeling money and support to more radical and less politically driven Salafists in Egypt and Syria helping these groups compete with the Muslim Brotherhood."[506]

In addition, perhaps the United States is finally waking up to the financing of Islamic State militants. The Counter Extremism Project, a nonpartisan group, is tracking the existing and potential financial support for Islamic extremism. So far they have identified Qatar, Turkey and Saudi Arabia (all US supporters!) as governments who have failed to prevent private individuals from making donations to terrorist groups. Along with support derived from brutality, stealing and

---

504 James L. Gelvin, *The Arab Uprisings*, pp. 26, 93.
505 Scott Stewart, "Defining al Qaeda," Stratfor Global Intelligence, October 18, 2012.
506 "Coping with the Islamist Threat," Stratfor Global Intelligence, January 4, 2013.

criminality, "nonprofit entities and private individuals in the United States and elsewhere have supported various extremists groups."[507]

The Daily Beast reported Kuwait, Qatar and Saudi Arabia, three major allies of the US, have dual agendas in the war on terror. Even before ISIS was known on the front pages, they were receiving support from these Gulf State countries. Money laundering was especially taking place in Kuwait where the country has emerged as "financing hub for charities and individuals supporting Syria's myriad rebel groups." The article notes, the US Treasury is aware of this relationship, but their general response is one of a "collective shrug." Even former Saudi Ambassador to the US, the darling of the DC cocktail circuit, Prince Bandar bin Sultan, told Secretary of State John Kerry this is what Gulf leaders had to do in light of the failed US policy in Syria and Obama's failure to strike Assad after his using of chemical weapons.[508] The icing on the cake is the White House hosting a Summit on Extremism and the statement made by a State Department spokesperson that "Extremism (not naming radical Islam of course), is generated by the lack of jobs." Do we have a problem here?

But the good news is Kaddafi has joined Osama bin Laden in death, while his country at this writing is still teetering between several factions. Egypt, after ousting President Mubarak, held elections where the Muslim Brotherhood and the more radical Salafist party received the most votes. General Al Sisi deposed President Morsi, head of the Brotherhood. Apparently, the military could no longer stand by and watch Morsi turn the country into a radical Islamist State. Some believe these "spontaneous democratic grass root movements" were inspired if not organized by Islamists. It was all a cover to take power. Some like Bernard Lewis argue it may be a "one man, one vote, one time" event referring how Islamists use the democratic process of elections one time to gain power so that they can then rule by Islamic law.[509]

Time will only tell in the above countries. Perhaps, by the time this book is published the answers will be self-evident. Until then the reality continues that Islam is back; though Osama bin Laden is dead, his ideology lives, and in the final analysis ideology is the enemy in this war. As Ambassador Gold sums up, "unless

---

507 Anne Gearan, "New Group Plans to Spotlight Secret Funding for Islamic State Militants," *The Washington Post*, September 20, 2014.
508 Josh Rogin, "America's Allies Are Funding ISIS," *The Daily Beast*, June 14, 2014.
509 Bernard Lewis, *Faith and Power*, p. 60.

the ideological motivation for terrorism is addressed and indeed, extinguished, then the war on terror will not be won."[510] Husain believes winning this war lies with the country that started it, Arabia. "Reforming the home of the Islam would be a giant step toward winning against extremism in this global battle of ideas."[511]

Conclusion

The journey we have taken through three major faith traditions is now complete. The religious group case studies have revealed how each of the religions cited have used the name of their God and/or religion, their sacred writings, and their previous histories to vindicate violence. The next section will address the "uncommon commonalities" of these religions. Uncommon because they would not be expected at first blush. Common because the groups share certain behavioral and intellectual phenomena. We will then look at how these religions differ and whether a true moral equivalency exists. Many today issue the sound bite "there is no difference between Osama bin Laden and Timothy McVeigh." Is this true or not? If not true, then how do they differ? Finally, some thoughts will be provided sharing the author's views about Countermeasures.

---

510 Dore Gold, *Hatred's Kingdom*, p. 225.
511 "Saudis Must Stop Exporting Extremism."

CHAPTER ELEVEN
Unlikely Bedfellows: Uncommon Commonalities

While nothing is easier than to denounce the evildoer, nothing is more difficult than to understand him"[512]

—**Fyodor Mikhailovich Dostoevsky**

In the big picture of Religious Terrorism up to this present time, eight common characteristics stand out. I call these the *uncommon commonalities* of religious terrorists. They are unlikely bedfellows. But in worldview and behavior they are remarkably similar. First, they share a unique kind of mythology.

---

512 Quoted in *The Sociology and Psychology of Terrorism: Who Becomes a Terrorist and Why?* Rex A. Hudson, Federal Research Division, Library of Congress, September 1999, p. 16.

Golden Age Mythology

I am using the word *mythology* not in the traditional sense of something not true or factual. As used here, it means whether true to history or not, one's perception of history is determinative and useful in providing a romantic vision of past glories. In Jacques Ellul's classic work, *Propaganda*, myth is "the all-encompassing, activating image . . . such an image pushes man to action. Eventually, the myth takes possession of a man's mind so completely that his life is consecrated to it."[513] The myth then becomes fodder for cultivating desires and ambitions to return to better times in the past.

To some Israeli militant settlers within the Kahane movement, the glories of ancient Israel play a critical role in their thought and life. What partially drives these movements is a longing to restore the lost kingdom and territory of Kings David and Solomon, especially during the first Temple period when Israel ruled from Lebanon to the Sinai and from the Mediterranean to the Euphrates (See Genesis 15:18 for boundaries promised by God). To these Jewish settlers, there is no "West Bank" or Palestinian people, only "Judea and Samaria," the Biblical names for what is now called "occupied territory" by the Palestinians and most Arabs. To restore these ancient boundaries is paramount in preparing for the advent of the Messiah and the "end of days."

Looking back to some previous time in history is amazingly common in the American evangelical movement today, in spite of the prophetic gurus who are looking ahead! The *Purists* want to restore the church to what it was in the first century when, they say, the persecuted church was the strongest, most faithful and committed. Of course, when I read the New Testament, I don't exactly see a *pure church*, but a church filled with the same problems and sins we face today. (Read Romans and I Corinthians for a start.) Some Christians are trying to get back to the Reformation and rebuild Calvin's Geneva. To them this was the period when the Protestant church was the most vibrant, Biblical and pure. A time that must be restored! Other evangelicals look to the early colonial period of Puritanism. My wife and I once knew a couple who insisted on having their young children sleep with them in the same bed simply because they had read somewhere it was what the Puritans did! Obviously for them, this was one of the keys to a more spiritual family time. Others look to the 1950s

---

513 Jacques Ellul, *Propaganda*, Vintage Books, 1973, p. 31.

"Father Knows Best" culture when the church and society in general was the strongest.[514] Catholics are still somewhat split between the Council of Trent and Vatican II. Vatican II brought significant changes in its attitude toward Protestants and the traditional views of Mary and the Mass. But now there is a fundamentalist Catholic resurgence that wants to restore the Latin mass and again view Protestants as "heretics."[515]

What all these perspectives share is a belief that true spirituality lies somewhere in the past. Within the Christian Identity and Reconstruction movements, it is easy to justify a militancy going back to the Crusades when Christians used the sword to defend Christianity against Muslims; or to see defending innocents by force of arms as granted by Just War theory! For each, a history exists to justify their actions. The only difference lies in dates! Much has been said about the "Golden Age of Islam." Many tributaries, including Jewish and Christian ones, contributed to the Golden Age of Islam. Though dates vary, and early tributaries predate mine, many date it from the Crusader fall of Jerusalem in 1187 to the invasion of the Levant by Napoleon at the end of the seventeenth century. However, as noted earlier the glory years started in Baghdad in the eighth century and probably peaked around the fourteenth. This reign of Islam over North Africa, the Middle East, East Asia and the Balkans lasted over 600 years. These were the glory years when Islam triumphed and Christians were defeated and subjugated under the rule of Islamic conquerors. Al Qaeda, ISIS and others want to restore this empire, reinstitute the Caliphate and make Sharia the law of the land. This Islamic Golden Age vision plays well among those who believe the West has corrupted, supplanted and destroyed Islam.

It is correctly observed that each of these faith groups looks back to a period of its history to justify its militant views. This *commonality* is one of many factors that characterizes those who do violence in the name of God . . . they share a golden age myth.

---

514 See my book, *The Christian Family in Changing Times*, for a further development of these Christian family myths. Baker Book House, 2002.

515 At the Council of Trent, Protestants were declared heretics. At the first Vatican Council Trent was reaffirmed. But at the second Vatican Council Protestants were declared "errant brethren" drastically changing the relationship between Protestants and Catholics. Officially, Catholics are under Vatican II administration but some in the Fundamentalist movement want to return to Vatican I and Trent.

Perception of *Theft of Culture*

Human nature is consistent in that when things are not as we would like them to be, we must find someone to blame. This second commonality among religious terrorists is they have a built-in psyche of blame for their failure or defeat. If these faith groups once experienced a *golden age* and it no longer exists, then it begs the question as to what happened. Rather than doing the hard analysis of historical and cultural examination, it is easier to say, "If we were once a glorious religion, and now we are not, then someone must have stolen our greatness."

For Kach and the Jewish radical movement, the clear thief is the liberal secular Labor party. From their perception this party has little concern for the rights of existing settlements and their theological commitment to a *Greater Israel* consisting of the West Bank. In the extreme, they believe putting the Jewish nation at risk justifies a violent response and even murder in the name of God, the assassination of a Prime Minister. As these religious militants see it, the secular State has no real justification in calling itself a Jewish State, because the secularists have either stolen its Jewish soul or by their laws prohibited it from moving in that direction.

Many American Christians use the same argument about their own government. Whether they are Christian Identity adherents, reconstruction evangelicals, or just plain *good 'ol boys*, what they share is contempt for liberal, secular politicians. They offer arguments that liberal secular humanism has destroyed our schools, made a tyranny of political correctness, and are constantly coming after their guns. As one militia member said recently, "We don't need our guns for hunting but to protect us against the government!" Over time, the names have changed as to who the real thief is, but in these groups there are always names. Years ago they were Bill Clinton and Janet Reno, now it is President Obama and company. If our nation is not what it used to be, then someone is at fault. We need the thief to explain the reality of its demise.

There seems to be a trend here. As I come to Islamic militants, they too believe someone stole the glorious Islamic culture. Clearly, the same enemy is argued: Western, godless, materialistic, addicted to sex, imperialistic America. These attributes of the West have stolen the soul of Islam. As Sayyid Qutb decried, "The problem is the West, the solution is Islam." To the ideologues of radical Islam, it is the West that has corrupted the world, subjugated Islam and spewed out all the Hollywood sensuality, legitimizing gay relationships and filling the culture with pornography that destroys families and traditional values. To protect itself against this disease, the only recourse true Islamists see is to strike back at the source . . . for them it is justifiable war!

Heroic Founder/Leader

Very few of us are one hundred percent intrinsically motivated. It is takes someone from the outside to stir our imaginations, give us an interpretation of what is wrong and inspire us to action. This is the role heroic founders/leaders play for our religions and the individuals who follow them. Religious zealotry is usually driven by actual or symbolic-heroic leaders. All the religious groups studied in this work demonstrate this reality. Judaism was founded by Heroic leaders: Abraham, Joseph, Moses, Joshua, David, and the Prophets all provided leadership and direction to pursue the One True God amidst pagan hostile gentile nations. Time and again, against the spiritual decline of the nation of Israel, Jewish prophets were raised up who spoke the *Word of God,* summoning His people back to faithfulness. These voices, written down, became the Sacred Scriptures of Torah with the rabbinic commentaries to follow called the Talmud. The Heroic leadership of these characters today provides the inspiration for modern Jewish radicals like Rabbi Meir Kahane, Rabbi Zvi Kook, and Dr. Baruch Goldstein. Today, they still inspire the settlement and Temple movements. Jesus Christ, of course, founded Christianity. Claiming to be the Son of God, Son of Man, and the Jewish Messiah made him a threat to the governing leadership. But instead of becoming the leader of a political revolt against Rome and the Jewish leadership, he taught as no one ever taught. He was a leader unlike any other in history. He rode a donkey not a horse, voluntarily gave himself up to an unjust death and gave his disciples a commission to take his message to the world. His sermon on the mount seemed strangely counter-cultural, and in his life and teaching he seemed more pacific than revolutionary. However, followers of Christ centuries later believed and acted differently. Popes and kings justified the Crusades, "taking the cross" while also taking the sword to defend Christendom and regain access to the Holy sites in Jerusalem. Whole national armies would fight what they considered "Just Wars" in the name of Christ during the European Thirty Years' war, and the Puritan Oliver Cromwell would use the sword and his Christian convictions to justify the English Civil War. Each of these events was sold to commoners as a righteous conflict by heroic leaders who were able to inspire their countrymen and armies. Times have not changed. Today, a new phenomenon has emerged called *leaderless resistance*. Timothy McVeigh and Eric Rudolph and Major Nidal Hasan were not part of any organized local group. Often called *lone wolves*, they were radicalized or self-recruited while being leaderless. This view fails to look in detail as to how ideology of even dead leaders (Kahane, Schaeffer, Richard Butler or Sayyid Qutb, Anwar Al-Alawaki[516]) can influence individuals through their writings or the internet.[517]

Just as the supremely heroic leader of Jesus Christ founded Christianity, so it was with Islam. Both Christ and Mohammad, when called to their mission, faced a major source of conflict from the leadership of the day. But unlike Christ, Mohammad took the sword to advance his message. His followers took the Crescent and Sword even further. By the seventh century, Islam had conquered North Africa, the Middle East, Spain and half of France. Names like Saladin the Great, the conqueror of Jerusalem, Suleiman the Magnificent, the conqueror of the Balkans, and Mehmet II, the conqueror of Constantinople are the heroic leaders of Islam. They are cherished and honored as we value the heroics of George Washington, Robert E. Lee, George Patton or Dwight Eisenhower. Of course, some called Osama bin Laden the new Saladin fighting the Crusaders and Jews, and he is now viewed as a heroic martyr still leading though dead!

Radical movements have leaders; heroic ones who do spectacular things. The ISIS leader Abu Bakr al-Baghdadi currently inspires and recruits followers to take his message further and act upon it. Their actions are extremely violent where beheadings have become common. Their attitudes and actions leave no room for neutrality

Polarized World View

I have a category of people who really bother me. I call them individuals who live in the *subjunctive mood*. This, of course, is a grammatical term which is the opposite

---

516 Al Awaki is the American born cleric who was an Imam in Falls Church, Virginia before going to Yemen and becoming an influential member of Al Qaeda in the Arabic Peninsula. He was killed by a drone strike in September of 2011. Federal law prohibits the killing of Americans without due process, and this targeted strike against an American citizen raised many eyebrows about assassinations and International law.

517 See ISIS' latest publication online called Dabiq; Dabiq is the site in northern Syria where the Ottomans defeated the Mamluks in a sixteenth century battle to establish the last Caliphate before Al-Baghdadi's Islamic State, "Dabiq: IS 'Caliphat's' Latest Magazine," www. pakistantoday.com, July 10, 2014.

of the *indicative* mood. The indicative mood is the mood of reality or facts. The subjective mood is the mood of maybe, often translated or communicated as *should, would or could.* In the world of militants and those who do violence in the name of their religion there are no maybes. Everything is absolute. In other words, terrorists have a polarized worldview. The color grey does not exist!

The same commonality is found in extremist Judaism. To the likes of Rabbi Kahane, there existed only two worlds . . . the one secular, liberal, compromising Labor government and their followers, and the other: the religious, Torah keeping, faithful individuals dedicated to seeing all of God's law carried out with restoration of all ancient territory. Not much middle ground! Those willing to compromise land for peace (like Rabin) are considered traitors to the Jewish cause. Those who are willing to put their faith in action by resisting the Palestinians and taking the land even through violence (justified by Rabbis), are the faithful, true believers. They are the ones who will usher in the Messianic age.

Christianity has the same version in the extreme. The New Testament describes two classes of people: believers and nonbelievers. The believers will go to Heaven and be with Jesus, the unbelievers will face eternal punishment. To Protestant evangelicals, there is no middle ground or Purgatory . . . no second chance. We either accept Jesus as our Savior or die in our sins. We either walk with Jesus or we are of the world. We walk in the light or in darkness. This absolutist dichotomy creates a polarized worldview and makes one somewhat set up for a heroic leader's call to action and decision. To prove we are not of the darkness but of the light, we are asked to perform some act . . . an act defined, of course, by some leader. Therefore, when a preacher says, "something must be done about the innocent slaughter of unborn children," one might conclude what needs to be done is to take a shotgun down to the local abortion clinic and prove to be a person of the light! This may be overstated, but as a former pastor myself, it places a great responsibility upon a preacher to make sure not only that his exposition of scripture is clear, but also what a reasonable application or action should look like for the listeners. This is why I think the New Testament writer James says, "Let not many of you become teachers . . . knowing that as such you incur a stricter judgment" (James 3:1).

Islam follows the same logic. There are only two kinds of people, Muslims and everyone else (Infidels), the classic *us* versus *them.* Yes, Jews and Christians are considered *people of the book,* but this tolerated category as shown earlier only means they are of secondary status to Muslims, called dhimmis. There are only two kinds of worlds, Dar-al-Islam (where Islam rules) and Dar-al-Harb (the world of warfare). Nothing in between! Muslims will gain Paradise by being faithful and if their good works outweigh their bad or if they die as martyrs. (Children under the Islamic law age of innocence and those mentally deficient are exempted and given Paradise.) Non-Muslims will face hell fire! Only Muslims can make pilgrimage, everyone else is banned from the holy sites. To be a faithful Muslim is to pray five times a day and practice Sharia law. Those who do not are not true Muslims and are considered traitors to their religion. Iranian expatriate Amir Taheri[518] confesses, "The Party of Allah (Hizballah) admits to no doubt and no speculation."

It does not recommend thinking, but "repeating the Truth as revealed once and for all in the Holy Book." Consequently, what Ibn Taymmaya, Sayyid Qutb, the Muslim Brotherhood and Osama bin Laden have in common (along with the other religions) is this common trait of a polarized world-view. What this means for all the extremists in these faith groups is that there is no room for compromise, middle ground, critical dialogue or discourse. To be in the middle is to be nowhere, a traitor to both sides, and one guilty of not being a true believer. This is one of the major problems facing and solving the Palestinian issue! In addition, what often drives one to these extremes is the feeling or reality of being marginalized.

Experience of Marginalization

As a Christian living in a secular society I often feel marginalized. As a military chaplain, I have experienced unspoken marginalization at times. In a meeting we were once talking about suicide, a major issue facing the military services today, and I brought up the resource of a personal, practicing faith is a major preventer of suicide. I remember the looks around the table, particularly from some in the mental health community or the gung-ho tough-guy warriors. I could see immediately I had violated the protocol by putting issues of faith into the discussion. The evil-eye stares said clearly "this is not appropriate to the discussion."[519] One might think

---

518 Amir Taheri, *Holy Terror: Inside the World of Islamic Terrorism*, Adler & Adler, 1987, p. 233.

519 The U.S Army bought into a "Resiliency Program" designed by an Ivy League University which made it very clear Chaplains were not to be involved in the training program. One might have thought issues of meaning and purpose in life as derived from religion might give one hope to continue on and be more "resilient"! But unfortunately in the military some believe we can't talk about that or include religion as a part of the discussion about what makes a person "resilient"!

a true faith in God might give meaning and hope for a despondent person! God forbid, says the committed secularist!

As noted previously, Israeli right-wing militants started out on the fringe of their society. Early on, Kahane was viewed as crazy, but now bumper stickers display "Kahane was right"! The secular government of Israel did not grant due respect to the religious right and thus marginalized them from the political process. Even when Meir Kahane was duly elected to the Knesset, the government banned his party from the coalition and eventually completely outlawed the Kach party. When Begin, the first religious Prime Minister, was elected the religious parties believed their commitments would be honored. However, at Camp David the religious right felt betrayed when he gave back the Sinai and Gaza to make peace with President Sadat of Egypt. Of course, PM Rabin, as noted, completely ignored the religious right and did not take them seriously. He was gunned down by one who felt marginalized by the mainstream Israeli society and finally acted upon it.

The voices of the American religious right are often portrayed as ignorant, uneducated, Bible and gun-toting extremists. Some may be, but for most, they are middle class American citizens who love their country, kids, and Jesus. Yes, some may be extreme or at least viewed that way by the media, but the question perhaps is why they have been attracted to the extreme right. The experience of being a seriously religious person in twenty-first century America is often an experience of being marginalized. We can't pray or have a Bible at public schools. Of course, no crosses on government property (Arlington Cemetery still excluded, thank God)!

Were Timothy McVeigh, Eric Rudolph, and a host of others in the militia movement marginalized? They certainly weren't mainstream . . . they did not exactly belong to a Presbyterian or Episcopalian church or the local Lions Club! Whether by choice, circumstances, or cult community, the ones who have done violence are those who feel disenfranchised by their government, mainstream churches, or society at large.

Sayyid Qutb, when he returned from his study in America, found Egypt a mere image of what he saw in the US. His native country was moving swiftly toward the Western values of secularism, materialism and sensuality. His Islamic faith no longer fit the country of his origin. He experienced this sense of marginalization. The sense deepened the more he pursued what he deemed was a purest form of Islam. He was disenfranchised by President Nasser, jailed and finally executed while in prison. His writings detail his permanent resentment toward both the West and his country that had failed to take his Islamic faith seriously. Osama bin Laden, after he returned from the Soviet war in Afghanistan, also felt marginalized by the time-honored custodians of the most holy places in Arabia. When the Royal family refused his offer to use the Mujahidin against Saddam Hussein in Kuwait he felt betrayed. Instead of accepting his help, the Saudis basically hired mercenaries from the United States to protect their land and rid Kuwait of Saddam. To bin Laden, it was defilement of the most holy land of Saudi Arabia. Being disenfranchised by his own government, he turned to violence against them, the West and Israel. The result was 9/11! The Saudi Royal family was viewed as corrupt by bin Laden and he openly called for their removal if not destruction. They had lost their legitimacy in his eyes.

Delegitimized Authority

How governmental authority becomes legitimate is beyond the scope of this book. However, in past history we have moved from the divine right of kings (powers who became *Royal* simply because they won a battle someplace and then argued that it was God's will), to constitutional monarchies, to democratic republics with elected officials. However governments came to be, they continued to exist by some element of consent by the governed that deemed them legitimate. A commonality observed in all terrorist faith traditions is there is a line that gets crossed somewhere in the mind of the individual terrorist or group. The line is where a governing power is no longer viewed by the individual as having legitimate authority over their life. Delegitimization then leads easily to justification for removal, revolution or assassination of the ruler.

More than anything else, the assassination of Prime Minister Rabin was due to his loss of legitimacy within the religious Jewish community. As mentioned in previous chapters, many were bantering about talk of a *Moser* and *Rodef* being placed upon their leader. Rabin was threatening to sink the Jewish ship by his concessions of giving up the West Bank and Golan Heights for the sake of peace with the Palestinians and Syria. He had marginalized the religious and they in turn delegitimized his authority. With apparent rabbinic justification and approval, delegitimization put him in a category of being worthy of removal by death. Mission accomplished by Yigal Amir!

Soon after President Clinton's election, I went to my office on a National Guard Base. Upon entering the front door, I noticed the picture frame where the Commander in Chief's picture goes was vacant. I thought, correctly, the new photo was not yet available. Weeks later when I walked through the door I noticed someone had put a picture of Hillary Clinton in the frame where the President's photo should have been. I laughed and didn't think much about it until I went into my Commander's staff meeting. When he heard about the photo he was furious and immediately sent a person to retrieve Hillary's photo.[520] We then got an earful about "respecting" our Commander in Chief no matter who his wife was and how we needed to keep our personal beliefs to ourselves.

What this illustrates is how even in our conversation and small actions we can delegitimize authority. Some airman used his or her personal views about Hillary Clinton to delegitimize the office of the President of the United States. My commander would not stand for it. As reported previously, the militia movement in America often delegitimizes our government accusing them of anti-religious bias, allowing religious rights to be violated, trying to overturn or get around the Second Amendment, and not protecting the unborn. The Montana Freemen have taken this to the extreme by saying the only legitimate government authority is that of the County Sheriff. Theologian Francis Schaeffer in his *Christian Manifesto* argued when a government does not protect the unborn, it loses its legitimacy and Christians are obligated to demonstrate civil disobedience.

In the Iranian revolution, the Shah of Iran had so lost his legitimacy that an aged cleric living remotely in France could begin a revolution by cassette tapes. By the time he arrived back in Iran, the popular revolt willingly accepted him as the legitimate ruler of the country. The same is the case with the Muslim Brotherhood, Al Qaeda and other extreme Muslim groups. Some of the Gulf State rulers are still somewhat under siege by popular street movements originally called the *Arab Spring*. Though this *Spring* failed, the Arab street still rages against their leaders' tyranny and lack of liberty for individuals. These uprisings accuse their existing governments of being illegitimate because they have failed to meet the democratic or Muslim standards for rulers. The Arab Spring, though viewed as a thing of the past, may not be completely over. No one is able to predict the outcome. As of

---

520 Of course, as of this writing, Secretary Hillary Clinton's name is being offered as a possible candidate for the presidency in 2016. So the picture in the frame may have been prophetic or wish fulfillment!

this writing Egypt has been taken over by a military dictatorship; Yemen, Libya, Iraq and Syria are all in chaos. Afghanistan may fall to the Taliban (again) after all American troops are gone. But one thing is certain: Osama bin Laden viewed the Saudi royal family as corrupt, tyrannical, spoiled, hypocritical and not worthy of rule. Their lavish lifestyle and whoring princes were an embarrassment to Islam. Though bin Laden is dead there are many more who share his view. With the new Saudi King Salman and a new generation of leaders no one really knows the future of this key Middle East country. For many in these faith groups, movements like these are signs pointing to a coming apocalypse.

Apocalypticism

When the Temple compound was secured by Israeli troops in the 1967 war, Rabbi Shlomo Goren, head of the military Rabbinate, ran to the Mount blowing a Shofar (ram's horn) with a Torah scroll under his arm. He then told Major General Uzi Narkiss to immediately blow up the Mosque of Omar (Dome). His argument was if they did not do it then, it would be impossible later. Narkiss refused. The rabbi's argument centered on the reality that if Jerusalem was back in Jewish hands, and Temple Mount under their control, "redemption was at hand."[521] The interpreted message of Rabbi Yehudah Kook given on May 14, days before the war broke out, and later viewed as prophetic, promoted the idea that May 14 began the countdown to the end of the world. What is driving much of the terror activity in the Israeli right wing is the belief that the end of days is upon them. The footsteps of the Messiah can be heard, and the only thing standing in the way of His return is the Temple Mount being held by an Islamic Waqf (the leading cleric who administers the mosque in Jerusalem), who refuses to let Jews walk on the holy ground. To those on the Israeli radical right, it is desecration of the Name (of God), and only their actions to restore the Temple will bring full redemption to the nation. Apparently for some, action means . . . by any means possible!

Even a 1999 paper produced by the American Air Force listed concerns over a nuclear weapon falling into the hands of an Israeli right-wing militant group: "Could Gush Emunim . . . or others, hijack a nuclear device to *liberate* the Temple Mount for building of the third temple? Chances are small but could increase as radicals decry the peace process." Quoting another source, the paper stressed the

---

521 Gorenberg, *The End of Days*, p. 101.

"possibilities of, and the need to guard against, a religious right-wing military coup, especially as the proportions of religious in the military increase."[522] For these, the times are apocalyptic. As Gorenberg concludes, "apocalyptic agendas have no room for Israel as a normal country."[523]

It is well known the former Iranian Prime Minister often spoke in apocalyptic terms. Many in the West did not regard his statements as sincere but only typical Middle East rhetoric. Remember the same was said before 9/11 about the sayings of Osama bin Laden! Mahmoud Ahmadinejad's first appearance before the United Nations saw him open with a prayer for "the hasty return of the Mahdi." The Mahdi, as noted earlier, is a person who according to Islamic Shia tradition will appear in the last days, and is a direct descendant of the last Mahdi, Muhammud Abu-lkasem or the Twelfth Iman. This Hidden One will be revealed prior to the Last Judgment and will conquer the world for Islam. Ahmadinejad in other public messages also alluded to the task of all Muslims "preparing the way for the advent of the Mahdi and his conquering of the world." He added, "A great event will lead to all mankind's salvation." As of 2014 Israel was estimating that Iran was actively pursuing and is almost ninety percent complete in building its nuclear weapons program. However now that the US has made an agreement with Iran, everybody is waiting to see what's going to happen. That, mixed with statements like, "Iran must become the platform for the appearance of the Lord of the Age," makes one wonder what Ahmadinejad's real plan was? Did he really believe the "event" that will kick off the age of the Mahdi is an apocalyptic nuclear blast? Of course, Ahmadinejad is now gone, and it is not yet clear whether the new Prime Minister will follow in his footsteps or take a different course.

Intelligence writer George Friedman argues Al Qaeda was also seeking a nuclear weapon with the possibility that either Iraq or Pakistan might provide a weapon.[524] So, on both sides of the Shia (Iranian) and Sunni (Al Qaeda) Islamic divide, these two groups were, and maybe still are, actively pursuing weapons of

---

522 Lt Colonel Warner D. Farr, US Army, "The Third Temple's Holy of Holies: Israel's Nuclear Weapons," The *Counterproliferation Papers*, Future Warfare Series, #2, USAF Counterproliferation Center, Air War College, Air University, Maxwell Air Force Base, Alabama, September, 1999, p. 21.

523 Ibid., p. 240.

524 George Friedman, in *America's Secret War*, states, "Strong evidence was emerging about close links, and some hints of nuclear collaboration, between Al Qaeda and the ISI (Pakistani Intelligence)." p. 217.

mass destruction capable of ushering in an apocalyptic event that would prove the superiority of Islam over the world. In fact, noted prophecy author Grant Jeffrey says the goal of this "Third Great Jihad" is to "develop and use nuclear, chemical and biological weapons to annihilate the enemies of Islam."[525]

As mentioned earlier, the ISIS official magazine, called Dabiq, reminds Muslims that this is the place mentioned by "Muhammad's companion Abu Hurayrah where "Roman's invaders are defeated, paving the way for the armies of God to expand and defeat Satan." Rome meant both the actual Byzantine Christians, and the symbol for all Christian, non-Muslims.[526] Geronberg summarizes, "For Muslims, Jerusalem is the arena of the apocalyptic battles, and capital of the perfected world."

Bassam Jirrar, a leading religious teacher and writer in the West Bank, says succinctly that Islam began in Mecca and Medina and will end in Jerusalem."[527] We all hope these opinions are wrong!

No one has taken the concept of the Apocalyptic further than Christians. In fact, the Greek word "apokalupsis" is the first word found in the book of "Revelation" from which the word is translated into English. Of course, Revelation is the last book of the Christian New Testament. These writings of the Apostle John's revelation or vision concern the end times including fierce judgments from God and the ultimate victorious return of Christ. Hence, throughout Christian Church history the book of Revelation has contributed theories about the identity of the Antichrist, and the timing of the Christ's return. To those in the Christian Identity movement, the Antichrist is often identified with the "ungodly leaders" of the Federal Government. (In my lifetime, mostly democratic presidents, Carter, Clinton and now Obama.) For the more Anti-Semitic groups, they see the evil forces identified as a Jewish cabal who controls the world through media and banking conspiracies. (New World Order). But for most in mainstream evangelical circles the establishment of the nation of the Israel in 1947 was the trigger point that put us in the last days. "The last of these last days" will culminate with a seven year treaty made by an Antichrist figure who makes peace in the Middle East. For three and half years the peace is successful. At the end of that time the treaty is broken and all hell breaks loose. A great tribulation begins followed by an all-out attack on Israel by a confederation

525 Grant Jeffrey, *The Next World War*, Waterbrook Press, 2006, p. 63.
526 "Dabiq: IS 'Caliphate's Latest Magazine.'"
527 Gorenberg, *The End of Days*, p. 191.

of nations led by Russia (called Gog and Magog in Ezekiel 38). At some point in the battle Christ returns, saves the nation of Israel and the world, and establishes his earthly reign. At that point believers in Christ share in the inheritance of his kingdom while the unbelievers are judged accordingly. Many disagree on the details, but overall, this seems to be the general thrust.

Christian Reconstructionists believe they must prepare the way for Christ's return by re-establishing the Ten Commandments and righteous living as law of the land. Therefore, abortion, pornography, and gay marriage are high on their list of social evils to be fought against. Many evangelicals believe their unconditional support for the nation of Israel is the critical key for the return of Christ. That's why many financially support the building of the Third Temple to enhance the return of the Messiah. Prophecy buff Chuck Missler is quoted as saying "Understanding where the Temple stood is a major prerequisite to any ambition to rebuild . . . the implicit purpose of probing beneath the Mount, even without moving a stone, was to hurry the End."[528] Of course, all this theorizing on the Biblical books of Ezekiel, Daniel and Revelation eventually leads to speculating about the exact timing of Jesus' return. We have observed the letdown of Harold Camping on his date setting of June 21, 2011, for the Rapture of the Church. What date setting does is increase the motivation toward apocalyptic thinking. And apocalyptic thinking increases the likelihood that some will respond to the message with acts of violence to hurry the end. Religious terrorists share some sense of urgency to do what they do! But there is one more commonality among these terrorists.

Divine Favor/Benediction

As developed in an earlier chapter, a basic uniqueness of the religious terrorists over against the old political left-wing terrorists is their sincere belief in the divine. The truly religious terrorists actually believe they will gain some favor with their God or divine representative by performing the violent act. They seek divine benediction for their actions. As shown throughout this book, each case study has demonstrated this reality. This is what separates the true believer from the madman. The madman does not need justification for his violence. He may be driven by his own personal demons, but sending a message to someone, someplace to find favor with them is not in his conscience. Even street gangs operate more on the religious terrorism

---

528 Ibid., p. 126.

model in this regard. Their acts of violence are often done as proofs of allegiance or initiation rites.

The disciples of Meir Kahane and other right wing Israeli radicals like Yigal Amir have publically revealed they would not have performed their violent acts without some rabbinical benediction. In fact, Jewish law forbids the taking of lives without the exception of having a pronouncement of a Rodef and Moser by rabbinic authority. Remember plans to blow up the Al Asqa mosque were called off simply because the rabbinic authorities would not give their benediction to it. Claims to make Yigal Amir, (PM Rabin's assassin), a lone, crazed gunman fails upon this examination of the role of rabbinic authority.

Certainly, within the Christian community a doctrine of civil disobedience exists. As noted previously, even scholars like Francis Schaeffer and Dietrich Bonhoeffer believed there are certain points when the Christian teaching of "turning the other check" must be overridden by the practical realities of evil. For Bonhoeffer, it was the evil machinations of Adolf Hitler that sent him underground, covertly trying to speak out and work against the Nazi regime. For Schaeffer, it was the evil of abortion as the murder of innocents. Faith in action must sometimes use the sword (violence or resistance) in order to save lives or secure a more just society, so they argue. Certainly this was the case with Eric Rudolph who saw himself a soldier in the Army of God, acting to protect the lives of the unborn, and demonstrate against what he saw as a severe evil to our society . . . openly gay clubs. Rudolph openly confessed he was doing his acts in the name of God. Divine authority was his justification. Those who murder abortion doctors argue innocent lives have been saved by destroying the agents who would murder thousands. Scriptural authority offers them benedictions like, "keep far from a false charge, and do not kill the innocent or the righteous, for I (God) will not acquit the guilty" (Exodus 23:7). They then see themselves acting as God's agents on the earth.

Islamic Jihadists have taken the element of divine favor to an art form. They sincerely believe they have Allah's ultimate justification in offering up their lives for the sake of Jihad. They receive a free ticket to Paradise by their martyrdom, when the rest of the Muslim world must await the final judgment. Palestinian poet Mahmoud Darwish exalts the honor of choosing one's death: "Do you, gentlemen, and specialists in genocide, wish to deprive me even of the liberty of choosing my death?"[529] Of course, there is also the lively promise of seventy-two brown-eyed virgins! Those living in the West, by supporting Jihad financially or rendering other kinds of material support, also receive a divine benediction for their acts. Amir Taheri points out, "adding to the number of believers and reducing that of the infidels is one of the most important duties of the militant fundamentalist."[530] So Muslims offer up their lives for Jihad acting on the instruction of their Imams who offer Koranic justification for the violent acts. The individual Jihadi believes he or she has the very benediction of Allah. They see themselves as holy warriors, no different than the uniformed military of the United States. They call it war . . . maybe so should we!

The above eight *uncommon commonalities* help define and delineate what makes the religious terrorist unique and as a result, far more difficult to understand than the mere political terrorists of past decades. These religious terrorists view the world differently, and act accordingly. But it also helps to understand how the individual mind of the terrorist operates. What is surprising about the next list is how most of these contributing factors are found to a lesser extent in most believers, regardless of the religion. The difference then lies in the matter of extremes.

Contributing Factors within the Mind of the Terrorist

Most alert readers have observed these contributing factors several times. Here, they are illustrated as to how the mind of the terrorist works. First, all the religious groups studied held their beliefs based upon the revered authority of their *Sacred Literature*. Jewish extremists are greatly influenced by the Torah and the Talmud. Their minds are formed by authoritative passages of Holy Scripture. So too, for Christians! The final authority for evangelicals is the inspired Word of God. Those wanting to justify violence or resistance in the name of God must find scriptural authority in either the Old or New Testaments. For Catholics, it is both their scriptures and Catholic tradition that can be used to justify the protection of life. Of course, for Muslims, the Koran is the final revelation from God and most accurate since it "corrects" all previous revelations made in the Jewish and Christian Bibles. In sum, the religious terrorists noted in this book "use" their sacred writings to justify violence. The opinion of this writer is, many of these

---

529 Quoted in *Holy Terror*, p. 101.
530 Amir Taheri, *Holy Terror*, p. 31.

"uses" are illegitimate, contrived and taken out of context or manipulated by their leaders. Some verses in fact mean what they say! As Mark Twain supposedly once said, "it's not what I don't understand in the Bible that disturbs me, it is what I do understand."

The second contributing factor is the role of the *Holy Man as Leader/Interpreter*. All groups have leaders who both interpret the world and the sacred writings: individuals like Meir Kahane, some Christian Prophecy televangelists, and Osama bin Laden. Most religious adherents don't "connect the dots" on their own. They don't see who the enemy is, or what they should do about it. Many are not familiar enough with their own scriptures to make connections between what is going in the world and what they believe their Bibles have to say about it. This is the role of the "Holy Man" who will guide and inform the unlearned. It took Sayyid Qutb to articulate what was wrong with Islam and what to do about it; it takes people like Hal Lindsey and Jack van Impe and their "Intelligence" reports to let Christians know what is really going on behind the daily news. It took Rabbi Kahane to declare things that no one else dared to speak about Palestinians. Even though much is discussed today about "leaderless resistance," every religious terrorist has a leader somewhere who functions as ideological guru. Though dead, they still live in print, on the Internet or are alive on cassette tapes CDs, DVDs and videos. Remember the American Al-Awaki created the radical Islamist magazine *Inspire* on the internet, and it is still available though he is dead.[531] Alive or dead, they continue to inform and inspire the mind of the terrorist. Major Hasan was a disciple of Al Alwaki!

Submission of the Individual and *Suppression of Critical Thought* is next. Cult psychology at some point takes over, and the devotee willingly allows his mind to be taken over by the ideology of his mentor. I have had discussions with fellow Christians on various points of Biblical prophecy, and at some point they do not want to hear my questions or critique of their views. Their minds are made up. Likewise, whether in the Madrassas in Pakistan or a fundamentalist church in Washington DC, the goal is often mere recitation and memorization. Critical thought is not encouraged or allowed. A Muslim professor in Lebanon was thrown out of a four-story window and killed by his students. His crime? He merely raised a question about the possibility that Mohammed might have used other sources

---

531 One issue praises Osama bin Laden, saying, "We are all Osama," Spring, 2013, Issue 10.

for the Koran and not direct recitation from Allah. So much for critical thought! Traitors are often looked upon as worse than infidels simply because they were once in the cult and by leaving have betrayed the secrets. Once someone claims to know all the truth, there is no room for further discussion. This is common in the mind of religious terrorists.

The fourth factor that contributes to the mind of terrorists is a belief in a *Hierarchy of Values.* In other words, some values have greater moral and ethical importance than others. For a pro-life activist, the value of protecting life (of the unborn) is of greater importance than obeying the law. To save the lives of the many takes precedence over the prohibition of murdering one. Thus, it's the hierarchy of values that sets one up to perform violent acts that seem murderous to most. Another illustration is that obeying God takes precedence over the killing of innocent civilians. Yigal Amir saw himself as obeying the higher value of "saving the Jewish nation" in the name of God rather than obeying the Jewish and Israeli law against murder. In this regard, he was unrepentant and believed he had done the right thing. Timothy McVeigh argued the same way. He saw himself as a good soldier fighting against the evil government who had killed innocents at both Ruby Ridge and the Waco compound of the Branch Davidians. In his mind, soldiers are exempted from normal civilian laws. In combat, the military ethic transcends civilian jurisprudence. (This is obviously not true: during World War II the Nazi Nuremburg trials confirmed "following orders" was not a legitimate defense). Khalid Sheikh Mohammad, the 9/11 mastermind, argued the same. He saw himself a soldier in the army of Allah, and as a soldier believed there are no noncombatants. All infidels are the enemy and worthy of death unless they convert. The terrorist mind is developed around a hierarchy of values.

The fifth factor goes directly to theology: that of *External Divine Will.* This one is difficult because it can be so controversial. I still remember taking my first MMPI (Minnesota Multiphasic Personality Inventory). To get into graduate school everyone had to take it, I guess to see if we were crazy or not. I remember the difficulty of answering the question "Does God speak to you?" As a Christian, I believe God speaks to us in many ways, but I knew if I said, "Yes" to the question, I would be viewed as a borderline psycho! Such is the problem with this factor. Religious terrorists believe or are taught to believe there is a true external divine will. They do not necessarily actually hear a subjective voice in their ears but believe God has revealed his will in some objective way . . . for most it us in the Sacred Scripture. This means God has a specific will or purpose He wants to see accomplished in this world. It means His will is external to mine; they are not one and the same. It follows then, if I desire to be obedient, I must align my will with His will and seek to accomplish His will on earth. For Christians, it is rooted in Jesus saying to his Father, "Not my will, but Thy will be done." It is also part of the prayer our Lord taught us, "Thy will be done on earth as in Heaven." In Islam, the will of Allah is determinative of everything that happens. If the Koran says, "Make war on the unbelievers and hypocrites," (66:9) then this is the will of Allah. If the Torah delineates the geographical dimensions of the Promised Land, then this is the will of God for the Jewish nation. The true believer will seek to fulfill the divine will.

The final factor that forms the mind of the religious terrorist is that of *Belief in Divine Calling*. Again, this is a theological factor the nonreligious do not understand or think relevant. But in each of the religious groups studied the factor is present. The belief functions to make the adherent take the final step toward performing some action. Since there is the belief in divine will, the final step is when the person believing God specifically does something in His name. Believers understand this: they routinely encounter specific demands outlined in scripture or while listening to sermons in mosques, synagogues and churches. When the preacher reads a scripture passage like "Love one another" and says, "This is what God asks of us," the final step for the Christian is to accept the admonition and do something to manifest love for his fellow man. The same dynamic happens when a Jewish rabbi says, "we must protect God's promised land" or the Imam says "we must take back our civilization" or a pastor says, "We must stop this evil secular government from taking away our guns." The final action by the listener is the conclusion and application about what God wants him to do!

As mentioned earlier, most of the factors above are common among most religious believers. I value the role of the Sacred Scriptures (Bible) in my own life and have been profoundly influenced by several mentors. I appreciated and accepted their insights and understanding, yet I don't believe I ever submitted my entire being to their every word. I embrace the reality of an external divine will over my life and desire to conform my life to that will. In this regard, I believe

God has a calling on my life to do His good will on earth. I also believe in a hierarchy of values. Protection of innocent life for me is a higher value than truth telling. Yes, if asked in Nazi Germany if I was hiding Jews in my household, I hope I would have lied to protect their lives. Though I do not want to take any human life, if I come home and find someone beating or raping my wife, I would stop them by whatever means possible (fist, knife, baseball bat, or gun). But if I agree with these contributing factors, does this make me a religious terrorist? Of course not! There is quite a difference between beliefs and behavior. This is what disturbs me about the often quoted phrase about "hate speech." Speech is simply thoughts and beliefs put into words, and the last time I checked, speech was still protected by our First Amendment. Though I am often offended and disturbed by some speech, I do not believe it should be prosecuted as a crime. It is easy to label people's conversation we don't agree with as "hate speech," but until they act upon their speech it is not crime.[532] The same is true for religious people who often use speech to express their views but would never engage in criminal or terrorist behavior. In short, not all who believe these things are terrorists or prone to engaging in some violent behavior. But everyone in this study who has conducted terrorist operations holds convictions similar to these factors. There lies the rub!

It now may be helpful to identify a spectrum of extremist involvement that demonstrates where a religious person begins his spiritual journey is not necessarily he they might end up. The following pyramid diagram best illustrates this movement.

---

532 Though a valuable resource on radical groups in the United States, the Southern Poverty Law Center in a recent edition of the *Intelligence Report* routinely categorizes people like Glen Beck, Michele Bachman, Ollie North and Rand Paul as promoting "hate speech." What is surprising is the organization often lists groups that criticize Muslims as "hate groups" while in my over ten years of subscribing to the report they have never listed any militant Islamic group as at a hate group including Hamas, Al Qaeda, the Muslim Brotherhood, or Hezbollah. See *Intelligence Report*, Southern Poverty Law Center, Spring, 2011. Postscript: After writing the previous note, the Fall, 2011 Intelligence Report issue arrived which focused on "Ten Years After 9/11." For the first time the issue revealed how "Jihadists Aim to Radicalize Muslims Already in America." The article names names and groups. A change for sure! However, though the individuals are called "terrorists" and "extremists," the term "hate group" is still nowhere to be found in the article. In fact, the article before "Ten Years After" agrees with a *New York Times* article about Lebanese Christian author, Brigettte Gabriel where she is called a "radical Islamophobe." To say the least, this is an interesting juxtaposition before reading about the serious threat from Islamic homegrown Jihadists!

A Spectrum of Extremist Involvement

At the bottom of the pyramid are what I call *Sympathizers*. These are the ones who share the ideology, goals and commitments of the larger organization or movement. At this level it could be your average churchgoer, synagogue or mosque attendee. They faithfully attend weekly meetings, listen to sermons, and will even agree with those who espouse more radical views. But they do not consider themselves militant. They just sympathize with the cause. This is the group from which most recruitment takes place.

The next level depicts an elevated level of commitment. These *Committed Devotees* are the ones who begin to attend additional meetings or small groups. They might write checks to support a cause or read extremist literature given to them or go online to get more information. They might give other kinds of material support to those planning direct action attacks. (housing, use of vehicles, credit cards etc.). They are more than mere sympathizers and are directly involved in supporting people or actions that can lead to terrorist attacks.

Level Three is where things get serious. These are the *Sincere Activists* or true believers. These are the 9/11 hijackers, the Timothy McVeighs, the Yigal Amirs, and abortion doctor killers. They believe the cause is just and right based on the propaganda and believed ideology and are the ones who dedicate themselves to performing acts of war against their enemy. But notice these are not on top of the pyramid. These are the foot soldiers in the fight, not the generals. These are the ones who either get caught planning the event, are killed performing the attack or are brought to criminal or military courts after the fact. They are the ones who are willing to pay the ultimate price of their lives for their causes. But there is another level above them.

These are what I call the *Politicos*. These are the individuals who see which way the wind is blowing and can change direction to jump on the bandwagon when necessary for political survival. I put people like Yassar Arafat, Saddam Hussein, some of the Israeli Prime Ministers, rich Arab Gulf state leaders and Christian conspiracy theorists in the category. They realize political power, publicity and/ or money is to be had by supporting radical causes. They are not necessarily true believers in the religion but realize they must talk the language and be seen praying or doing religious things to gain favor with the true adherents. In this sense, they become key power brokers for militant religious causes while living a totally different lifestyle in private (Saudi Royals who fund mosques and then jet off to Monte Carlo to enjoy the pleasures of gambling, women and alcohol; and some Christian televangelists and marketers who make tons of money off their sermons, CDs, and other merchandise like selling gold and survivalist resources).

On top of the pyramid sit the *Ideologues*. These are the ones who concern me most and in the long term do the most damage; simply because they influence so many by their ideas. They drive the entire terrorist enterprise. Ideologues may be far removed from the fight, and in fact are often dead. (Kahane, Bin Laden, Prophecy gurus, Qutb, Pierce). But their influence is still felt. They are the silent voices behind the scenes that rarely come to justice for their radical ideas. The author of *The Turner Diaries*, William Pierce, wrote this alarming racist book cloistered in a comfortable mountain top home. He apparently never acted on his beliefs yet produced an ideological treatise having a profound effect upon Timothy McVeigh.[533] McVeigh was the sincere activist, while Bill Pierce pulled his strings. Pierce died having never been brought to justice for his influence. His only weapon was the pen! For years, Osama bin Laden was listed as Number One on the FBI's most wanted list. Ayman Zawahiri was Number Two. In my opinion, they should have been reversed. From my study, I always viewed Zawahiri as the far more influential ideologue and strategic thinker and bin Laden as the fluent,

---

533 McVeigh's sidekick and co-conspirator Terry Nichols when arrested had a copy of *Hunter*,
    Pierce's sequel, where a lone extremist acts on behalf of the white supremacist cause. *Hunter* is
    written under the pen name of Andrew Macdonald, National Vanguard Books, 1989.

public face, tactical activist and soldier. Now that bin Laden is gone, Zawahiri is Number One![534]

Ideas are powerful and have lasting consequences. Egyptian author Walid Phares in *The War of Ideas* writes, "People of faith believe that all religious ideas come from the divine. In contrast, many social scientists believe that humans create religious ideas. Regardless, one fact remains unchallenged: ideas are at the center of religions; man-made or divinely inspired, they have moved people throughout history to change the world, their achievements seen by proponents as progress, but by opponents as catastrophes . . . they are the real engines of history."[535]

There exists today an often-quoted sound bite: "there is no difference between an Osama bin Laden and a Timothy McVeigh." The sound bite is paraded out regularly on talk shows like *The View* and others complete with adoring nods to its truthfulness. From the contents of this chapter a good argument could be made that these "uncommon bedfellows" are proof positive confirming the talk show sound bites. However, the next chapter will engage this question. Is there a moral equivalence among these terrorists? Are these various religious faith groups equally prone to use violence or are some more potentially violent than others?

---

534 Peter Bergen says, "It was bin Laden who set the group's strategy," but his observation is concerning the 200 or so committed soldiers of Al Qaeda prior to 9/11. In a military organization, this is more like an army captain commanding at most a company or battalion level organization. See Bergen's *The Longest War*, for details, p. 89, Free Press, Peter L. Bergen, 2011.

535 Walid Phares, *The War of Ideas*, Palgrave Macmillan, 2007, p. xiii.

CHAPTER TWELVE
Are All Terrorists and Religions the Same?

"Religion is always a factor in the complexity of war . . . simply because religion deals with the ideology of life, death and violence."[536]

—Seminar on the World & Religious Affairs: Afghanistan, Pakistan, & Beyond

"One would be hard-pressed to find a nation that respects religious freedom and also poses a security threat to the United States"[537]

—William Inboden

---

536 Quoted during a lecture on "The Religious Dynamics of War and Peace," Seminar on the World and Religious Affairs: Afghanistan, Pakistan and Beyond, Armed Forces Chaplain Corps College, Ft. Jackson, SC, April 12, 2010.

537 William Inboden, quoted in a paper "Religious Freedom in U.S. National Security Policy," Report on the Georgetown Symposium, Berkley Center for Religion, Peace & World Affairs, Georgetown University, October, 2010, p. 6.

Many Americans either don't see a difference between a Timothy McVeigh and an Osama bin Laden or they just accept the sound bite blather often promoted by uninformed talk show hosts. We may be approaching a time when we will be the least-educated people on the globe about religion or at least how to think about religion without gravitating into sentimental stupidity. As a military chaplain, I was always called upon to give a "Cultural Awareness Briefing" whenever we had troops deploying (even before 9/11). It was the chaplain's responsibility to brief the cultural and religious issues that might be unique to the host country . . . particularly when deploying to non-Western countries. These briefings were short, usually just a list of do's and don'ts, with a little religious history of the country thrown in. After 9/11, I thought things would change since this Global War on Terror was certainly, in one way or another, far more about religion than anything we had seen in previous wars. But I was wrong. Early on, we just kept doing what we always did with just a few do's and don'ts about Iraq and Afghanistan. We added some material on the differences between Shiites and Sunnis but that was about it. Finally, after almost seven years at war, my service (Air Force) saw the need to incorporate teaching on religion to their early and mid-career officers . . . but how to teach it? Religion is a subject the military does not do well, and there were sensitivities about having chaplains be the religious experts, teachers and advisors to commanders.[538] So it took almost seven years into the war for the various branches of the military to sort out how they were going to deal with religion when this war had all kinds of religious elements to it.[539]

The above paragraph illustrates how naïve, uninformed and ignorant we are about the role of religion in our modern world. As the famous proverb goes, "There is a way that seems right to a man, but the end is the way of death" . . . literally in this case (Proverbs 14:12). Without serious, careful analysis we fall into the trap of thinking all terrorists are the same, and there is no difference among religious people. So, is a bin Laden or Al Baghdadi no different from a Timothy McVeigh? The question raises an interesting assumption. One

---

538 More reliance on the role of "culture" (read religion) was placed in the hands of contract Anthropologists, not Chaplains!

539 The Chaplain Services differed on this subject. The Navy leaned forward and viewed their chaplains as the key religious consultant to commanders, even going out and meeting with tribal leaders. The Army would only allow this in certain circumstances. The Air Force official position was that chaplains are not allowed to go "outside the wire" because their main duty was ministry to Air Force personnel "inside the wire."

good thing came about with 9/11. That day liberated us from the faulty view saying, "All religions are beautiful and peaceful." This view generally excluded Christianity and made it the classic illustration of murderous warfare with its Crusades, Inquisitions, and European wars; in the eyes of some extreme left-leaning academic theorists. Perhaps even the Holocaust as conducted by German Christians might be included! (I would point the reader to a truly outspoken Christian, Dietrich Bonhoeffer, whose courage in the face of Nazi terrorism would be more in line with my own views and those who were truly Christian in the Nazi German nation.) I call this outdated view *The Benevolence of Religion School*. It is best known in some of the state university religion departments, and is notoriously accepted by wide-eyed freshmen who have never experienced a violent act. However, after 9/11 the more popular *Moral Equivalency School* emerged. At least I had not heard the term used in reference to religious terrorism before that fateful day. Now, it is commonly attached to almost anything viewed as repulsive, offensive or hateful. Therefore, even the Tea Party movement is sometimes put into the same category as McVeigh and bin Laden. Those who disagree with this extreme analysis are also labeled terrorists! Such is how the moral equivalency argument works. My simple answer is: McVeigh and bin Laden are two completely different animals.

McVeigh was your classic loner with no community support except for a couple of old army buddies. Osama had massive community support from his Wahhabi mentors, Gulf state Arabs, the Taliban, Sunni Pakistanis, and fellow Soviet war mujahidin in Afghanistan. Though raised Catholic, Timothy McVeigh belonged to no organized religion nor held any organizational memberships. On the other hand, bin Laden was a seriously devout Sunni Muslim committed to living under Sharia law. McVeigh did embrace Christian Identity doctrines, which led him to his racist, antigovernment and pro-gun rights beliefs, but he was anything but religious. Bin Laden fully embraced Saudi Islamic Wahhabism emphasizing a return to the purist form of faith established by Mohammed. The Oklahoma City bombing was at most a conspiracy of three (McVeigh, Nichols, and Fortier). Bin Laden's organization was likened to Holy War Inc., patterned after a corporation with very strict lines of authority and chain of command.[540]

---

540 See Holy War Inc., by Peter L. Bergen, for this evaluation. Free Press, 2001.

It was estimated during his time in Afghanistan, Sudan, and Pakistan, Osama trained over 100 thousand mujahidin. How one can compare this massive force to three lone individuals is beyond belief.

Fundamentally, McVeigh was a poor young man, living off the land supported only by his former army buddies. Even when he attended gun shows he did not sell the radical racist book he loved, *The Turner Diaries*. He gave it away! Bin Laden was incredibly wealthy, having inherited millions from his billionaire father. He used his inheritance money not only to set up training camps in Sudan, Afghanistan, and Pakistan but used it to pay salaries, provide hospital care, and improve civil infrastructures in these countries. McVeigh was a community college drop-out, while Bin Laden was a graduate of King Abdul Aziz University majoring in Public Administration and Engineering. McVeigh's "axe to grind" was directed primarily at President Bill Clinton and the Janet Reno Justice Department. He saw his terrorist act as payback for the Justice department's fiascos at Ruby Ridge and killing of the Branch Davidians in Waco. Bin Laden's "axe" was much larger. He would be targeting all the symbols of the United States and Israel for their power, intervention and occupation of the Islamic Holy lands. He issued two fatwas (96, 98) clearly delineating his ambitions and strategic goals. Most of the world ignored these!

McVeigh's anti-US government contempt was rooted in his hatred of the Clinton Administration. Bin Laden held in contempt all things Western as spearheaded by the United States. In sum, McVeigh in no way could be classified as a religious terrorist because though raised Catholic, he held no particular religious beliefs. Bin Laden was thoroughly religious, regularly quoting the Koran as justification for his actions. McVeigh had no similar justifications. Most of his ideology, even the design for his fertilizer bomb, was taken from *The Turner Diaries*, certainly not the Bible. Conclusion: in no way can an equal comparison be made between these two terrorists. Though both saw themselves as soldiers, and both were war veterans, McVeigh performed a mere criminal act but was not a religious terrorist. On the other hand, Koran-quoting Osama bin Laden prided himself in being motivated by his religious understanding and commitment. So the moral equivalency argument does not exist. There is, however a more intriguing question on the subject.

Why does the media and popular culture want to believe a moral equivalency exists? Does this assumption grant some strange comfort in believing all terrorists are the same? Or in the face of events so beyond the pale of explanation, they retreat to this simplistic position of lumping anyone who does violence into the same category. Only they can answer! One point is clear though . . . Timothy McVeigh and Osama bin Laden are both dead. Here, there is equivalence!

Aren't All Religions the Same?

From the previous historical section of this book it was observed there are many differences in the religions studied.

First, terms need to be defined. I will be using the term *Absolutist* to mean how certain faith groups believe they have all or most of the Truth . . . this is Truth with a capital T. Absolutists see very little if any Truth outside their particular faith group. The term *Universal* means the religious faith is given for all people in the world without exception, and consequently everyone should be asked to believe it. The words *expansionist* or *propagative* carry the moral necessity to expand the faith community via the means of recognized messengers. In this sense, the individual believer has a commission from the divine to communicate the message to others. The faith should not be kept within the particular faith community but should be expanded to those outside. The word *Global* implies the moral imperative to take the message to the entire world . . . these are not local or regional religions but global in nature!

There is not room in this book to deal with Eastern religions such as Hinduism, Buddhism and Shinto, but we can note they are rarely absolutist except when a particular cult leader like Shoko Asahara makes it such: Imperialistic Japan's Shintoism being the exception to the principle.

The revelatory Monotheistic religions (Judaism, Christianity, and Islam) tend to be more absolutist. Only two are both absolutist and universal: Christianity and Islam. Both are under a compulsion to extend their faith to the world. In this sense they are truly world religions. Judaism originally was under a Biblical mandate to be a "light to the gentile nations" (Isaiah 42:6), but for most of its history it has not sent out missionaries.[541] Fundamentally, Judaism is a racial religion and the national religion of Israel. As noted earlier, the justification for violence by Kahane

---

541 In the New Testament, Gentile converts to Judaism are noted (Acts 10:1-2). They were called "God-fearers" like the Roman centurion, Cornelius.

inspired groups were defended as "defensive" preemption to save the Jewish nation. But this violence was rarely exported outside of Israel.[542]

The revelatory religions of Islam and Christianity are most expansive and propagative. They have global imperatives. The Koran's teaching about Dar-al-Islam and Dar-al-Harb clearly depicts the necessity of propagating the faith to the entire world. Mohammed's message must be extended to the world of warfare and unbelief (Dar-al-Harb) in order to establish world peace (Dar-al-Islam). According to this logic, world peace will not exist until the world accepts Islam! As Imam Zuhri recently noted quoting Kanzul Ammal (even before rise of ISIS) "black flags will emerge from Khorasan (area around Afghanistan) so when they descend from the mountain passes they will do so for the sake of Islam. Nothing will hinder them except for the flags of the non-Arabs which will come from the West." Further, Abu Huraiah predicts, "When black flags emerge from the east nothing will be able to stop them till they are planted in Aelia" (Arabic: Bait-ul-Maqdis).[543]

The phrase refers to the Temple Mount or Dome on the Rock in Jerusalem! Almost nightly, the black flags of ISIS in Syria and Iraq are shown on television screens all over the world.

Likewise, Christianity is under a mandate from its Savior Jesus Christ to take his message to the entire world. The last words given to his disciples were "Go into the entire world and preach the gospel to every creature," (Mark 16:15). The imperative is often further understood that Jesus will not return until everyone in the world has heard this gospel and had an opportunity to respond (See Mark 13:10). So within Biblically rooted Christianity there exists a contingent element of end time expectation.

Obviously, this places Islam and Christianity on a collision course. In fact, it was Samuel Huntington in his classic work, *Clash of Civilizations*, who argued this futuristic scenario. He pens in 1996, "Some Westerners, including President Bill Clinton, have argued that the West does not have problems with Islam but only with violent Islamist extremists. Fourteen hundred years of history demonstrate otherwise. The relation between Islam and Christianity . . . has been stormy. Each

---

542 During the Soviet era, Kahane did plan attacks on Russian Embassies due to their anti-Semitic treatment of Jews throughout the Soviet Union.

543 "Hadith Explanation, "Black Flags of Khorasan are Madhis," www.dailyhadith. adapticsolutionsinc.com, 23, April, 2013.

has been the other's Other."[544] He goes on to point out that the enemy of Islam is not the CIA or DOD, but the West as a whole, simply because Western civilization with its Christian base believes its culture is superior to any other. Likewise, Islam is "convinced with the superiority of their culture and are obsessed with the inferiority of their power."[545]

What is further amazing is that Osama bin Laden agreed with Huntington. In a post 9/11 interview with Al Jazeera, bin Laden was asked, "Do you support the *Clash of Civilization* argument put forth by Samuel Huntington?" He answered, "No doubt about it . . . Jews and Americans are drugging Muslims while talking about world peace." Author Peter Bergen, who interviewed bin Laden, adds about this exchange, "The battle is inevitable but Islam believes it will win in the long term."[546] The logic of these statements is inescapable. If true, and I believe it is, the greatest potential threat for each of these religions (Christianity and Islam) is the threat of each other. Additional logic could argue that these two universal, absolutist, propagative religions are potentially more prone to violence than other faith groups. But another consideration must be made.

Contemporary Christianity does not argue for, nor believe in holy war. As noted earlier, Jesus was a determined nonviolent resister of the status quo and did not submit to the temptation of having world power (Matthew 4:8-10). He taught "turning the other cheek" when slapped, never physically defended himself or carried a weapon. He willingly laid down his life. He instructed his disciples to live the same way. One writer says, "To be sure, the New Testament uniformly teaches that we are never to use violence to promote or defend our faith."[547] The author does go further and points out Christians would eventually practice violence as members of the military but then, as normal citizens serving their Emperor. In fact, the Apostle Paul instructed the Roman church "to be at peace with all men" (Romans 12:18) and in all probability was encouraging them to be subject to the ungodly, tyrannical Emperor, Nero (13:1). Early Christians likewise were overtly pacifist, refusing to serve in the Roman Army due to the requirement of swearing allegiance to Caesar as divine while honoring all the pagan gods of Rome.

---

544 Samuel P. Huntington, *The Clash of Civilizations: Remaking of the World Order*, Touchstone, Simon & Schuster, 1996, p. 209.
545 Ibid., p. 217-18.
546 Peter L. Bergen, *The Longest War*, Free Press, 2011 p. 92.
547 Mark Galli, "Wielding the Sword," *Christianity Today*, February 4, 2002, p. 80.

It wasn't until the reign of Constantine in 313 AD when Christianity was legitimized and Christians began to openly serve in the military. Just War theories of the Greeks and Romans were "Christianized" by St. Augustine and St. Thomas Aquinas, which gave emperors a Christian justification for the use of violence.[548] But it wasn't until the Crusades the concept of holy war was attached to Christianity as declared by Pope Urban II in 1095 AD. In fact, prior to this time the word *holy* is hard to find related to Christian warfare. Even the Cistercian abbot, Bernard of Clairvaux, never used the word *holy* in his clarion call to take arms against the infidels. Writing to the young warriors of England, France and Bavaria, he calls upon them to "take the Cross, fight without danger to their souls, and find indulgence for all the sins they confess."[549] The term h*oly war* is not found in the letter.

The concept of *holiness* in this writer's opinion developed from the time of Pope Gregory VII (1073-85).[550] St. Augustine did not give us a doctrine of holy war, but as Brundage argues, "the roots of the holy war idea . . . are more of ancient German heroic traditions."[551] It was a leap from defending the holy places or shrines in Palestine to the concept of holy war as perhaps borrowed from Islam. Even Pope Urban did not use the term. During his stirring public oration at Clermont, France (Nov 27), crowds of clerics and lay Frenchman interrupted the pope with cries of "Deus le volt," God wills it. So what began as a call in aiding their Eastern Christian brethren being attacked by advancing Turks, (a defensive war) soon gravitated into what we would probably call today a "Just War."[552] After all, Christian lands were taken over by Muslim invaders, and with the loss of the Holy Land, Christians were harassed or prevented making from pilgrimages. As such, Christians saw it as a righteous or Just War and recovering lost territory for the work for God.[553]

---

548 Just War Criteria usually stated as: 1) Just cause 2) Just intention 3) Last resort 4) Formal declaration 5) Limited objectives 6) Proportionate means 7) Noncombatant immunity. Robert G. Close, editor, *War: Four Christian Views*, InterVaristy Press, 1981, p. 119.

549 Quoted in *War and Christian Ethics*, Arthur F. Holmes, Editor, Baker Book House, 1975, p. 90.

550 James A. Brundage, Medievalist scholar, says, "The principal inventor of the holy war idea was Gregory VII," p. 104.

551 James A. Brundage, *Holy War and the Medieval Lawyers*, Editor, Thomas Patrick Murphy, Ohio State University, 1976, p. 103.

552 In the words of Brundage, "Every holy war, to put it another way, was a just war; but not every just war was a holy war." *Holy War and the Medieval Lawyers*, p. 117.

553 See for this background, Steven Runciman, *The First Crusade*, Cambridge University Press, 1980, pp.41-51.

Holy War has not been the theological justification for violence for most of Christian history. Often, princes and kings used Just War criteria to argue for "defensive" or "preventive wars" and in time got translated into holy wars. There were many "religious wars" but these were mostly religious wars between differing Christian rulers and state churches. They might better be called wars of national religion or political ambition (example: World War I, where both sides thought they were fighting a holy war against each other).[554]

Today, most would see World War II as a Just War since the United States was attacked by Japan, and Germany was trying to destroy our allies in France and England. But I don't recall anyone calling it a holy war. Some could argue the first Gulf war was a humanitarian Just War to liberate the Kuwaitis from Saddam Hussein. Others claim it was a war about national interest . . . oil! But no one called either a "Holy War." Today, the willingness, if not necessity, of using military power as an instrument of policy by our national command authorities usually centers on humanitarian or national interests (Granada, Panama, Serbia, Kosovo, Somalia, Libya, Syria).[555] Again, I don't know anyone who has called these wars, "holy." The most one could argue in using military violence to stop the killing of innocents or genocide is *Just Cause*, not holy war. Sometimes it takes greater violence to stop violence, and in this sense Just War criteria could be applied. But the point is clear: no one today calls these wars, *Holy*. The Christian experience in holy war is based primarily on one medieval episode and a series of Crusades, most of which went badly.

---

554 The "Christmas Truce" of Dec 25, 1914, was a unique pause between two warring Christian nations. Both the English and German soldiers called a truce in the middle of the conflict and celebrated Christmas together complete with caroling, gift exchanges, playing football and a shared Christian mass. This was only possible because of the shared Christian convictions on both sides of the enemy lines. However, once the higher commands found out about the event they commanded a return of hostilities and viewed those involved as traitors. In the opinion of this author, this event and the entire war ended the dominance and credibility of Christian Western Civilization!

555 "Wars of necessity" are often driven by the media rather than clear foreign policy or what is in the US national interest. The author while at the USAF War College heard a noted cable correspondent speak. The individual had covered the first Gulf war and our intervention into Somalia. When asked by a student officer why they didn't go into Rwanda rather than Somalia where there was a far greater crisis involving genocide, his sincere answer shocked us all. He said, "because we couldn't get into Rwanda . . . We were told we would be shot if we did, so we went into Somalia and covered that story." The footage from Somalia created so much pressure on public opinion finally President Bill Clinton "had" to respond by sending in our troops to stop the humanitarian crisis." When I heard this, I said to myself, "My God, we are doing foreign policy by where the press can get a camera!" It is more true today than then.

Originally, Pope Urban II declared assured salvation for those taking the Cross to secure Christian pilgrimages to the Holy Land, and/or dying in the pursuit thereof. Most Catholics, Protestants and evangelicals do not believe this doctrine today. In fact, most would say it was heretical then and still is. No one today believes a person gets saved or has his sins forgiven by going to war or dying in battle! Gratian, a mid-twelfth century monk and canon lawyer, believed "war was morally wrong and sinful." This was his baseline or first principle for Just War theory.[556] Besides, just because a Pope or King declares a war to be just or holy, does not mean it is!

But the reality remains: Islam has always had a doctrine of holy war or Jihad, and the current view among its radical adherents is that Paradise and seventy-two virgins await the Holy Warrior. There is no comparison between Islamic Jihad martyrs and Christian martyrs. Islamic martyrs blow themselves up and take as many with them as they can. Christian martyrs are those willing to die for their persecuted faith rather than convert or take arms against their enemies. Basically, a Christian martyr is defined as "one who prefers to die rather than deny his Christian faith."[557] He or she dies alone or with others not willing to deny Christ! Islamic martyrdom and Christian martyrdom are not comparable nor can be made into moral equivalence . . . there is no equivalence to be found!

American Christians have no national or state church, no Protestant pope, or a uniform view about the use of violence. The spectrum of Christian views ranges from strict passivism (Quakers, Amish, some Brethren, and Mennonites) to hard line armed religious patriots willing to defend their perceived loss of liberty against an intrusive government. Anyone challenging what they consider their God given rights justifies resistance. In between are Christian conscientious objectors, military noncombatants, and nonviolent resisters. All argue a view based upon their understanding of Christian Scripture and tradition. In short, Dinesh D'Souza observes, "Christianity in all its history has never had suicide bombers and neither has Judaism, Hinduism or Buddhism."[558] Practicing Baptist, Methodist or Catholic terrorists simply do not exist!

---

556 Brundage, *Holy War and Medieval Lawyers*, p. 107.
557 J.D Douglas, General Editor, *The New International Dictionary of the Christian Church*, Zondervan Publishing House, 1974, p. 638.
558 Dinesh D'Souza, *The Enemy at Home*, Doubleday, 2007, p. 91.

So to summarize the clash of these religions and civilizations I return to Huntington. As noted in his term, the greatest "clash" takes place between religions or civilizations that are Absolutist, Universal, Expansionist, and Global. This places Islam and Christianity at a standoff at a most precarious stage of history. Both religions believe their religion is superior to the other and are under a command from their founder to take the religion to the world. Thus, conflict should surprise no one. Dr. Eric Patterson, professor at Georgetown University adds, "Religious conflicts generally last longer and suffer more casualties than secular conflicts.[559] This implies the "War on Terror" will last longer than most of our wars that had clear beginnings and ends. CNN analyst Peter Bergen called the war on terror "The Longest War" in his most recent book.[560] This insight is not good news for either the religious or non-religious. However, it does underscore the reality we are facing. The war on terror or whatever the government wishes to call it[561] is not a conflict of civilizations at all. It is a conflict of religious convictions rooted in religious and theological ideology. Short version: it's the Battle of the Books (Koran and the Bible)! If our leaders don't recognize this element of conflict, they will never find a way to end it. Sun Tzu, the philosopher of war, had it right saying, "Know the enemy, know yourself; and your victory will never be endangered."[562]

Today we are very aware and prideful in our superior military capabilities, but we don't have a clue about who our enemy is and how to engage them. As noted earlier, our own State Department does not "do" religion, yet without religious understanding it is difficult finding workable solutions. Recent statements by the State Department seem to imply that the only thing terrorists need to be pacified is a good job. Even if it is "nuanced," this cure in no way fits the illness. If religion is the problem, then it is also the solution! It would seem our national leadership has backed itself into an absolute futile axiom of American diplomacy: religion is a private matter and therefore should not be discussed within official circles. This is to the dismay of religious people around the world and especially those in Islamic countries. For fear of offending, or not knowing how to engage this delicate subject, we project ourselves as religiously bankrupt or worse, atheists! Even former

---

559 Dr. Eric Patterson, Seminar on the World and Religious Affairs, April 12, 2010.
560 Peter L. Bergen, *The Longest War*, Free Press, 2011.
561 The Obama administration avoids using the term terrorism and instead calls the former GWOT (Global War on Terrorism), Overseas Contingency Operations (OCO).
562 Samuel B. Griffith, Sun Tzu: *The Art of War*, p. 129.

Ambassador Madeleine Albright admitted the blinders she had on prior to 9/11. She confesses, "Like many other foreign policy professionals, I have had to adjust the lens through which I view the world."[563] A recent Pew Research poll found Americans want to see more religion being addressed in politics![564]

The current Administration is reluctant to use the word *war*. But as a *non-war* conflict it looks even to the most naïve observer like an *all-out war*. Using terms like *overseas contingency operations* or refusing to give operations a name may score some political kudos with isolationists, but it does not help define who the enemy is. (The Administration finally conceded and gave the ISIS war an operational name: Inherent Resolve. Now the combatants can add another campaign medal to their uniforms!)

While teaching a course on Religious Terrorism at the USAF War College, a student in my class was a senior officer from one of our partner Arab countries. He was most likely a blood relative to his country's royal family or at least a close friend of the family.[565] Of course, he was Muslim. Through most of the course, he was silent even when we addressed the subject of Islam. He wrote his final paper on "The Western Misperception of Jihad." Basically, he argued Jihad in the Koran is always "defensive." When he defended his paper in class, many took issue with him including a US Army officer who had served in the Middle East for many years. At the end of the course, my Arab student lingered behind and spoke to me saying, "I didn't agree with much of what you said in the course, but I was encouraged by your willingness to discuss religious issues. In my country, every discussion is religious, but you are the only one this year who openly spoke about your faith . . . I wanted to thank you for that." I was surprised, shocked and ashamed this high ranking Arab officer could spend almost a year in "Christian America" and not have anyone speak to him about religion . . . his or theirs! This confirms what Karen Armstrong espoused saying, "But when Muslims look at Western society they see no light, no heart, and no spirituality."[566]

So the illustration raises an important question for the book. If few want to call religious terrorism a new kind of war, how can this viewpoint be turned around?

---

563 *The Mighty & the Almighty*, pp. 8-9.
564 Noted in www.worldmag.com, "Good religion is good for politics," D.C. Innis, October 13, 2014.
565 In most Arab Gulf states the officer corps is composed mostly of princes of the royal family or close friends of the family. This way loyalty to the reigning authority is secured!
566 Karen Armstrong, *Islam: A Short History*, p. 157.

What are some countermeasures to be adopted in order to more seriously engage this conflict of religious ideologies?

Religious Terrorism Countermeasures

The term *Countermeasures* should not be confused with the term *Counter-Terrorism* or *Anti-Terrorism*. Counter-Terrorism is a term used for the offensive measures taken by the CIA, FBI, DOD or Homeland Security. Anti-Terrorism involves the defensive approaches in protecting potential targets like military bases, or security screening tactics at airports. Countermeasures are things we can do with a view to the more strategic level of warfare. Current military approaches divide military engagement into *tactical, operational*, and *strategic* levels. Tactical is the lowest level, which involves the nuts and bolts of how a particular operation will be carried out. This is the level of what Seal Team 6 did in killing bin Laden. The Operational level involves all the planning, mobilization and utilization of personnel and airframes to pull off the tactic. At the Strategic level, this is the highest level dealing with our National Security Strategy; StateDepartment goals, International Relations and Administration Foreign Policy. My countermeasures are not military but ideological and focus primarily on the Strategic with a few Tactical suggestions. Ideologies can never be destroyed by drone-launched Hellfire missiles!

Full Ideological Engagement Strategic Ideological Level

First, a Full Ideological Engagement is needed. Hisham Melhem, Washington Bureau Chief of Al-Arabyia, comments on Arab civilization, "Obama with great reluctance is stepping into the chaos of an entire (Arab) civilization that has broken down." He goes on to point out the reason for this failure is all the tried Arab ideologies . . . the colossal ideological failures of: Arab nationalism, in its Baathists, and Nasserite forms, various Islamist movements, Arab socialism, rapacious monopolies. All these have led to continuous bloodletting between Sunni and Shia which in five years has seen a quarter of million people perish."[567] Middle East warfare is not only about Israel and the tensions between Jews and Palestinians, but also the much larger ideological conflict inside the Muslim world itself. It is this ideological conflict that is much harder to understand and shed light on because of the long standing neglect by leading political leaders. British Prime Minister

---

567 "The Barbarians Within our Gates," September 18, 2014, www.politco.com/magazine.

David Cameron's remarks to the United Nations hit the mark clearly; "Defeating the ideology of extremism that is the root cause of this terrorism is absolutely necessary so that we win the battle of ideas."[568] He did not offer any steps in how to defeat this ideological enemy, but at least he defined it and expressed the realism and necessity of the battle. This is far more than our own State Department and Executive branch has expressed.

One problem may be our society has become too specialized in almost every area. As noted earlier, there are huge gaps between Religious Studies programs, Political Science departments, and approaches to International Relations, Professional Military Education and National Security Officialdom. Serious religious study should be brought into all these fields without compromise. Full Ideological Engagement means first of all, political correctness must be put to death. True ideological engagement grants every person's beliefs are allowed to stand as is without compromise. If both Christianity and Islam believe their religion is superior to the other, then discussion should be allowed on the merits and demerits of each in order to compare claims. When the Soviet Union was our feared enemy, Radio Free Europe and others broadcast daily the message of freedom simply because we believed our ideology and way of life was superior to theirs. It was a war of ideas and we countered it. But what are we doing to counter this ideological threat? George Freeman of Stratfor succinctly states, "A military strategy to defeat Jihadists is impossible. At its root, the real struggle is ideological and that struggle simply cannot be won by Hellfire missiles."[569] If we fought the Soviet Cold War threat on the ideological battlefield, why not now? Because political correctness rules the day!

So far our propaganda war against ISIL or ISIS has been limited to leaflet drops from specially equipped F-15 fighter jets. At a cost of $1 billion, 60,000 leaflets have been dropped depicting Islamic State recruits standing in line at an Islamic Recruiting office. The man at the front of the line drops his ticket with the number 6001 on it.[570] It is part of the psychological operations program of the Pentagon. The State Department has also aired videos demonstrating how many Muslim fighters have died in the conflict. These attempts may have some effect of

568 "Defeating Islamic State Speech," David Cameron, September 25, 2014, quoted in *Defense News*, www.defensenews.com, September 29, 2014.
569 George Freeman, "Hellfire, Morality, and Strategy," Stratfor Global Intelligence, February 19, 2013.
570 "U.S. Drops Propaganda Bomb on ISIL," Tom Vanden Brook, *USA Today*, March 26, 2015.

the radical fighters to discourage them, but the graphic videos and cartoons do not touch the ideology that is at the heart of their extremism.

If radical Islamists believe we are infidels and their religion is superior to ours, should not we respond in kind and engage at the ideological level? Even after the killing of Osama bin Laden, with the celebrated victory laps, "his poisonous ideology and other varieties of radical Islamist thought thrive on the Internet."[571] Bin Laden still lives in the Internet sermons of Anwar Al-Awlaki (now deceased), who was a critical influence on the Boston Marathon bombers and Major Nidal Hasan, the Ft Hood shooter.

So where is the defense of our own, and the polemic against theirs? Most likely it doesn't exist because *officialdom* does not feel comfortable with religious ideological engagement.[572] Dr. Patterson, Georgetown University professor, admits, "Religious variables have largely been left out of the traditional international relations scholarship, in part because they are ideational in nature rather than material."[573] One way this can be accomplished is by inserting theologians and learned clergy into some of the prestigious DC think tanks. These should be conservative (not in the political sense) *text scholars* (Christian theologians, Jewish rabbis & Islamic Imams) who are competent about the use and misuse of religious texts, since sacred texts are used to justify violence. Let's face it. For most serious Christians, Jews and Muslims it's about their book! Remember: It's the Bible and the Koran, dummy!

The theologically illiterate are often caught up with simplistic justifications for violence as instructed by sometimes equally illiterate mentors who use sacred texts for their arguments. Thus, introducing text scholars into the fray with National Security analysts sheds important light on understanding the terrorist. Like Madeleine Albright's experience, Doug Johnston a Public Policy expert confirms, "Foreign policy practitioners in the United States, for example, are inadequately equipped to deal with situations involving other nation-states where the imperatives of religious doctrine blend intimately with those of politics and economics . . . this

---

571 Joseph J. Collins, "End of the War on Terrorism," *Armed Forces Journal*, June 2013, p.33.

572 Canon Andrew White gave the term *officialdom* where he articulated its four presuppositions. They are 1) Religion as a private matter as derived from the Enlightenment. 2) Separation of Church and State as derived from the Peace of Westphalia. 3) Risk Aversion about religion because religion is always a problem. 4) Official solutions driven by top-down formal structures and money. Seminar on World and Religious Affairs, April 30, 2010.

573 Eric Patterson, "Religion, War and Peace," paper presented at The World and Religious Affairs Conference, Ft. Jackson, April 30, 2010.

has led to uninformed policy choices, particularly in our dealings with the Middle East."[574] It is truer today than when Johnston wrote these words! Text scholars in public policy debates might change this approach to critical issues involving religion. Muslims like Zuhdi Jasser would welcome this in demonstrating options in the interpretation of the Koran. As he so acutely states, "If militant Islam is the problem, then moderate Islam is the solution."[575]

However, to say or believe one's religion is superior to someone else's goes against the grain of what many believe about pluralism. But this is not correct. We have a prime example of true religious pluralism in the American military chaplaincy. Somehow, since the founding of our country, the military chaplaincy has incorporated into its corps chaplains of almost every denomination (all the Christian ones, Jewish, Islam and now Buddhist). When meeting with other chaplains, I was regularly in the presence of chaplains with whom I disagreed, sometimes strongly, and them with me. But somehow, we extended to each other the "privilege of being wrong" and "respecting differences" for the common good of supporting our troops. We were not there to create uniformity or agreement but serve the greater good of ministry to those in our care, while protecting the religious liberty of all those in uniform. But in the process of extending and accepting this diversity something else took place. We better understand each other's world of ideas and faith practice. Somehow, this happened without killing each other! This model of ideological diversity without compromise has seldom been looked at for possibilities on a much wider scale. There is something very affirming in being able to say to a fellow chaplain, "I think you are wrong, and I believe my views are better than yours, but I accept you and need you as a fellow professional in ministry."

Full Ideological Engagement also means putting to death the Secular approach to the Public/Private sphere. Someone once said the most religious country in the world is India; with Sweden as the most non-religious. Unfortunately, America is a bunch of Indians (India) ruled by Swedes! Micklethwait and Wooldridge profoundly observe, "Washington's diplomats and think-tankers remained locked in their Westphalian box[576] obsessed with balance of power or pursuit of economic

---

574 Doug Johnston and Cynthia Sampson, Editors, *Religion, The Missing Dimension of Statecraft*, Oxford Univ. Press, 1994, p. 5.

575 See chapter eleven in his book, *A Battle for the Soul of Islam*.

576 The Peace of Westphalia in 1648 ended the 30 years of European religious/national wars and is marked as the beginning of the modern Nation State era. As a consequence of this peace,

interests or clash of secular creeds." They also point out former Ambassador Madeleine Albright commenting about her tour of duty "as recalling no American diplomat ever speaking in depth about the role of religion in shaping the world."[577] Is it any wonder we were so blindsided by 9/11 when we did not even have the tools or platform to engage in serious religious dialogue? Maj. General Michael Nagata as commander of American Special Forces in the Middle East even tried to get out of this box by putting together an unofficial brain trust. He brought individuals from outside the DOD and State Department, (Business professors, marketing experts and such) in order to try to understand the "hybrid terrorist organizations" he was facing. His stated premise was clear: "we do not understand the movement, and until we do, we are not going to defeat it . . . we have not defeated the idea. We do not even understand the idea."[578] His conclusion? General Nagata praised the effort but admitted, "I do not understand the intangible power of ISIL." Just maybe he might have been better informed by inviting experts on religion in the Middle East or Imams to help him understand what is going on. It seems the totally rational secular approach does not provided the needed insight.

This *Secularist Failure in Foreign policy* has created an approach whereby religion and religious actors were not taken seriously which resulted in little understanding of the Islamic world. As noted by Armstrong, "politics is no secondary issue for Muslims. We have seen that it had been the theatre of their religious quest. Salvation did not mean redemption from sin, but the creation of a just society."[579] However, a secular approach does not match the reality of what is going on especially in the Middle East.

America with most of the world is very religious, when one gets out of the major East and West coast cities. (With the exception of Western Europe for good reasons.)[580] Most of the world does not live by the public/private realms artificially created by secular-materialist philosophies that began after the Peace of Westphalia in 1648. The "Edict of Toleration" that the Enlightenment inherited turned into

---

"Tolerance of other religions was made official while maintaining the concept of National State Churches. Some argue this is the beginning of the concept of separation of Church and State.

577 John Micklethwait and Adrian Wooldridge, *God is Back*, Penguin Books, 2009, p. 358.

578 "In Battle to Defang ISIS, U.S. Targets its Psychology," Eric Schmidt, *The New York Times*, December 28, 2014.

579 Armstrong, *Islam*, p. 134.

580 After two world wars on their soil plus 30 years of religious wars before that, "God" and religion have become largely irrelevant categories!

a complete separation of Church and State, and relegated everything religious to the private realm if at all. Consequently, "Christmas wars" rage whether mangers and Christmas lights can occupy "Public space"! But the authors quoted previously reveal, "Oddly, America's problem . . . is its refusal to admit how much religion is part of public life. For once religion is part of a conflict; it must also be part of the solution."[581] It is also important to note how totally secular ideologies proved to be just as murderous as the older more religious societies. Think Hitler and Stalin![582]

It was the genius of our American founders who made the first statement of the First Amendment, freedom of religion (Freedoms outlined in the First Amendment cover religion, speech, press, assembly, and petition of grievances). By abolishing the establishment of a state church, it left society with an open market for religion. Congress could neither show favoritism to any religion nor prohibit any exercise of it. In opposition to the Constitution, some would say Congress today has established the state church of secularism, while prohibiting the free exercise of many religious practices (prayers, teaching religion, wearing religious symbols, hiring practices in religious schools). Originally, this was not the case. Without a State Church, religious freedom exploded producing new denominations, organizations, even cults . . . all protected by a free market concept of the First Amendment. Toleration and respectful acceptance of the "other" was not always the case and took time to develop. But it was the concept of religious freedom that created the pluralism and diversity, our founders envisioned. This is what Islam needs to rediscover and move toward in our present age.

Return to Ideology and Culture of the Islamic Golden Age

The second countermeasure grows out of the first. As one teaching history at the university level, I have gained great respect for the Golden Age of Islam. Simply, it was a time of unprecedented scholarship in science, medicine, philosophy, architecture, astronomy, mathematics and the arts. It was a time when Islamic, Jewish and Christian scholars were allowed to cooperate, research, debate and philosophize about the world. Even when Ferdinand II, Christian king of Castile (Spain) won victories over Muslim Cordova and Seville, he re-consecrated its historic

---

581 Wicklethwait and Wooldridge, p. 364.

582 Hitler had no real use for the church except to Nazify it, and in so doing created his own secular Nazi Church. Stalin, of course, made atheism the law of the land until World War II when he gave limited freedom for church attendance again. Hitler's Holocaust on the Jews and Stalin's Gulags on his own people illustrates the utter failure of pure rational secularism.

Great Mosque and prayed there every day of his life. When buried, his monument was inscribed in Arabic, Hebrew and Latin.[583] Tolerance went both ways! In the opinion of this writer, and as noted earlier, the end of this period marked the significant decline within the Islamic empire. What is rarely acknowledged is that this Golden Age did not end due to Western intervention but by more puritanical and absolutist Islam. Hisham Melhem reveals, "The great city of Cordova, one of the most advanced cities in Medieval Europe, was sacked and plundered by a Muslim group (Al Mourabitoun) in 1013, destroying its magnificent palaces and its famed library."[584] Many Islamists like bin Laden, Zawahiri, and Qutb have blamed the West for this decline. But what is needed is for Islamic scholars to revisit their own Golden Age to see what kind of philosophical ideas and academic culture brought about their high civilization.

A pluralism of ideas was not only tolerated but also encouraged by their Islamic leaders in Baghdad and Cordova, the two main learning centers of the Caliphates. When the city of Toledo returned to Christian hands, it became a center for European Christians coming to Spain to learn from Arabized Jews, and Muslim scholars even experiencing Christians performing their liturgy in Arabic.[585] Rubenstein sums up the educational novelty of Toledo expressing, it was a time when "sitting at a table together were bearded Jews, tonsured Christian monks, turbaned Muslims and dark-haired Greeks pouring over manuscripts written in Syriac, Aramaic, Hebrew, Arabic and Greek.[586] Imagine this happening today?

Contributions of Persian culture, Greek philosophy and Indian mathematics were all part of the curriculum of Islamic studies during the Golden Age.[587] If returning to this Golden Age is what Islamists want, the answer surely lies in what created it in the first place. But it seems easier to simply blame the West for its own demise. In many respects, their advances helped create what we now call the West! It is important then for Islamic leaders to revisit the Golden Age at the strategic level and put tactical shoe leather on the implications of this recognition. Bloom observes the reality of where Islam is today saying, "There are no Muslim Andalusians (Spain) visible anywhere in the world today. The Iran of the ayatollahs

---

583 Noted in Maria Rosa Menocal, *Ornament of the World*, p. 200.
584 "The "Barbarians With in Our Gates," Politico.
585 Ibid., p.143.
586 Richard, E. Rubenstein, *Aristotle's Children*, Harcourt, 2003, p. 12.
587 See *The House of Wisdom*, by Jim Al-Khalili, for a comprehensive study on how Arabic Science created the Western Renaissance. Penguin Press, 2011.

and the Afghanistan of the Taliban may mark an extreme ideology, and even Egypt is now not much of a culture of tolerance."[588] Bloom made this statement in 2002. Egypt under the short-lived Muslim Brotherhood presidency had even less tolerance of Christian Copts, Jews, and other Muslims who disagreed with them. It is the opinion of this writer, a full return to this period would pull the Islamic world out of the faulty Sharia-Solution Cycle so many have adopted . . . a solution that only leads to more poverty and a lower standard of living. By every measure, Arab professor James Gelvin explains, "on a scale measuring the quality of political and social life, not one Arab state provided a high 'stand of human welfare' to its population"[589]This cycle is illustrated below:

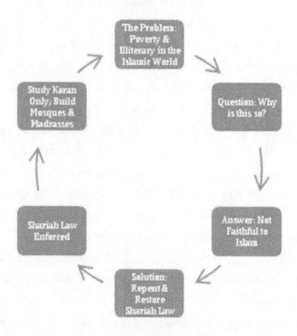

Islamic Cycle of Reasoning

The cycle depicts the reasoning of many Islamic "scholars" who argue the solution to their problems of poverty and illiteracy is to repent of unfaithfulness and return to a full implementation of Sharia law. After al-Nasser's policy of secular Arab Nationalism failed to bring about prosperous conditions Armstrong clarifies,

---

588 Harold Bloom in the Forward to *Ornament of the World*, p. xiii.
589 James, Gelvin, *The Arab Uprising*, p. 6.

"People felt that the Muslims had failed because they had not been true to their religion."[590] Without going back and restoring the elements which created their own Golden Age, they are left with this reoccurring cycle of poverty and illiteracy. The United Nations Human Development Report of 2001 is quoted as saying "the majority of the Islamic world lies in the middle to low categories of human development which include poverty, literacy and status of women."[591] The report does not mention Sharia law as the problem, or the solution! (Both would be viewed as politically incorrect). However, as D'Souza affirms, "The real divide in the Muslim world is between Islamic radicals and traditional Muslims."[592] The traditionalists make some accommodations on Sharia, but the radicals view them as not truly faithful. Thus, the radicals enforce Sharia law as the ultimate sign of faithfulness, which only continues the poverty/illiteracy cycle. Without returning to the Golden Age where openness to truth outside the Koran is embraced, this cycle of poverty and illiteracy will continue. In sum, Professor Peter Mansoor, Chair of Military History at Ohio State University states emphatically, "Jihadists want to restore the glory of the Islamic golden age without understanding what made it golden in the first place.

Moving Beyond "Hate Group" Language

A third countermeasure looks at the overuse and misuse of the term *hate group*. Webster defines *hate* as an "intense hostility and aversion; or extreme dislike or antipathy." Therefore, all of us who hate traffic or have an intense aversion to broccoli could technically be classified as a hate group! Those who use this term are using the wrong word for a human condition that cannot otherwise be solved. Hatred has reasons. Behind every element of hate exists some rationale for the hatred. Former FBI agent Mike German humorously quips, "Individuals who do violence without any reason are not terrorists but psychopaths . . . terrorists are not psychologically abnormal."[593] Likewise, terrorist researcher Anne Speckhard confesses, "The terrorists I have studied were not insane. Instead they were rational actors considering their choices within the context of their religious beliefs."[594] This

---

590 Armstrong, Islam, p. 143.
591 www.YesPakistan.com.
592 D'Souza, The Enemy at Home, p. 93.
593 Mike German, Thinking Like a Terrorist, p. 49.
594 Anne Speckhard, Talking to Terrorists, Advances Press, 2010, p. 773.

is a significant statement in light of the reality that Dr. Speckhard did personal interviews with over 400 terrorists, militants, family members and friends of terrorists.[595] Bruce Hoffman, another long standing researcher, affirms "terrorists are surprisingly normal in many ways and surprisingly human."[596] Just calling something a hate crime will never get rid of the problem. In the context of this book, the focus has been on the American Christian Identity movement and the sometime Neo-Nazi racist views of militia groups. So let me ask some questions:

First, do these right wing militia groups espousing racist hatred concern me? Yes! Are they prone to violence? Yes! Are they morally equivalent to Al Qaeda, ISIS, Boko Haram, Al Shabab, Al Qaeda in the Maghreb, Al Nursa, and Al Qaeda in Yemen? No. Here is why. They are mostly reactionary movements responding to particular political concerns or perceived threats coming from the political left.[597] As such, their numbers and groups rise and fall depending on the political climate. Their view is basically that of limited government, state sovereignty, white supremacy, individual rights, and especially gun rights. When they have used violence their targets are not random but usually selected against specific law enforcement, African American churches, synagogues, mosques or abortion clinics. (The 1996 Olympic bombings might be considered an exception although Rudolph thought the Olympic park was a gathering of mostly gays.) These acts reflect generally antigovernment and racist beliefs.

Take Jarad and Amanda Miller, who after shooting two Las Vegas police officers point blank in a pizza buffet restaurant, pinned a note on their bodies declaring their revolution. In addition, they placed a Gadsden flag (used by the Tea Party) on one body and a Nazi swastika on the other. They then went to a nearby Walmart, shooting into the air and ordering everyone out. After killing one customer who drew his licensed firearm, they shot him and waited for the police. Jarad was wounded by the good Samaritan, and when a SWAT team arrived Amanda shot her wounded husband and then shot herself. Both died. Scott Steward of *Stratfor* says, "Their beef was not with other restaurant or Walmart patrons, but with the

---

595 Dr. Speckhard also admitted some of those interviewed were "psychologically disturbed," p. 773.

596 Bruce Hoffman, *Inside Terrorism*, Columbia University Press, 1998.

597 Southern Poverty Law Center reports attacks on mosques but does not confirm who the perpetrators are. What is clearer is the arrest of four militia members in Georgia who plotted bombing Federal Government buildings, and the murder of law enforcement using ricin poison. *SPLC Report*, Winter 2011, p.3.

authorities." He concludes, "Their domestic terrorism remains a persistent threat even when the suspects seem a little unstable or delusional . . . but tends to be a low level one like the Millers who operate as lone actors or small groups."[598] In fact, FBI statistics of hate crimes for the year 2011 showed 46.9 percent of these were motivated by racial bias; 20.8 percent were motivated by sexual orientation while those motivated by religious bias accounted for 19.8 percent.[599] These are certainly horrible crimes, but they do not rise to the level of religious terrorism as defined in this book. In addition, I am not aware of militia or patriot groups exporting their views to the world at large. In fact, many find a "brotherhood" in European Neo-Nazi groups, but here the ideology is coming the other way . . . from Europe to the US!

So what is the countermeasure in regard to these groups? Hatred, as a condition of the human heart, can only be changed from within. In my Christian theology, it is accomplished by the transforming power of the Holy Spirit of God. Jesus made it very clear that "theft, murder, hatred, anger, and lust all are issues of the human heart. Unfortunately, activist groups look to the legal processes to remedy these deep seated issues of the heart. But change is possible and does happen. I have seen this change come through the use of plain dialogue and dispelling of erroneous views. I have had conversations with individuals in these various "hate" groups and have spent time answering their questions, refuting their conspiracy theories, and presenting what I consider genuine Christianity. Most had never heard these arguments because they are so ideologically driven by Identity leaders and racist literature. Few had even a rudimentary understanding of Christianity or any religion. Once they "see the truth," their views begin to moderate. Some convert to true Christianity and see the error of their racist views. Others just melt away back into mainstream society. Calling individuals "members of hate groups" only provides organizations like the Southern Poverty Law Center with legal justification to dismantle organizations or prosecute individuals. I don't disagree with this, but it does not go far enough. It is the same as taking out an Al Qaeda leader from a drone-launched Hellfire missile. It results in one less terrorist but continues to enrage those left behind and may be useful as a recruiting tool. It also does not in any way address the ideology that inspires these "Holy Warriors" and "Patriots."

598 Scott Steward, "Domestic Terrorism is No Joke," Stratfor Global Intelligence, June 12, 2014.
599 "FBI Releases 2011 Hate Crime Statistics," U.S. Department of Justice, Federal Bureau of Investigation, December 10, 1012.

Awareness of the Enemy Among Us

Great concern exists about community sleeper-cells and grass root Jihadists. So awareness about these is critical as a countermeasure. First, there is significant difference in the two groups. Sleeper Cells, as a term, is a holdover from the Cold War when intelligence agencies (both US and Soviet) embedded agents for long periods of time. In short, they were embedded to do nothing! They waited for years just gathering intelligence but rarely becoming operatives. Stratfor believes "there are no sleeper Jihadist cells in the US currently."[600] A current debate is ongoing from where the greatest threat is coming. Each of these still use the term *sleeper cell*, however the better terms are *grassroots Jihadist* and *lone wolf*. Some believe Al Qaeda-connected sleeper cells are still in the US. Another school of thought says the sleeper cells have been discovered, disbanded or indicted. Another school says Al Qaeda's strategy and its franchises are now e-driven, utilizing radical websites to foster violent ideology creating lone wolf home grown terrorists, also called "self-radicalized."[601] In this view, Al Qaeda has "morphed" from its centralized organization to now asserting itself in local actor networks.[602]

Others believe mosques are at the forefront of recruitment making local Imams the ultimate source of Jihadist ideology. One unnamed National Security officer told me, "Behind every Jihadist is a mosque, madrassa and imam . . . there are no purely self-radicalized." All these could be true. But a couple of things are clear: when anyone takes a trip to Pakistan, Yemen, Libya, Somalia, Eastern Turkey or Syria as a "vacation" or to visit relatives or friends, awareness flags should go up.[603] These are the current training grounds for Jihadists. Secondly, the controversial Patriot Act allowed federal agents to investigate mosques for intelligence purposes.[604] If

600 "Understanding Sleeper Cells," *Stratfor Security Weekly*, September 18, 2014.

601 One expert says Jihadist movements can be divided into three basic elements: the Al Qaeda Core, regional Jihadist franchisees, like Al Qaeda in the Arabian Peninsula, and grassroots operatives who are radicalized, inspired and equipped by the other two elements. Scott Stewart, "Why the Boston Bombers Succeeded," Stratfor Global Intelligence, *Security Weekly*, April 23, 2013.

602 See "Al Qaeda on the Run? No way, say experts," Oren Dorell, *USA Today*, Aug 6, 2013.

603 I wrote this section even before the Boston Marathon bombing where one of the two bombers had recently returned from visiting relatives in Dagestan. The FBI interviewed him before he went as having possible terrorist connections.

604 There was great outcry at the Bush Administration for the passage of the Patriot Act. However, what gets lost in the outcry is that the Act was passed legally by Congress, which included Senator Harry Reid, opposition Democrat. It is claimed the new intercept program prevented the deaths of almost 3,000 people. See Ronald Kessler, *The Terrorist Watch*, pp. 133-5. However, at the time of this writing it seems Congress is divided on the issue, those

the statistic is true that fifty to eighty percent of the clerics in American mosques were trained in Saudi Arabia, this is reason enough to take seriously what is being said in the Friday sermons. Dore Gold maintains, "Half the mosques and Islamic schools in the United States were built with Saudi money,"[605] and Craig Unger states directly, "many of the biggest and most powerful Muslim organizations in the United States are run by Wahhabi Islamic fundamentalists.[606]

If this justification is not enough the Pew Research Foundation found twenty-five percent of American Muslim men ages eighteen to twenty-nine believe "suicide bombings could be justified . . . these attitudes in turn are generated by Imams who preach Jihad and hatred in American mosques and in postings on the Internet according to FBI sources."[607] So what is going on in these mosques should concern us, especially when the threat is underplayed like it apparently was after the Benghazi attack. Several months after the attack, there was another attack on the BP natural gas facility in eastern Algeria by the same Al Qaeda connected group. A National Security expert concludes, "Thus, we cannot afford to be lulled into a false sense of security that *lone wolf* attacks are not a product of Al-Qaeda recruitment and support."[608]

In October of 2011, Obama's Justice Department was given further powers for "data mining" of vast stores of information on suspected terrorists. (Of course this did not prevent the Boston Marathon bombers.) Additional guidance was given to FBI counter-terrorism agents to go undercover in suspected mosques. Approval and oversight for these investigations comes from a newly created Sensitive Operations Review Committee or SORC.[609] Obviously, civil liberty groups see problems with undercover agents in religious places of worship.

I am not totally comfortable with religious undercover work as important as it may be; simply because it seems to sacrifice the cherished value of freedom of speech and worship for a security concern. Recently, while speaking to a church

---

praising the program now say the controversial program prevented 50 terrorist events. In 2013 two prohibitions were added to the Patriot Act: the prohibition against bulk acquisition of electronic communications and the acquiring of content. Congress is holding investigations and hearings on the National Security Agency spying on Americans without specific warrants.

605 Dore Gold, *Hatred's Kingdom*, p. 149.
606 Craig Unger, *House of Bush, House of Saud*, p. 203.
607 Kessler, *The Terrorist Watch*, p. 203.
608 Joshua Sinai, "Al-Qaida Threat to US Not Diminished," *Defense News*, April 23, 2013, p. 21.
609 Massimo Calabresi and Michael Cromley, "Homeland Insecurity: How Far Should We Go?" *Time*, May 13, 2013, p. 22-28.

group, I commented on how I didn't think I would want an FBI agent listening to my every word in a sermon on Sunday morning. Afterwards, the pastor came up to me and said, "I would love it: if he was not a Christian he might become one, and if he was already a Christian he would be blessed by the message!" But I lean on the side of civil liberties based on the American Constitution and the Fourth Amendment guaranteeing the security of our "persons, houses, papers and effects and against unreasonable searches and seizures without a warrant." Recently, the Mayor of Houston attempted to subpoena five pastors' sermons, emails and texts for use as evidence in "bias" investigations concerning alleged comments against LBGTs. This seems to be a new wrinkle in the war on terror. Now pastors' sermons are not only subject to political correctness but can be construed as hate speech or at worse, a crime. So the debate continues.

As noted earlier, community awareness has led to arrests and disruptions of groups simply by local law enforcement doing routine police work (McVeigh & Rudolph). Individuals have also reported to law enforcement those with extremist beliefs and/or indicating potential actions within their own faith communities and/or local communities. These are front line grass root defenders such as neighbors, store clerks, landlords and motel managers who find themselves in positions to come across or notice someone doing operation planning. Remember it was an alert street vendor who first noticed Faisal Shahzad, a naturalized US citizen from Pakistan, leaving his parked van at the New York Times Square that was set to explode and kill passers-by (May 2010). These are some of the real heroes in the war on terror because they are willing to jump out of their cultural-religious safety zones and turn informant against someone who is suspicious in their own faith group. This by itself might have prevented the Boston Marathon bombing if the university friends of the Tsarnaev brothers might have been more observant and willing to inform authorities. This is the wisdom behind the current New York City Police program that has been adopted by the Office of Homeland Security: "If you see something, say something."[610]

We face simple statistics. Our official counterterrorism measures are limited. The FBI has around 14,000 agents, and after 9/11, 2500 to 3,000 agents were assigned to counterterrorism.[611] Besides, to do 24/7 surveillance on one suspect can

---

610 Referred to by Scott Stewart, "Fighting Grassroots Terrorism: How Local Vigilance Can Help," Stratfor Global Intelligence, August 3, 2011.
611 Scott Stewart, Ibid.

sometimes involve 100 agents on the ground and air. So the importance of local citizen awareness is critical. If one sees the importance of jumping outside their safety zone to meet this challenge, it is equally important as a countermeasure to "Welcome the Stranger."

Welcoming the Stranger

Remember Sayyid Qutb? He came to America to study American education and return to Egypt. However, what he saw in America did not appeal to him. In fact, he concluded America was spiritually bankrupt, racist, sex and alcohol crazed, and materialistic. From this experience, when he returned to his homeland he was convinced "The West is the Problem, and Islam is the Solution." We don't know much more than what he writes, but he does reference going to church in Greeley, Colorado. He records being put off by the sensual dancing he observed in the church recreation halls, and loud blast of guitars and drums. We don't know what kind of church he attended or whether he ever attended a worship service. Perhaps he only attended some recreation dances. But what I wonder is if he ever saw true America, and especially true American Christianity?

Having probably spent too much of my life in the higher education environment, I recall who was usually left on campus during long vacations and holidays: International students! During my college years, they lived in the dorms, did not join fraternities or sororities, and over Thanksgiving and Christmas holidays usually were the only ones left on campus. I now wonder if they ever had the opportunity to get into American homes and make friends with American families. If not, mostly American television and the longhaired, shabbily dressed roommate who shacked up with girls on the weekends formed their perception of America! Today, the ubiquitous electronic media, ridiculous "reality" shows, rampant pornography, and even more scantily clad co-eds could drive a more extreme perception. It would not surprise me if many of our Muslim visitors today come to Qutb's same conclusion, like the Boston Marathon bombers, Tameran and Dzhorkhar Tsarnaev.[612] The West indeed is the Problem!

So the countermeasure is simple. As Americans we need to embrace the strangers (those unlike us), have them in our homes, take them to our churches

---

612 The Chechen brothers conspired in the Boston Marathon bombing, April 16, 2013, killing 4 and wounding several hundred.

if willing, and expose them to what true American values are. They need to hear from us, that we also are not pleased by the glorification of wealth, sports, beauty, the hottest gadgets and sexual exploits. And that these are not the Judeo-Christian values that built our nation. We too have an enemy and the enemy is Western materialism, sensuality, secularism, humanism, agnosticism, and atheism. We, like them, do not want our families destroyed, our faith marginalized, or our morals corrupted. Embracing others, who could potentially become our enemies, is an important countermeasure and fundamental to Christian teaching.

A student recently asked me how I could have served in the military being a committed Christian while obeying Jesus' words about loving our enemy (Matthew 5:44). First, I replied: "Jesus isn't playing a game with us. He acknowledges in the passage "we have enemies!" In fact, when he said this, Rome was the enemy of all Jews, and in a short time, some in the Jewish leadership would be seeking ways to kill him. Even one of his own disciples, Judas, would be the conspiring agent toward his death. However, some Christians I know have their heads in the sand on this point. They mistakenly think nothing really bad will happen to them. Or "an enemy" is just someone at work with a cantankerous attitude. Worse still are those who believe "if we think we have enemies, it is just a faulty concept in our heads!" Jesus, by his clear words, affirms enemies exist. Then the question, for us, his disciples, is how we should respond to those trying to kill us? He says, "Love them." As noted earlier, I have felt my life threatened several times by a variety of people, but I never want threats like these to stop me from welcoming and embracing those who may not believe as I do. Loving, by my definition, means continuing to treat them as human beings made in the image of God and not demonizing them to the point of reducing their humanity. This is what happens in warfare when we must demonize the enemy in order to be able to kill him. This is not an easy task and can be frightening to the point of being persecuted for it. Love in this sense when the Army medic renders care not only to the wounded American of an attack but also the terrorist who tried to kill him. Likewise, as chaplain it means providing a Koran, wash basin and prayer rug for a captured Prisoner of War. It seems counterintuitive and it is, but I believe it is what love of neighbor and enemy means. Equally, as a part of our commission to love the stranger, a logical outgrowth of love is to seek reconciliation where possible.

Seeking Reconciliation Where Possible

This last countermeasure is the hardest and sometimes least reported when successful. Was there any press coverage of the religious solidarity movement in Egypt? All that was shown in the West were the violent demonstrations by mostly Muslim Brotherhood supporters after the ousting of President Morsi. On July 26, 2013, a rare event took place. Christians publically ate with Muslims during the end of Ramadan fast; church bells rang in support of the Muslim fast; an estimated 40 million people took to the streets and crowded into Tahrir Square; there were few incidents of violence, no petty theft or harassment of women![613] Reconciliation between warring factions has been successful in the Balkans, South Africa, Australia and the Middle East. However, little is known about one of the very successful attempts to reconcile warring religious factions in Iraq. In January of 2007, then President George W. Bush announced in his State of Union address the initiative of sending an additional twenty thousand troops to Iraq (called the Surge). Under the new commander, Gen David Petraeus, the Surge would focus on the counterinsurgency tactics of winning the hearts and minds of the Iraqi people. By September of the same year, Petraeus reported most of the objectives were accomplished. By July of 2008, official reports listed the fewest number of both American and Iraqi casualties since the beginning of the war in 2003. In other words, the Surge was viewed a political and military success. However, this was not the complete story.

Along with the Surge, June 11-13 of 2007 brought about a delicate meeting of fifty-five Iraqi religious leaders, facilitated by the Iraq Inter-Religious Congress. This reconciliation initiative was a watershed event including nongovernmental organizations, the multinational forces, Iraq, the US Department of Defense and the government of Iraq national peace initiative. Army Chaplain Colonel Michael Hoyt, as key leader in the event and Command Chaplain for the multinational force said, "this was the largest representation of faith groups

---

613 Email letter from Ramez Atallah, General Director, The Bible Society of Egypt, Aug 2, 2013.

and geographic dispersion from north, south, east and west in Iraq in thirty-seven years."[614]

From this group of influential clerics, who only days before were plotting attacks against each other and the coalition of forces, a significant Accord was produced. During long hot days at the Al Rasheed Hotel in Baghdad, they came together at great risk and signed a Religious Accord that was historic. The Accord, signed by all parties, including representatives of Ali al-Sistani, Chief Shia leader and Muqtada al Sadr, leader of Sadr Army, pledged complete and the first religious support of the Iraqi government. It rejected terrorism and the use of sectarian violence. It publically "renounced Al Qaeda by name and made the spread of arms a criminal act."[615] This historic accord held sway until 2012 when sectarian violence again erupted as a result of the US withdrawal of forces. It is hoped some critical lessons were learned from this reconciliation Accord initiative. Though violence has returned and Baghdad is almost surrounded by the ISIS forces, the Accord illustrated reconciliation was possible between warring religious groups. If possible once, maybe again!

Peter Maki, Executive Director of the Center for Conflict Relief and Reconstruction, records lessons learned from the Baghdad Accord. First, religion cannot be ignored but must be incorporated into any peace-making process. However, regrettably, secular governments are slow in their willingness to recognize the power and influence of religious leaders. Second, "legitimacy" in the Middle East is based on family history and tribal accomplishments, not education and individual accomplishments as in the West. This means once we engage someone we must remain committed to them. If we don't, they easily become our enemies rather than our friends. This is the lesson we obviously did not learn after leaving Afghanistan to the Taliban after the Soviets left! We wanted no long term commitment to the country. Will it be any different when we leave again? Third, diplomatic relations tend to be *risk-adverse*: a perspective that dealing with religion is filled with the most risk being irrational, with outcomes difficult to measure. Therefore, it is much safer to "not do religion."

---

614 "Seeking a Way Forward Through Inter-Faith Reconciliation in Iraq," June 25, 2007, www.army.mil/article/3794.

615 Berkley Center notes, "Religion and World Affairs," USAF Chaplain Conference, April 2011. Listed 22 Sunni clerics, 11 Shia, 4 Kurdish, 2 Christian plus 2 Council Representatives. Signing ceremony included Anglican Canon Andrew White, Ambassadors from the UK, Italy, Denmark, General Petraeus and Prime Minister Nouri Maliki.

Fourth, in the West we are so used to communicating via email, texting, phone and faxes we fail to recognize tribal societies do not function this way, even when they have the technology. "Cups of tea" and face to face discussions are the only way to gain enough trust that conflict resolution can be accomplished. In conclusion, what Maki calls for is "a comprehensive approach that does not ignore the role of religion and instead incorporates its unique power in the process of peacemaking."[616]

One morning I walked to the Student Union to get a cup of coffee and overheard two students in what sounded like a heated conversation. I saw two Middle East students both of whom I knew, in a deep, lively Middle Eastern style conversation, full of strong voice inflections and hand gestures. One was from an Arab country, the other from Israel. After I purchased my coffee I went over to their table and put a hand on each of their shoulders. I said, "Do you know what is going on here?" They both looked at their professor with perplexed expressions. Apparently, they were so deep in their "discussion" they weren't aware of how they were being perceived. I finally replied, "The solution to the Middle East . . . that's what going on here!" Debating, disagreeing, even getting a little agitated, but there they were, at the same table, eating together without killing each other. This is where reconciliation begins.

The Baghdad Accord came about by getting all the senior religious leaders in the same room for three days. They didn't agree on whose religion is superior, or whose political party should be in power. No one probably changed any of their theological commitments. But for a brief moment in time, they saw the futility of violence and realized they had to be part of the solution. There would be no peacemaking without them, no matter how many troops the Coalition brought into the country. In this example, they found common ground in just renouncing violence. As I pen these sentences, my heart is broken when I hear that Baghdad is surrounded, with Sunni ISIS forces attacking the Shia strongholds, with most Christians fleeing. It makes me think about what could have been!

In the example of my two Middle East students, their reconciliation went even further. The Arab was raised Muslim, and the Israeli Jewish. Both were brought to a point in their lives where each saw the futility of past choices of action. My Jewish

---

616 Points summarized and quoted from "God and Politics: An Inside Perspective on Religious Peacemaking in Iraq," www.centerforconflictrelief.org.

friend had dabbled in sixties Marxism, extremism, and Jewish mysticism before he found peace and solace in seeing Yeshua (Jesus) as His Jewish Messiah. His Arab friend had become disillusioned with the Palestinian Liberation Organization but still hated Jews and Israel. On the opposite side of a border, he too found in Christian teaching a reality he had not experienced in Islam. So as in the Biblical narrative of Esau and Jacob these "brothers" were reconciled though still wrestling. Their common ground came through seeing themselves as fellow Christian brothers. In reality, they still debated the hot issues about the role of Israel, Jews and Arabs in the world. But this modern day Muhammad had not become a member of Al Qaeda, Hamas or Hezbollah. Likewise, Eliezer had never joined the Israeli radical right like Kach or the Kahane movement.[617] Both were ostracized by members of their own family and persecuted by some in their former faith groups. Many will scoff at the thought that belief in Jesus made the difference here, but it is reality . . . unfortunately, a reality that officialdom does not want to admit or embrace.

Conclusion

The historical analysis in the previous chapters looked at various religious groups who have used violence in the name of their religion. Now it is time to ask the fundamental question, "Which group poses the most clear and present danger to the United States and our world? Beginning with Israeli right-wing religious extremism, I tried to demonstrate how Jewish violence was limited to the nation of Israel. It centers on the Palestinian West Bank conflict between Jews and Arabs and settler opposition to the liberal non-religious Israeli leadership. The "land" ideology as driven by the Jewish religious right's claims to the land is not relevant anywhere else in the world. As such, it seems to this writer, Israel is the final hope in the long history of anti-Semitism. Current FBI statistics from 2013 demonstrate that even in "safe" America, Jews are "the most frequent victims of religiously motivated hate crimes."[618] So, in a Jewish State, they argue, they have a right to their own land. Likewise, Israeli militant violence has not been exported, though some could argue the conflict could plunge the larger world into chaos. But so could many conflicts around our world today.

---

617 Both names are made up to protect personal and family security of the individuals who still live on separate sides of the Middle East conflict.

618 Is it time for the Jews to leave Europe?" Jeffrey Goldberg, *The Atlantic*, April, 2015, p.73.

Religious conflicts in the Eastern religions are usually isolated within countries with divergent religious sects. As such this violence is localized and not a threat to the world unless they go nuclear (think Kashmir, between Pakistan and India). Likewise, I do not consider American Christian Identity a relevant religiously-driven threat. It may be a threat to law enforcement, minorities and certain religious groups, but the violence performed is criminal in nature driven by radical political-ideological-conspiratorial concerns. It therefore needs to be prosecuted as such . . . a crime. Christian Identity doctrines have never been a part of mainstream Christianity or any recognized denomination. Other than abortion doctor killer Paul Hill, who was an active Presbyterian, there has not been any across-the-board violence by a mainstream religious group in America. Even Mark Potok of the Southern Poverty Law Center revealed in 2013 that radical right violence was "political" in nature coming from a "neo-Nazi gunman, an "active-duty military member," and a "white power student" plotting an attack against black and gay classmates.[619] These are terrible events with a senseless loss of lives, but they do not rise to the level of religiously inspired terrorism. What I am more concerned about is the so-called "stonewalling" by the Obama administration on things like the Fast & Furious gun fiasco, Benghazi, IRS targeting, and the obtaining of cell phone records on reporters and average citizens and cover-ups by the Veterans Administration in dealing with those who have put their lives on the line for this country. Perceptions of this kind, whether true or not, breed possible violent reactions from the radical right whether political or religious. However, it is my belief Christian Identity adherents, no matter their vitriolic rhetoric and activities, will not bring down America or the world at large.

This leaves Islam. I agree with many quoted in this work, that Islamic Jihadism is the new global ideology. ISIS has certainly made it clear by the beheadings of American and British citizens; it is at war with the West whether we realize it or not.[620] This is the ideology that must be attacked primarily. But as noted, this ideological battle few see as relevant or "safe" to engage. As revealed about the two Boston Marathon bombers, one source states, "there is likely only a small chance that authorities will discover a formal link between suspects and state sponsors . . . Any link will likely be ideological rather than

---

619 Mark Potok, "The Year in Hate and Extremism," *Intelligence Report*, Spring 2013, Southern Poverty Law Center.

620 See editorial by Stanley Orman, "War is War," *Defense News*, September 22, 2014.

operational."[621] If we don't recognize this threat and call it what it is . . . war, we have no hope in defeating it. When few call this conflict war, we end up being defeated by political correctness that gives advantage to if not establishment of Islam.

When Christian children cannot wear a cross at school or carry a Bible for fear of offending Muslims something is wrong, especially when educators are expected to "accommodate" the religious dietary needs and dress of Muslims in the same schools. Religious freedom must be equal for all and not just protected for a few. If religion is to be accommodated it must be accommodated equally without discrimination or not accommodated at all. In the military arena Muslims are accommodated with private places to pray, provided prayer rugs, wash basins and Korans (All at government expense). But so are Christians and anyone who wants to exercise a demonstration of their faith. (Though now at Air Force Base Visitor Quarters, Gideon Bibles are no longer allowed to be replaced in rooms . . . interesting because they were never at any cost to the government!) The only caveat is these religious accommodations must not interfere with mission accomplishment. It's up to commanders, not chaplains, to make that decision. I wish our educational community would see the value of this approach.

Individual Muslims are not the threat, but they must be more ideologically engaged with those more radical; it is the radical Jihadist ideology of a few that creates the threat. As noted before, the conflict between Christianity and Islam is a battle of the Books: The Bible versus the Koran. Here is where the ideology (theology) for both faiths begins. This aspect when ignored only creates more confusion. Koranic ideology mixed with what Speckhard calls "the lethal cocktail of connection with a terrorist group (face to face or online), some personal vulnerability, and social support," can make the threat become virulent.[622] However, what is the reality of this "few?" Current estimates of the number of Muslims in the world are around 1.6 billion. If only one percent is radicalized into a Jihadi ideology that puts their numbers in the millions! This by itself is cause of great concern. Further, Al Qaeda trained tens of thousands in the training camps in Afghanistan, Sudan, and Pakistan.[623] In many places, the additional threat of

621 Stratfor Global Intelligence, 2013 Intelligence Summary, "Boston Bombing Suspects: Grassroots Militant from Chechnya," April 19, 2013.
622 *Talking to Terrorists*, p. 9.
623 "Why the Boston Bombers Succeeded," Scott Steward, Stratfor Global Intelligence, April 23, 2013.

the loss of religious freedom for non-Muslims is a concern. (Egyptian Christian Copts, Syrian, Iraqi and Palestinian Christians and Jews) But the main enemy is the ideology of violence as interpreted, articulated and applied from the Koran. When radical Imams encourage the imposition of Sharia law on Muslims and non-Muslims who don't want it, serious questions are raised in a free society. Another enemy we face is when religious freedom and toleration is no longer defended under the Constitution by our elected and uniformed officials. This also is a critical war that must be won.

For most adult Americans, 9/11 is a distant memory. The feelings of outrage, shock and intense fear are now lost in getting back to our routines. At least when the Japanese hit Pearl Harbor the entire country was mobilized, and almost everyone, even those who had been anti-war, came around to embrace the war and fight. The war concluded with a defeated Germany and Japan, signing an unconditional surrender. World War II was a war . . . a real war! But today we fight these seemingly "dirty little wars" where no one really knows how they started or if they will ever end. Even after the catastrophic events of 9/11, few called the "War on Terrorism" a real war. For the few who understood the religious complexity of the conflict, and called it what it was, it seems we chose to fight the war with weapons we like to use. Therefore, it becomes a war between Daisy Cutter bunker busting bombs and box cutters![624] A war where Umar Addul Mjutallab puts explosive material in his underwear to bring down a commercial jet, while the "controller" of a remotely piloted vehicle sitting in an air conditioned Nevada van puts a precision missile on a target in Yemen. As Mjutallab is escorted to jail, the UAV controller goes home to his kid's soccer game. Such is what this war on terror has become and how we choose to fight it. One commentator recently expressed the view that ISIS is much more than a terrorist group, or even an insurgency. He comments: "It has an army in the field, one that has routed regular units of the Iraqi national Army, they take and control territory, run banks and set up hospitals." His conclusion? "It is no longer a war on terrorism, but war on a standing army!"[625] At least he is calling it by the right name . . . war. It seems our own American President not only denies this reality, but in his denials has wandered into the dangerous territory of

---

624 Daisy Cutters are the bunker busting bombs dropped from Air Force cargo planes in Afghanistan to kill or drive Al Qaeda from the caves in Tora Bora. Box cutters were reportedly used by the 9/11 hijackers to kill the flight attendants and pilots on the four 9/11 airliners.
625 "No Longer a War on Terrorism," William R. Hawkins, *Defense News*, March 16, 2015, p. 21.

being considered a *takfir* (apostate). Graeme Wood in his widely reported article states, "Western officials would probably do best to refrain from weighing in on matters of Islamic theological debate altogether. Barack Obama himself drifted into *takfir* waters when he claimed that the Islamic State was *not Islamic*, the irony being that he, son of a Muslim, may himself be classified as an apostate, and yet is now practicing *takfir* against Muslims. The idea of non-Muslims practicing *takfir* elicits chuckles from Jihadists: "Like a pig covered in feces giving hygiene advice to others," one tweeted.[626]

However, this book has tried to offer a different understanding about religious terror and set a different course for defeating terrorism. If religion has been a consistent source of violence throughout history, then the solution is not to ignore it but explore it and utilize its unique resources. As mentioned several times, "if religion is the problem, it must also be a great part of the solution." Canon Andrew White, one of the key players bringing about the Baghdad Accord, stated succinctly, "When religion is good, it is great . . . but when it goes wrong, it goes very wrong."[627] Unfortunately, as of this writing, the good Canon White is surrounded by ISIS who would like to kill him for just being an outspoken Christian in Baghdad. For him, religion gone very wrong is at his doorstep. For the few who call religious conflict "war," the need exists to deploy from our arsenal more than just military and legal weapons. Those in power cannot overlook the spiritual dimension of humankind due to political correctness, sheer ignorance or avoidance. In a sense, we must understand the "fanatic." Lee Harris concludes, "It is due to the fanaticism of such men that empires have been toppled, religious traditions uprooted and destroyed, cultures turned upside down. That is why this kind of fanaticism must be taken seriously, and why its dramatic return to the world stage cannot be ignored. If we wish to understand our era, we must neither deny fanaticism, nor simply condemn it from our own ethical perspective. We must, above all, grasp its logic and power.[628]

The countermeasures listed above are only starting points to think about national security issues in much broader and deeper ways. But this will take time

---

626 Graeme Wood, "What is the Islamic State," *The Atlantic*, March, 2015, p. 94.
627 Quoted in *God and Politics*, Peter E. Maki.
628 Lee Harris, *The Suicide of Reason: Radical Islam's Threat to the West*, Perseus Basic Books, 2007, p. 205.

and training; we need to learn how to deal with religion and engage religious leaders so that they seek peace rather than violence.

King David, Israel's heroic warrior, had so much blood on his hands his greatest ambition was denied in building a house for God. The privilege would go to his son Solomon who was a man of peace. Perhaps it was from this rejection King David learned (the hard way) there were other alternatives. He wrote a psalm encouraging the other approach: "Depart from evil, and do good; seek peace and pursue it" (Psalm 34:14). When Jesus was taken captive by those arresting him in the Olivet garden, Simon Peter, one his disciples, took out a sword and sliced off the ear of the High Priest's servant. Jesus tells him directly, "Put the sword into its sheath" (John 18:11). This was in spite of earlier telling his disciples to sell their outer clothing if need be to obtain a sword (Luke 22:36). When two swords were produced (strangely hidden up to this point) he said, "It is enough." The question of what is "enough" weaponry echoes through the corridors of history.

The outrageous fortunes of terrorism are upon us.

I do not believe radical Islam will destroy America or Western civilization. I agree with Scott Stewart that terrorism of any kind is not an existential threat to the United States.[629]

Even though the stated goal of radical Islamists is to establish a global Caliphate, many clerics and Imams cringe at the thought. At its worst, the beheadings of Christians and others by ISIS is a tactic of fear. Its goal is to make us fearful. If we feel unsafe, then they have accomplished their first aspect of their goal. However, the real game changer is the big IF. If ISIS, Al Qaeda, Kach, or an American militia group ever obtained a nuclear weapon, then we face an existential threat equivalent to Armageddon.

In the movie *The Man in the Iron Mask* (1998) the aging three Musketeers are debating whether they should take arms or not. Aramis says, "When we were young men and saw injustice we fought it." D'Artagnan answers, "Now we know some problems cannot be solved with a sword." Athos responds back saying, "And some cannot be solved without one." It takes informed wisdom gained from the past and good intelligence in the present to discern which direction to take. The religious people of the world can either continue to be part of the problem or part of the solution. Ultimately, it is up to us as to whether it is time to sheath or draw

---

629 "Is Terrorism an Existential Threat," Scott Steward, *Stratfor Security Weekly*, February 5, 2015.

the sword! But the sword of military force can only go so far. As Scott Steward so clearly admits, "There is no military solution to the Jihadist threat: It is an ideological problem and must be addressed on the ideological battlefield."[630] But what does it mean to engage ideologically?

This writer concludes, it is the sword of the Spirit as found in the Christian Scriptures, carefully examined and expounded that cuts much deeper into the hearts of men and women, friend and foe. It's not just a matter of quoting scripture passages to justify what we already want to do; but serious study and application of Biblical principles. In other words, if it is a battle of religious ideas then other (better) religious ideas must come from somewhere; ideas that attack, answer, and demolish the hostile ideologies threatening civilization, our Constitution, and way of life. As a Christian, I have experienced with numerous individuals confirmation of this reality. The New Testament's Apostle Paul wrote: "We do not war according to the flesh (material), for the weapons of our warfare are not of the flesh but divinely powerful (Spiritual) for the destruction of fortresses, destroying speculations against the knowledge of God" (II Corinthians 10:3-5). If what we are fighting is a religious/spiritual battle, then it will demand spiritual resources to counter it. That for me is the Sword of the Spirit as found in the Word of God (Ephesians 6:17). But as Hamlet acknowledged, "there lies the rub." How do we apply a spiritual sword to flesh and blood realities on the ground? If we are not wresting against flesh and blood, how then do we respond to those who are flesh and blood seeking to do us harm? I do not believe this argues for holy war against Islamic radicalism, Jihadism, extremism, or whatever the term du jour is. This was tried before. It might argue for applying historic Just War criteria to terrorism justifying armed conflict, but what is the reasonable end state we seek? Or we can continue on the standard path of justifying the sword whenever our national or political interests are violated . . . interests as defined by whom, and interests that change with the political wind?

The range of historical "Christian" options as noted earlier run from sheer passivism to radical military activism. Whether we use the Sword of the Spirit in a personal way (engaging people every day in the normal course of life) or a more militant fashion (joining the military, National Guard, FBI or CIA), the requirement on the Christian is the same: We are to pray for our enemies and those

630 Scott Steward, "Responding to a Chronic Terrorist Threat," Stratfor Global Intelligence, October 9, 2014.

who persecute us (Matthew 5:44), pray for our elected leaders (I Timothy 2: 1-2), and seek to be at peace with all men (Romans 12:18). As being witnessed almost daily in Egypt, Iraq and Syria, there must be a willingness to die for our faith rather than deny our Lord under the threat of conversion. These are the true martyrs described in Heaven by the Apostle John (Revelation 6:9, 20:4), not suicide bombers who blow themselves up to obtain a heavenly reward. As Christian citizens we also have the First Amendment right to petition our government to fulfill its Constitutional duty in protecting the security of its citizens and defending the nation against all enemies, foreign and domestic. See the Preamble to the Constitution: "We the people . . . to insure domestic tranquility, provide for the common defense," and Article II, The Executive: "to preserve, protect and defend the Constitution of the United States." Maybe that's why the historical oath of office ends with "So help me God."[631] So help us, Oh Lord, in this battle!

---

631 The United States Air Force recently deleted this statement in the oath as a requirement, Kristin Davis, "'So help me God' not required," *Air Force Times*, September 29, 2014. P. 15.

An Open Letter to My Religious Readers

We who embrace religious convictions and take the practice of our religion seriously place ourselves in a unique category. Atheists, agnostics, and secularists will never quite understand us. But that is okay, I don't expect them to understand me or share the value of my faith. My concern lies with the need to clean up our own religious household. So here are a few personal recommendations that might cause us to recognize extreme attitudes within our own camp.

First, my understanding of the Truth and the Truth itself are not necessarily synonymous. This means I can be both right and little wrong at the same time. Realizing this opens me to further dialogue, discussion and perhaps a little self-doubt.

Secondly, the beliefs and practices of the religious leaders who mentored me might also be right and a little wrong at times. I can still embrace and respect them for their influence on me, but question some of their views without being unfaithful to God. All human beings are fallible but only God is perfect.

Third, so far all end time date-setting prophecies have been wrong. But this does not mean none will ever come true. My point is: as believers we need to exercise caution in prophetic details and time-tables, without discarding a Scriptural hope of the Christian Second Coming or the Jewish first coming of a Messiah.

Fourth, all beliefs do not have to be acted upon. If I believe a righteous life is the best way to live, it does not follow that it is my religious duty to make all men righteous (the way I define righteousness) whether they want to be or not. There should be no coercion in religion, as the Koran states. Persuasion and example make the best converts. Jesus said, "Follow me." Some did, others didn't!

Last, the two most critical questions for religious people are *who* determines who speaks for God; and *who* gets to decide what God wants from His followers?

As religious people we are all carriers of potential extremist attitudes that when acted upon can lead to violence. Frustration with the existing order plus extremist ideology plus the right personal circumstances can push someone into committing violent acts. My hope is this book has allowed you to see whether you might yourself harbor the beginnings of attitudes that led some people into terrorist attitudes and behaviors. It should clarify in your mind how easily we can cross a line between being a faithful religious follower to one willing to commit violent acts in the name of God.

Robert Michael Hicks
July, 2015

About the Author

Dr. Robert Hicks is a retired Air Force Chaplain of 32 years and currently Adjunct Professor of History at Belhaven University (Orlando). He holds an undergraduate degree in Psychology, two Master's degrees (Theology & National Security Studies) and a Doctor of Ministry Degree. Post Doctoral work includes studies in Religion & History (Villanova, Rollins College) He has taught at four institutions of higher learning including the Air Force War College teaching on Religious Terrorism. He has served most major commands of the Air Force and Joint Army & Air Commands with the National Guard. He has traveled extensively overseas in both military and civilian capacities and consults on Terrorism and Mass casualty events. He is a published author of eleven books (one with his wife, Cynthia) focusing on men's issues and dealing with Post Traumatic Stress. He served at Landstuhl Medical Hospital (Germany) at the beginning of the War on Terrorism where he was the senior National Guard Chaplain caring for the combat wounded. Since

9/11, he has lectured and briefed on Religious Terrorism to local law enforcement, FBI, Border Patrol, Civil Air Patrol, First Responders, University groups, Churches, Denominational meetings, and Senior Military Personnel. Now retired, he has more time, freedom and availability to travel and promote his speaking, teaching and literary career.

Past book publicity has included more than 200 radio, television and bookseller appearances. He feels comfortable and experienced in connecting with audiences of all types including those of other faiths and nationalities. His published works include:

Uneasy Manhood: Oliver Nelson, Thomas Nelson Publisher

Failure to Scream, Thomas Nelson Publisher

Returning Home, Fleming H. Revell Company

Masculine Journey, NavPress Publisher

Feminine Journey, (Co-authored with wife) NavPress Publisher

Trauma: The Pain that Stays, Fleming H. Revell Company

Man of All Passions, NavPress Publisher

In Search of Wisdom, NavPress Publisher

The Christian Family in Changing Times, Baker Books

How A Man Faces Adversity, Bethany House Publisher

Husbands and Wives, (Contributor), Victor Books

Masculine Journey, also published in Dutch and Portuguese

Uneasy Manhood, Thomas Nelson Publisher (also published in Spanish)

9 781630 477851